Author Biography

Born in Middlesex England and raised in Hamilton Ontario, Canada, Fran L. Porter (B.Ed., M.A.) moved to Alberta with her geologist husband in 1974. She has spent the majority of her working life as a high-school teacher with the Foothills School Division, just south of the city of Calgary. Today, when they are not travelling the world, she and husband Andy (pictured below with her in Hawaii) still live in suburban Calgary on the edge of beautiful Fish Creek Provincial Park, where they love to say they enjoy a retirement abounding in the "three 'f's": friends, family, and fulfilment.

To Jean:
With thanks for
your support!

Fran

D1602527

When The Ship Has No Stabilizers:
our daughter's tempestuous voyage through borderline personality disorder

Fran L. Porter

CROSSFIELD
PUBLISHING

ISBN-13: 978-0968664650 (Crossfield Publishing)
ISBN-10: 0968664650

Cataloguing in Publication Data
Non-Fiction, biography, psychology
1. psychology/mental illness 2. borderline personality disorder 3. BPD 4. mentally ill/biography 5. mental illness/case studies 6. mentally ill children/biography 7. dialectical behaviour therapy 8. DBT

Edited by E. Tina Crossfield
Layout by Harald Kunze
Cover Illustration by Larry Stilwell
Font style Garamond
Manuscript prepared by Crossfield Publishing
2269 Road 120
St. Marys, Ontario, N4X 1C9
www.crossfieldpublishing.ca

Author's Note

The BPD testimonials quoted in this book are either composites or used with permission. Opinions I attribute to "my psychologist colleague" are gleaned from conversations held at various times with psychologists and/or guidance counsellors on the same teaching staff as I. Names used are real, except where, to protect anonymity, I specifically state that I have adopted pseudonyms.

Dedication

To my husband, Andy, for being my life jacket through it all. To my daughter, Lisa, and my son-in-law, Shawn, for never abandoning ship. To my precious granddaughter, Jaimie, who was so reluctant to give up the ship, even as it sank. And to Colleen herself, who has taught me more than she'll ever know.

Foreword

By Rev. Gordon Hunter

About a quarter century ago Colleen Porter crashed into my orbit like a meteorite. Elementary schools in Calgary do not have guidance counsellors, so when there are crises in the school, administrators (I was an Assistant Principal) work with students, parents and other professionals to find answers to problems. Colleen and I got to know each other soon after I arrived in Deer Run School, as she was wont to precipitate crises in her classroom, to the point that teaching and learning was compromised. The best way I could help the teacher and students in the class was to have Colleen talk with me while I attempted to discover what caused her misbehaviour and then come up with a plan to change that behaviour.

Colleen was very bright and we know that there was much good in her. That goodness now shines out though her daughter Jaimie, a talented and capable young woman. Colleen, though, used her genius in ways that were often manipulative and anti-social. I quickly discovered that this young girl, then in grade four, was a voracious reader, but that she read some disturbing books. Among her favorites were the dark tales of Edgar Allen Poe. Our discussions were fascinating, but I realized that I did not have the diagnostic skills to identify her problems, nor did I have the time and resources to treat the deviance. With the assistance of resource teachers, Colleen was referred to various programs within the Calgary Board of Education. None of them provided enough.

Through much reading, research and effort, Fran and Andy eventually determined that their daughter probably had borderline personality disorder. We don't know if Colleen's acceptance of such a label would have helped her, and of course we cannot return to Colleen's early days to experiment with possible solutions. Even today there can be no certainty that treating her for BPD would have made a difference, but it would have provided a starting point. And with this statement comes an acknowledgement that significant numbers of children may be mentally ill and in need of treatment: a fact about which there has been much denial.

We must admire the soul searching Fran and Andy have done, as well as their faith, their love for Colleen, and the sacrifices they made to keep their daughter safe. This fascinating biography has pushed the boundaries of research on borderline personality disorder. We are grateful to Fran for sharing Colleen's story and the effects of Colleen's behaviour on family, classmates, and others. The courage it took to write this book may mean that other parents in Fran and Andy's situation will have access to available resources and will be able to strategize with professionals to work effectively towards rescuing their children's futures. It is recognized that research in this area is at a relatively early stage. This work is an important step in moving that research forward and improving the lives of those afflicted with BPD and similar disorders.

Foreword

By Rev. Linda C. Hunter

I remember a little girl with a lovely head of hair framing a face with eyes that reflected intensity, curiosity, and wisdom beyond her years. I also remember a tormented and angry young woman who spun a tangled web of fabrication and deceit that became her reality and ultimately led her into the labyrinthine world of addiction.

Colleen Porter entered my life as a captivating child attending Sunday school and exited as a drug-dependent, broken woman. The journey between those two contrasting realities forms the content of this book. Make no mistake: Colleen was surrounded by people who loved her, especially her parents and her sister. Creative, artistic, and brilliant in so many ways, she was always ready to challenge the status quo of her world, especially when she encountered injustice. But she was unable to overcome the mental health issues that festered within her and drove her to dark places. That she was born into a family that adored and cherished her is the best part of her story, and it is shared with you here through the candid and beautiful words of her mother, Fran.

It takes courage to write a book that reveals the pain and helplessness accompanying mental illness. It takes courage to reveal the sorrow of broken promises and the anguish caused by the premature death of a beloved child. But this is a story also filled with tender moments of love and caring, as a family struggles to live in hope in the face of daunting challenges.

What you are about to read is more than just one family's journey through heartbreak. It is also an account of a devastating mental health disorder and its impact upon our society. It is a tremendously important book because it shines the light on a disorder neither easily understood nor much researched until recently. While offering a glimpse into one family's struggle to comprehend their daughter's dilemma and eventual destruction, it also dares throw open the doors on an illness long shrouded in shadows and mystery.

This book challenges us to end the cultural stigma that still surrounds mental health issues. Fran Porter, Colleen's mother, insists we take a stand to change our prejudices and fears. She asks us to become informed about how to help *ourselves*, so that we might push back the barriers of ignorance and open the human heart to healing and hope.

If even one person reads this book and experiences a life transformation, Colleen's family will know that her life and death has made a difference. I can only stand in awe of their determination, in the midst of pain and loss, to embrace optimism rather than despair.

Author's Introduction

I am numb yet raw, devastated yet relieved, crushed yet uplifted. How do I work through this emotional oxymoron? I write. From the moment I first put pen to paper, writing has been my solace, my refuge, and my therapy. So I do it now to honour the souls of the living as well as the dead. Catharsis is a need, yes, but greater than that is the need to feel her death was not in vain. Some meaning and moral must be taken from it. Some help for others must be found in it. Some relief and rebuilding for our precious family must be provided by it.

Two days ago at the start of this writing a phone call came, made by our elder daughter Lisa. My husband Andy and I had just arrived home from a church picnic featuring lovely weather, tasty food and great fellowship. We were in good spirits as we came in through the door to the ringing phone. Then, abruptly, the bottom dropped out of our lives.

Her younger sister Colleen, Lisa chokingly informed us, had been pronounced dead-on-arrival at Royal Columbian Hospital in New Westminster, B.C. Colleen had been transported there by ambulance in a state of cardiac arrest and attempts to revive her had failed. Our thirty-two-year-long battle to save our second child was over.

Wracked with sorrow and defeat, our first impulse was to close up our Calgary home and fly straight to Surrey to be with Lisa, her husband Shawn, and Jaimie, our thirteen-year-old granddaughter—Colleen's daughter—who has lived with Lisa and Shawn for the past two years. Family ought to stand together in crisis times like this, holding on to one another for support and comfort. Indeed, we offered to do exactly that without delay. But Lisa, a high-school teacher like her mum, said Shawn was being wonderful and Jaimie was already much calmer than when she'd first heard the news. We spoke to Jaimie. Through sobs she said, "I expected this. I just thought I had more time."

Bless their hearts; they are strong people, both of them. So is Shawn. And so, when it comes down to it, are we. Anyone dealing with Colleen and surviving the interaction has had no choice but to become strong. Parenting her, being her sister, being her brother-in-law, and being her daughter were all situations where indecision or cowardice simply would not do. In the pages that follow I hope to explain why. And I hope to put her to rest by talking seriously to others like her who can still get help.

Jaimie, as well as for my own cathartic need, this project is for you, sweetheart. Since you started to be old enough to understand, you have dealt admirably with the tragic truth.

May knowing the story behind what happened and the medical realities that made your mom who she was help you deal as admirably and as courageously with the rest of your life.

1. A Touch of Cerebral Palsy

In nineteen seventy-four Andy and I became parents for the first time. The birth of a child, as one colleague put it, is "one of life's biggies". And yes, we wanted to trumpet the news from the rooftops. We satisfied ourselves with phoning both sets of thrilled parents, then living in Hamilton Ontario, and telling all our closest friends. "Congratulations to you both," my dear mum applauded. "Parenthood involves a huge outlay of time, emotion and money. And it's worth every minute, every tear, and every penny." Her words brought a lump to my throat and I have never forgotten them.

Born in Calgary's Foothills Hospital, Lisa Michelle was beautiful. From the start she ate well, slept well, and thrived. Girlfriends complained about their babies' fussiness while feeding or restlessness when put down in the crib; I knew nothing of those. So far this parenting business was a cake walk.

So easy did we find it, in fact, that the decision to get pregnant again was a no-brainer. Our darling would have a little sister or brother, and we four would be the idyllic, close-knit nuclear family. Four years later Colleen Tamara was born, again in Foothills Hospital. And again, she was beautiful.

Both pregnancies were trouble-free. I had little morning sickness with either and I ate heartily and healthily throughout both. Neither Andy nor I are smokers, nor have we ever been. We drink socially if we're at a party, maybe two or three glasses of wine per month—though I couldn't even do that during either pregnancy. In short, we're a couple of nerds who fell in love in university, married right before obtaining our respective Masters' degrees, and, until retirement, pursued careers in our chosen fields lasting just over thirty years each. It doesn't get any more "ordinary solid citizen" than that.

Yet despite the similarity of my pregnancies and the identical "nerdy" environment in which the products of those pregnancies were raised, the two girls couldn't have been more different. Physically, Lisa and Colleen looked like sisters: peaches-and-cream complexions, large blue eyes, pert winsome smiles. Temperamentally, they were day and night.

When we took Colleen home I discovered, in spades, what those girlfriends of mine had been complaining about. Colleen was as restless and fussy as Lisa had been placid and content. She would startle visibly and violently when touched and would scream for hours at a time. Neither food nor rocking nor bouncing on the knee would placate her. Rare was the night when one or both of us was not up with her several times. Still, her six-week check-up caused no concern. She was eating well, gaining weight, and exhibiting normal responsiveness to her world. Some babies, the doctor shrugged, are just fussier than others. They usually outgrow it.

You're not supposed to worry as much with the second child. The first has trained you well not to be panicked by every little thing, so subsequent children reap the benefits. In our household that wasn't the case. The day Lisa first grasped the edge of the coffee table and pulled herself to her feet to begin taking tentative steps on her own, we cheered and celebrated. The day Colleen did likewise, both of us frowned. Her left foot didn't go down flat on the floor; she walked on tiptoe. As well, she carried her left arm pulled in close to her body at right angles, which made her gait awkward and clumsy. Around the same time her left eye began showing signs of being "lazy": wandering off on its own instead of coordinating with the movements of the right eye. Back to the doctor we went!

This time she got a much more thorough examination. The clinic we go to is the University of Calgary Medical Centre (then called the "Ambulatory Care Centre") affiliated with Foothills Hospital. Its advantage to patients is that it is a training centre for residents wishing to pursue Family Practice—so a resident-in-training will often do the first check-over and then a teaching supervisor is called in if anything warrants it. For Colleen, the teaching supervisor was called in.

"What I suspect," he told us carefully, "is some minor brain damage. It's so minor you can hardly call it brain damage: just a tiny area I could indicate on a brain diagram with a pencil point. Technically, she's got 'a touch of cerebral palsy'. I don't mean that to sound flippant but really, it won't seriously affect her life. That term conjures up visions of crippled hemiplegics or quadriplegics, but this is nothing like that. I'm going to refer her to a specialist at the Children's Hospital. The foot can be corrected and so can the eye, probably when she's a little older. She seems a normally bright, active child. If I had to guess, I'd say the level of disability we're talking here is maybe coming in last at the sports-day sprint event."

So reassuring were his words that the crushing phrase "cerebral palsy" was only a mild punch in the stomach. At that very time I had a quadriplegic student in my high-school French class who, despite his stammering speech, was bright, sociable, and well accepted by his peers. Peter's level of disability was far more serious than the description being applied to our Colleen. It meant the problem was minimal, practically non-existent.

The Alberta's Children's Hospital specialist readily confirmed this. Colleen was three when she saw him, and by then she was talking a mile a minute and showing no signs of stammering. She told him his ears looked like Mr Spock's on *Star Trek*. Right away they were laughing together like old buddies. He got her to identify some pictures he showed her and to solve some simple puzzles. All the tasks he gave her to do she did quickly and correctly. She was not just normally bright, he told us; she was *extremely* bright. "Take her away and bring me a child with a *real* problem," he joked.

Heartened by this news, we lost our fears. The eye seemed to be straightening of its own accord anyway and the heel cord in the left leg, given a minor surgical nick to make it thinner, stretched enough to allow her left foot to go down almost flat against the floor. Another minor surgery on the underside of the foot flattened the sole further, and a third surgery later, to insert a stabilizing screw into the left big toe, completed the effect. Throughout her recovery from each surgery she screamed endlessly, but recover she did. She still carried her left arm in close against her body, but that too wasn't as noticeable as she got older. By age five, she and Lisa had developed a large repertoire of interactive sisterly games that showed her to have a fertile imagination and reasonably satisfactory motor skills. So when Lisa piped up one day, "Mummy, Colleen is weird," I just giggled and assured her all big sisters think their little sisters are weird.

How, at that time, was I to recognize that my older daughter's comment was the portent of something far graver lurking in Colleen's future?

15

2. "Colleen is a Brat"

I have memories of Lisa at age four begging to be allowed to push the infant Colleen in the stroller and proudly chanting as she pushed, "I've got a little sister." I have memories (and photos) of Lisa carefully sitting down on our carpeted living-room floor and stretching out her arms, ready to hold and cuddle her baby sister.

And those memories, rife with fond nostalgia, are punctuated by the infant Colleen's piercing and constant screams.

I have no doubt today that she screamed because she was in neurological distress. Though medicine has made gigantic strides, there's still so much we have left to learn about the human brain. Andy and I had been told by the experts that the damage was insignificant and I no longer believe that. Whether related to the pencil-point "touch of cerebral palsy" or not, something else much larger was amiss inside Colleen's brain.

Not that I hold the experts to blame in any way. I think they did all they could. Just to confirm there were no tumours or masses they tried a CT scan (or CAT scan as it was still called then) of her brain when she was three but had to abort the procedure. She was exceptionally resistant to sedation and they couldn't safely give her enough to keep her still. My presence at her side and my efforts to soothe and coax her to keep still had no effect at all; she screamed and thrashed until the technician gave up and said, "It's no use. We'll have to try again when she's a bit older." Two years later, when she was five, I *was* able to cajole her into lying still and the results showed everything to be fine. A CT scan, however, only presents part of the picture. And MRI (Magnetic Resonance Imaging) or PET (Positron Emission Tomography) scans were still new enough back then not to be readily available. Even if they *had* been available, they would have been deemed unnecessary. And by the time they *were* available, Colleen was old enough that we were no longer in a position to insist.

Besides, her early childhood history, peppered with incidents of rebellion and defiance, still contains some very humorous and endearing stuff. Frenetically active, she always seemed to want to do a dozen things at once, as though she couldn't absorb her world fast enough. As she was learning to talk she jabbered—unlike Lisa, whose pronunciation was always precise and meticulous. Once, at the Calgary Zoo, I pointed out to Colleen some pink flamingos, enunciating the word "flamingo" for her as clearly as I could. Lisa, as a baby, had had trouble with that word and had not been satisfied until she'd mastered every syllable. Colleen simply blurted "flingo" and ran on to the next animal enclosure. Close enough was okay by her.

She was a rugged individualist, unafraid to stand up for her own rights. One day Lisa was out at the tennis courts in the park behind our house practicing some hits. Lisa's ball was suddenly seized and carried off by a dog belonging to a nearby couple. Our distressed older daughter came home crying and the fearless Colleen went right to her rescue. "EXCUSE ME, BUT…," she cried out at the top of her voice, "your dog has my sister's ball! She needs it back!" Charmed by such directness in one so young, the couple grinned and remedied the situation pronto. And they weren't the only ones charmed.

Contrary to many young children, Colleen never had the slightest fear of talking to strangers. Restaurants—though their bustle and noise sometimes irritated and upset her—were a favourite venue for her to demonstrate that lack of fear. One evening we were at Denny's with the girls for supper and Colleen spotted a man sitting directly behind her eating an enormous chocolate sundae. She turned around in her chair, gave a dimply smile and cooed, "*Hi*, nice man!" Andy and I nearly split our sides. In every aspect of her demeanour she was a miniature Mae West! The man was as charmed as we and laughingly offered to share. Needless to say, we were persuaded to buy her a sundae of her own.

Lisa was as shy with strangers as Colleen was bold. In restaurants she would hesitate to ask for ketchup or butter, and usually wanted either us or Colleen to ask in her behalf. Dispensing with such niceties as waiting for the correct waitress to come by Colleen would simply bellow, "EXCUSE ME, BUT…" at the nearest available server. It became her tag line: she was affectionately dubbed "Little Miss EXCUSE-ME-BUT".

Yet even as we admired her brashness, we felt vague stirrings of unease. Ralph, a colleague of mine, was going through a painful divorce from his wife Sue. One summer evening, Andy and I put steaks on the barbeque and invited him over. "Be gentle with poor Ralph," I told the girls. "And don't mention Sue at all. We just want him to enjoy himself and forget his troubles for a few hours." Lisa, ever sensitive to the feelings of others, wouldn't have dreamed of mentioning Sue. Little Miss EXCUSE-ME-BUT was a whole other story.

Scarcely had Ralph arrived and been poured a glass of wine before she clambered up onto the back deck clasping in a clammy fist several wild flowers she'd picked from the field behind our back fence. "Here," she said with that winsome grin, offering them to Ralph. "I call these *Sues*!" Appalled, I gagged on my own wine. But Ralph, to his credit, didn't miss a beat. Grinning back, he accepted the flowers, praising how pretty they were. Colleen looked distinctly disappointed.

On another occasion I had just finished washing and polishing the kitchen floor. Normally Colleen was moderately good about remembering to take off her outdoor shoes when entering the house but that day she stamped straight in, leaving muddy tracks all over the clean linoleum.

Scolding her and sending her back to remove the shoes, I had the niggling feeling she'd gone out and jumped in as many mud puddles as possible with the express intention of undermining my efforts.

"She's a real character," claimed the lady who ran the day care centre she went to during our work days. "When she wants a particular toy she doesn't believe in waiting her turn. Today she hit another kid over the head and just took it. That smile of hers is cute as the dickens, though. It's almost hard to discipline her."

I shook my head. "She doesn't learn such behaviour at home. I hope you *do* discipline her. We can't have her assuming that's acceptable."

"Oh, she knows full well it's not acceptable. Sometimes I think that's why she does it! And yes, she always gets a stern talking-to. As long as we discourage it here and you discourage it at home, she's bound to grow out of it."

We *did* discourage it at home, without success. While part of me rationalized that an assertive personality would stand her in good stead in this world, another part of me couldn't help feeling this was more than just assertiveness. Colleen was a bully. When she wanted something it had to happen and it had to happen *now*. If it didn't she screamed and flailed until it did. Sometimes she hit out at whoever was nearest or pounded the floor with her fists. Granted, instant gratification is a normal desire in young children but by the time she was three I could already see that most other children handled delayed gratification far better than she.

At three she had a leg cast for a few weeks following the heel-cord surgery. Twice while recovering at the Alberta Children's Hospital she kicked out at nurses with that cast, hitting one in the face when the poor lady bent over her bed and asked, "How are you feeling, sweetie?" Flooded with embarrassment I apologized. "She's just insecure," the nurse assured me. "She needs a good cuddle."

Yet cuddling was something else Colleen reacted to in a surprisingly unpredictable manner. Cuddling was never a cure for her distress. When we took her into our laps and held her, she would often push us away with vehemence and want to get down immediately. Or she would snuggle right in and hold on as though in danger of drowning. No happy medium seemed to exist; it was the one extreme or the other. As a baby, Lisa too had preferred snuggling at certain times and exploring at others; that in itself was not what baffled me. It was the *vehemence* that baffled me, the life-or-death, all-or-nothing attitude that Colleen seemed to have about everything.

"Me and Michael," she told me intensely (if ungrammatically) one day at age five, "are going to *wreck* the day care centre. They have a stamp. We're going to steal the stamp and use it all over the walls!"

"Bad idea," I responded and dismissed her claim. I shouldn't have. That afternoon when I picked her up on my way back from teaching my own classes, her supervisor said Colleen had had to spend "time out" standing in a corner as punishment for defacing public property. "Michael was just as guilty," the supervisor added. "He stood in another corner. I'll be speaking to *his* mother as well. We may have to charge you for some repair to the walls." The stamp was indelible.

As it turned out no issue was ever made about charging us. I confess to minimizing the incident in my own mind: two impish kids had committed a harmless prank. They should have been watched more carefully, shouldn't they?

Briefly, the mother of two of Lisa's schoolmates accepted the job of minding Colleen during the day in her own home but complained Colleen was far too demanding and quite destructive if she didn't get her way. By then the second surgery had been done on the underside of Colleen's foot and she again had a walking cast. The mother claimed Colleen kicked out in abandon with that cast, marking up walls, furniture, whatever was in her way. The mother herself was once kicked in the face (that again!) while putting a screaming Colleen down for a nap in the master bedroom. As well as refusing to nap, Colleen blew her nose copiously into the bed-sheets and pillows, requiring the mother to change the bed and launder all the bedding. Shortly thereafter this beleaguered woman tendered her resignation.

"Colleen is a *brat*!" Lisa used to declare angrily. "Why don't you *do* something?" At the time, I placated her by saying the bratty behaviour wouldn't last, particularly once Colleen started school. Given more inter-action and diversion to stimulate her bright mind, Colleen was bound to settle down, I felt, and stop causing such problems. I'm sure Lisa didn't believe me but I was equally sure at the time that I spoke the truth. School would be a godsend to a child like Colleen and she would no doubt excel there and find her niche very quickly.

I couldn't have been more wrong.

3. "Nobody's Idea of fun"

W̲e lived in the southeast Calgary community of Deer Run, an area predominantly populated by middle- to upper-middle-class working people with school-age children. Calgary, at that time, was undergoing a typical urban-sprawl issue that still prevails: the springing up of new young-family housing at its extremities and the simultaneous stagnation or decline of older established neighbourhoods located closer to the downtown core. Schools in those older neighbourhoods stood half empty while schools in the younger neighbourhoods bulged at the seams. Transporting some students by bus from these younger neighbourhoods to the half-empty schools was the logical solution. Deer Run's closest such school was in the community of Fairview.

We didn't want Colleen to be bussed to Fairview School, mainly because Deer Run Elementary was located just the other side of the green space behind our house and you could see its playground area from our back window. As a student there, she'd be able to walk to school and back once she was older. She would also develop friendships with the local kids and so have playmates that lived on our street or on streets nearby. So Andy got up at four-thirty in the morning on the registration day for her kindergarten year and went to stand in line at the door of Deer Run Elementary. It was "first come, first served", and we didn't want to take chances. To our great relief (at the time) she got in.

Lisa, at four years older, was attending elementary school in Queensland where we'd had our "starter home" before moving to Deer Run. Queensland is very close to Deer Run, and it made sense to leave Lisa in the school where she already felt secure and comfortable, rather than trying to get her transferred to the same school as her sister. In later years, we were to congratulate ourselves heartily on that decision.

Almost at once, Colleen's kindergarten days rendered her a standout in ways the rather prim and self-conscious Lisa would have found mortifying. Her clumsy gait had the other kids asking questions which she answered (according to her teacher) with obtuse and grimly over-dramatised references to her cerebral palsy. Not surprisingly the other kids shied away, the sole exception being her co-conspirator Michael, of daycare wall-stamping fame. Michael was the one who laughed the loudest and gave her the most reinforcement—again according to the teacher—on the occasion of her sabotaging their reading time.

"It was *deliberate* sabotage," the teacher related with a grin. "Colleen is very cute and very bright. She's probably headed for great things one day but right now she's a challenge in the classroom."

The sabotage story went like this: the teacher had seated the children in a circle on the floor around her own chair and had begun to read to them from a brightly illustrated storybook, showing her audience the pictures as she read. Colleen and Michael instantly engaged in a game of elbowing each other and causing a distraction. Shushing them and then separating them the teacher warned, "That's enough. We don't make noise in this room during reading time. It's a *rule*." The word "rule" was all Colleen had to hear. From the day she'd fallen out of the shopping cart because she stood up the moment I cautioned her to stay seated, she'd hated rules of any kind. She rose and made a prompt exit to the adjoining bathroom where she right away launched into a raucous song at the top of her lungs. Quite shocked, the teacher left the other children and went over to the bathroom. "Did you not hear what I just said?" she pointedly asked Colleen.

"Sure," Colleen replied, waving a hand towards the classroom. "You said we don't make noise in *that* room during reading time. *This* is another room."

I fully admit the story sent me into fits of mirth. What an amaz-ing—and amusing—child I have, I reflected with pride. I bet she'll be a lawyer someday! There aren't many kindergarten kids who would have thought up an argument like that. When I told Andy about it that evening, his reaction was the same. "We better start putting aside money for law school," he kidded. "She's very young to have such a legalistic mind. Maybe she'll be the next Clarence Darrow."

The only member of our family who didn't laugh was Lisa. I think it offended her moral sensibilities of what appropriate classroom behaviour should be. Lisa knew that she herself would *never* have defied a teacher in such a way; her awe of teachers persisted throughout her elementary school years and she was unable to understand why Colleen didn't have the same awe. What Andy and I saw as endearing spunk, Lisa viewed as further proof of a judgment she'd made in the past and still stood by: Colleen was a brat.

Perhaps even then, the child's unclouded eyes had seen things far more clearly than had the doting unwary eyes of the adults. Still without sufficient vocabulary to explain more precisely what she meant, Lisa had been trying for some time to tell us (and this became crystal clear to me in hindsight) that Colleen's actions weren't merely innocent and cute; they were *calculated*. From pre-school days Lisa had sensed that, and it had disturbed her profoundly.

Meanwhile, Andy and I clung to our naiveté. The next incident, which involved a telephone call in the middle of my last-period class from Colleen's after-school care centre, still amused me initially. Colleen, the supervisor told me, had swallowed a Lite-Brite peg and it was caught in her throat. They were taking her to Rockyview Hospital and I should meet them there.

Lite-Brite, as many will remember, is a child's game consisting of a backlit board into which various coloured pegs made of transparent plastic can be inserted to build multi-hued artistic creations. Colleen had recently asked me why the game was not recommended for very young children and I had replied, "Because they might swallow the pegs." The rest of that conversation had gone something like this:

"What would happen if they swallowed the pegs, Mom?"

"They'd probably have to be taken to hospital."

"Can the hospital people get the pegs out?"

"Yes, but it could be very dangerous if a peg got caught in a child's throat."

"Couldn't you swallow and swallow until the peg went into your tummy and then you'd just poop it out?"

"Maybe (*laughter*), but one can't predict what might happen. Plastic is very bad for you, and spending time in the hospital is certainly nobody's idea of fun."

The irony of that final statement hit me like the proverbial ton of bricks as I arrived at the designated floor and wing in Rockyview shortly after that conversation and watched my daughter perform in a squeaking rasp before an audience of several staff, including the attending doctor. Pointing at her throat, she nodded and smiled when asked if she still felt the article stuck there. Far from this being nobody's idea of fun, she was having a blast.

"I think you ought to know," the after-school care supervisor whispered, "that the children say Colleen *planned* this whole thing. She told them she was bored and wanted to see what it would be like to spend the afternoon at the hospital."

"Must be lodged in the vocal cords," concluded the doctor. "We'll have to go down into the throat and get it out of there." Hardly had he finished speaking before Colleen swallowed a couple of times and announced, "There. It's gone. It's in my tummy." She looked as though she were about to explode with mirth at a huge joke no one else understood. Indeed an X-ray showed the peg to be in the stomach now and therefore presenting no further cause for worry. The doctor's last words just before discharging her echoed those of Colleen herself a few days earlier: "She'll just poop it out."

Though Andy and I shared a laugh about the whole thing that evening, we agreed that life would definitely get a lot less tense for us once Colleen grew up a little. She was so bright she'd be bound to realize the potential dangers both of bucking the system and of indulging in high-risk behaviour. It would be only a matter of time, we were sure, before she settled right down, took the bit between her teeth, and began to shine as the remarkable person we could see she was. With pleasant anticipation we looked forward to that day.

Not until she was observed some time later walking around on the roof of our house did we begin to suspect that pleasant anticipation would soon give way to nothing less intense than dread.

4. "There has been an Accident"

The separation of Colleen and Michael after her kindergarten year was a wise move nobody would have disputed. Yet as time went on, it became apparent the two still saw each other at school and reinforced one another's rebellions at every opportunity. Almost wistfully Colleen would relate stories of the latest trouble Michael was in and the amount of time he spent at the Principal's office. That she admired and looked up to Michael was evident.

Simultaneously, another Michael of celebrity status began to enter her preoccupations. Michael Jackson's stage presence, mannerisms, and general over-the-top demeanour made him a favourite with Colleen, who spent hundreds of hours listening to his music while rhythmically rocking back and forth. Her love of Michael Jackson renders her identical to numerous fans of that era; her reaction to that love makes her very different. She started asking me pointed questions about her father's health—questions that boiled down to how long her dad might reasonably be expected to live! Andy had recently been diagnosed with Crohn's disease and had undergone a very successful bowel re-section procedure. Colleen seemed almost disappointed that the surgery had yielded such satisfactory results.

I believe now that, even then, she had started to learn how to mask her true feelings and her exceptional brightness made her very good at it. Her enquiries after her dad's condition I originally chose to interpret as a sign of care and concern over his well-being. Yet a part of me warned, from those earliest times, that I was kidding myself. Furthermore, the day arrived when I was confronted, whether I liked it or not, with a truer picture. In Lisa's presence Colleen piped up, "Mom, do you think maybe, if Dad dies, you could marry *Michael Jackson?*"

After a pang of initial shock, I smiled. There went my utterly charming child, acting the comedian again. She sure could keep us in stitches, that one, with her whacky wisecracks. Lisa, as usual, was not amused in the slightest—and there is certainly nothing wrong with Lisa's sense of humour! Again in retrospect, I think the question was appalling to my elder daughter's moral sensibilities. When I smiled, Colleen cackled with laughter, as though we two shared some *entre-nous* joke. Lisa merely glared. She saw my dismissiveness as an act of compounding Colleen's crime.

"Loosen up, Lisa," I ribbed more than once. "Where's your funny bone?" It did not for a moment occur to me that the skew might not be in Lisa's perception but in mine.

Elementary school was a tumultuous period for Colleen. Gordon Hunter, her Assistant Principal of those days, assures me she spent as much time in his office as did any of the troublemaking crowd. "In grade four she told me how much she enjoyed reading Edgar Allen Poe," Gordon relates. "It threw me for a loop, I'll admit. That a girl of nine could make head or tail of such advanced reading material as Poe was only part of my astonishment. The main part was her obsession with the darkness of Poe's subject matter. I never met a child as fascinated by evil and death."

Colleen's grade four teacher, Mary Ann Metcalf, concurred. "When she's not belching aloud and making other rude noises in class, she delights in telling stories in gruesome detail as well as in writing poetry that is in, uh, questionable taste. Like *this*, for example, which I intercepted yesterday." Grimacing, she unfolded a piece of lined notepaper and thrust it in front of us as she set the scenario. "One of the boys, I gather, whispered something off-colour about coming up with a definition for the word 'sex'. This was Colleen's creation."

Casting our eyes downward at the maligned paper, Andy and I read:

> *He has a dink, you have a tush.*
>
> *Put 'em together and push, push, push!*

As always during my daughter's early childhood, I was instantly overcome by a sense of how funny this was. "Not only does it rhyme but it *scans*," I giggled at Mrs Metcalf, unable to take seriously the direness in her tone. Like Lisa, though, the primary-school teacher refused to lighten up. Colleen had major problems, she continued to insist, and we, her parents, had better start addressing them.

It was not until Colleen's after-school care supervisor greeted me a few days later with a grave expression that I first experienced a twinge of genuine fear—only a twinge, mind you. I mean I'd been through this before with the wall-stamping business, right? No doubt my mischievous daughter had merely pulled some other childish prank. *What now?* I sighed to myself, reflecting on a tiring workday spent dealing with older kids' childish pranks and wistfully envisioning myself at home in a comfy armchair.

"Please have a seat in here." The supervisor indicated a small office. When I entered, she carefully closed the door. Evidently this was more serious than running amok with a stamp. I found that my hands had suddenly turned sweaty and cold at the same time.

She picked up some sheets of newsprint. The top one, I could see, was a childish drawing of a cozy-looking house with a smoking chimney. She held it toward me so that I was able to read the scrawl below it: *This is where I live with my mom and stepdad.* The second one was of two sticklike figures in skirts standing amid some grass and holding onto brightly-coloured flower bouquets: *Mummy and I are picking flowers in the garden.* In the third a man and a small boy stood together by a stream, each equipped with rod and reel: *My dad takes me fishing in the summer.*

"We asked the children to draw something they enjoy and then write us a brief explanation of their drawings," the supervisor related. "They like that. It's a fun activity for them. Most of the stuff we get back is like what I've just showed you. *None* of what we get back is anything like what Colleen drew." She took a deep breath. "I'm no expert, Mrs Porter, but I thought I ought to call you in here in private and show you her drawing."

It was not in the pile with the others but by itself in a folder on the desk. She removed it and handed it to me. What I saw made me feel as though I'd just had the wind knocked out of me.

Two cars had collided in the picture. They must have been going at great speed because, with a number of squiggly lines, Colleen had mashed them together so that the one was hardly distinguishable from the other. On the ground, in a sea of red crayon, prone figures assumed oddly twisted shapes.

The caption read: *There has been an accident. It's a bad crash and bodies are lying all over the road. There is blood everywhere.*

5. Not Normal

I consider myself to be reasonably well-informed on certain subjects. In Colleen's childhood mental illness was not one of those subjects. Vaguely I remembered reading somewhere that it ran in families. I could think of no one in my family who'd been talked about as mentally ill, and Andy could think of no one in his family either. Surely Colleen was just delightfully odd. We persisted in believing her eccentricities would disappear with time.

Besides, I took motherly pride in Colleen's high intelligence and her advanced reading level. What inspired the accident picture must simply have been her current Poe preoccupation. Her pert brashness I regarded as a cute, loveable quirk. The terms *normal* and *average*—synonymous with *boring*, I sometimes reflected—didn't even remotely apply to my younger daughter; nor did I want them to. *Exceptional* was a term that inspired fascination, and *exceptional* is what Colleen was.

On the other hand, though, I couldn't help comparing her reading choices with those of our elder daughter. No slouch herself when it came to reading, Lisa's preferences of youth ran the gamut from such material as Shel Silverstein's *The Giving Tree* to C.S. Lewis's *The Chronicles of Narnia* and Tolkien's *Lord of the Rings*. Charmed by the whimsical world of Dr Seuss and unashamed of how babyish it might seem to others, she even subscribed to a book club and purchased a series that included such kiddie classics as *The Cat in the Hat*, and *Green Eggs and Ham*. To this day, I believe, she keeps these and other treasures from her childhood on their own special bookshelf in her home.

For a time Colleen too was entertained by these but she soon outgrew her satisfaction with the kind of adventure they portrayed. She particularly embraced Poe, but also Stephen King, Anne Rice, Dean Koontz, and anybody else who majored in the creepy tale with the bizarre, unresolved, and/or super-grisly ending. Her tastes in TV and movies ran the same way; she revelled in the soap-opera hyperbole of *Days of Our Lives* as well as flicks like *Jaws*, *The Chain-Saw Massacre*, *The Amityville Horror* and *Nightmare on Elm Street*. Why did we allow our child, who had not yet even reached junior high, to watch that stuff? We didn't. She found ways to do it behind our backs, often cutting school in the process.

A few streets over lived a thin, pale-faced neighbour I will call Sandra.

Reclusive and not inclined to mingle with others, Sandra developed a friendship with Colleen based on their common love of the fare I describe above. Colleen would leave school, go home for lunch, and then make her way over to Sandra's place for the rest of the afternoon. Sandra was a single parent of young children and Sandra's TV was always on. She would put her kids down for their afternoon nap and then she and Colleen would settle in to watch either *Days of Our Lives* or one of the many videos she regularly rented. While they watched, they talked.

Right away of course, Colleen's truancy was brought to our attention. When we questioned her, Colleen was evasive at first but then told us about Sandra. Sandra and I had a meeting at Sandra's front door. "A lot of life sucks," was Sandra's reaction to my enquiries. "Colleen and I both realize that. I'm giving her someplace she can go when things get her down. She knows she can always hang out with me." It was not at all the exchange to settle a concerned mother's anxieties.

"During the school day, *school* is where she should be," I pointed out.

"But she has problems at school," Sandra objected. "I know what that's like."

"She won't overcome her school problems by not facing them," I persisted. "I'm not here to debate you; I'm here to let you know Colleen is using you as a hidey-hole, and I'm also here, as her mother, to ask you to please stop encouraging her truancy by letting her come into your house during the school day."

Sandra nodded in a non-committal manner. "Okay." Her verbal concession was unconvincing; a blinding flash of enlightenment brought me the realization that their friendship was a symbiotic one. In their co-dependence, they reinforced one another's sour take on the world. More than ever this made the bond an undesirable one. Yet I hesitated to flat-out request Sandra to end it when I knew Colleen had few friends and no other close ones.

The necessity to do so happened the day Sandra admitted to giving Colleen one of her Valium pills on an occasion when Colleen was feeling especially low. Evidently Colleen had gone over there with a box of chocolates (a gift I'd bought for a teaching colleague, the disappearance of which I'd attributed to my own carelessness) and had eaten those while watching a *Days* episode and saying, "School blows. I hate my teacher and I hate the other kids." Sandra tried to soothe her and one of the techniques Sandra herself always resorted to was Valium.

"It was just to mellow her out a bit," was the protest. "It won't do her any harm." I believe Sandra meant well and was honestly trying to help, but of course I couldn't allow the friendship to continue after that admission. In fact, as any mother would have, I bristled.

"How *dare* you give my daughter drugs!" A heat-wave of anger surged through me. "If you ever see my daughter again I'll press charges!" Needless to say, poor Sandra swore she was done and conceded she may have stepped over the line. (*May* have...!) But sadly, the world is full of Sandras if one wants to find them. And Colleen wanted to find them.

My putting the kibosh on the Sandra liaison caused predictable havoc. "You just know Sandra's a better mother than you are," Colleen stormed. "I *hate* you. I wish you would *die*!" She continued to rant and call me all sorts of other names but it was those two sentences that stung like salt on a fresh wound—sentences I never in a million years would have dreamed of uttering to my own mother or of hearing from my bright and beautiful baby. How had things come to this point and why?

I guess when you have children, you automatically expect their growing-up process to replicate—at least in part—that of your own childhood. Yes, there are ups-and-downs: teachers and schoolmates you wish you didn't have to deal with, your best friend in the world suddenly moving away, sly intimations of fun you're missing out on that beckon and intrigue, yet are too shady and scary ever to pursue. (You see what I mean about my being the quintessential nerd?) But at the end of every day, you know you can go back to a loving home where you are accepted, cherished and adored no matter what. That's how I had been lucky enough to grow up. Mum and Dad were bricks, always there for me and for my brother Brian. And subconsciously, that's how I had assumed things would be when I had a family of my own.

Not that I didn't empathize with my darling Colleen's troubles. My heart bled for her and the difficulties she had finding acceptance at school even though those difficulties often seemed to be of her own making, as though she intentionally went out of her way to be dislikeable to other kids. And I was very sorry about the Sandra relationship not being a more positive one (though not at all sorry I'd demanded Sandra end it) because everyone needs a soft place to fall. Maybe I even harboured some jealousy of Sandra, since *I* would have liked to be that soft place for my daughter.

In an effort to make it up to Colleen and to try to improve our relationship, I decided I would suggest she come with me every Thursday evening to church choir practice: a mother-daughter bonding activity. We attended Deer Park United Church in our own community of Deer Run and I loved singing in the choir there. Not only does music itself always raise my spirits, I find that people who enjoy singing are usually upbeat, energetic and happy. If I could get Colleen mingling with them, her general outlook on life was bound to improve. Besides, at choir she would readily see the difference between individuals like my choir mates and individuals like Sandra.

It was a short-lived experiment. Colleen was unfailingly reluctant to go, and when she got there she regaled anyone who would listen with how awful her life was. Of course kindness and sympathy toward her abounded, as did practical strategies on how she might work towards making things better for herself. But it was never enough for Colleen, and she took none of the strategies seriously. In fact upon returning home from practice, she would frequently disparage and ridicule the very people who had offered them.

The end came one Thursday evening as I was cooking supper right before setting off. Andy had just arrived home from work. Colleen had been on the phone with someone and she suddenly announced she needed "a drive over to a friend's place, *now*". "What friend?" I asked, getting no answer. "Choir is tonight," I said next, "and I'm in the middle of preparing dinner."

Colleen went into one of her worst tantrums thus far. She stamped her feet, pounded her fists against the kitchen cabinets, screamed and blubbered indistinguishable oaths of rage. Raising my voice above hers (which was certainly not the best way to handle it) I yelled, "Scream all you want; it won't do you any good! I'm making supper, then I'm going to choir—and you're coming with me!"

Colleen picked up a plate off the counter and threw it. I believe she was aiming at my head, but it missed and smashed to smithereens against one of the kitchen cabinets. Still ranting, she flounced up the stairs to her bedroom. Me, I collapsed into tears and began picking shards of broken plate off the counters and floor. Ever supportive, Andy helped me clean up and tried unsuccessfully to talk Colleen into coming down to eat with the rest of the family. Lisa, Andy and I ate a strained meal as a threesome, then Lisa retreated to her own bedroom while I approached Colleen's door with trepidation and knocked.

Loud eerie music issued from within—so loud I wasn't sure she heard my knock. I tried again without success, so I twisted the knob and entered. Colleen lay on her bed, rocking frenziedly back and forth to the music. Forcing calmness into my voice, I turned down the volume. "Colleen, I'm on my way to choir. How about you get yourself ready, and let's go."

She stopped rocking and glared into my face. With a cold fury that raised the hairs on the back of my neck she spat, "I hope you have a bad car accident on the way there and end up in hospital! And I won't come to visit you there because I *hate* you!" Horrified, I felt tears welling anew. Then suddenly, Lisa's arms came around me from behind and she was crying too.

"Colleen, what an awful thing to say!" Poor Lisa hugged me and sobbed, not knowing how else to help. Andy took over then, speaking sternly to Colleen, comforting Lisa, and encouraging me to alleviate my misery by going off to do some singing. There isn't a day when I don't count my wonderful husband amongst the true blessings in my life. Though I had little enthusiasm for it right then, I *did* follow his advice and it *did* help. Whether I had the right to do so or not, I escaped.

I recount this episode because the night Colleen's choir participation ended also marked the figurative removal—for good—of those rose-coloured glasses I'd so adamantly worn up to this point regarding my younger daughter's oh-so-charming refusal to be boringly average. That night, for the first time, I could no longer delude myself. The difference in makeup and temperament between the two girls finally slapped me across the face, forcing into my consciousness this distinctly horrible thought:

Our elder daughter is normal. Our younger daughter is not *normal.*

6. The 'I-Don't-Get-It' Syndrome

I recently read somewhere that one in five Canadians has some form of mental illness. That sounds very high to me, but friends and colleagues with psychology backgrounds confirm its accuracy.

Maybe even after shedding my rose-coloured glasses, I was still in some form of denial because, despite the number of troubled high-school kids I've taught over the years, I theorized that *all* teens are a little crazy and most eventually grow out of it. I still believe that to be true—for most. But possibly more of them than I realize *never* completely grow out of it and must struggle on a daily basis to cope with issues about which the majority of us never think twice.

One of those issues involves the ability to read body language. There is a part of our brain that understands and responds to subliminal "vibes"; hence, when we go for a job interview (for example), we can "read" quite clearly how positively, indifferently, or negatively we are being received by the interviewer. We leave the interview with a fair idea of what our chances are of being hired, or at least short-listed. Furthermore, we know instinctively by the interviewer's subtle gestures (an un-crossing of the legs, a shifting in the chair, perhaps a slight rising motion) when it is time for the exchange to end. What we call a "sixth sense" is something most of us take for granted—something we expect others to possess, just as they expect *us* to possess it.

That certain individuals have it far more strongly than others is something I know from experience. We call them the *sensitive* people. But suppose a person is born with that part of the brain not functioning at all? That person would have no ability to respond to anything except overt oral cues. That person would have to be bluntly told: "The interview is over. I'm finished with you. Now go away." Colleen was, I believe, such a person.

Sensitive people find non-sensitive people extremely irritating, which is something else I know from experience. As a classroom teacher I've overheard snide conversations between "normal" kids about those who just "don't get it". And, in the teacher's role, I've found myself annoyed at times by particular students on whom my looks or postures of disapproval are wasted. Those students "don't get it" unless I actually interrupt the lesson and say to them in so many words, "*Please* stop tapping on your desk with that pen while I'm talking!" Colleen was, I'm sure, such a student.

Given that this supposition is correct (and I can't positively know that on account of Colleen's rejection, even when it became available, of any medical or psychological help), her problems at school with both teachers and peers were entirely predictable. Deprived of the normal coping equipment most of us have—and aren't even consciously *aware* we have—she was definitely at a disadvantage.

When she was about eleven, I remember taking her to the doctor for some minor infection and sitting with her in the office waiting room. Amongst the magazines on the table, she found a joke book which she began reading aloud. I chuckled quietly at the punch lines and several other patients in the vicinity began to smile. But one middle-aged lady with hunched shoulders and a ravaged expression *didn't* smile. She held a wad of tissues in one hand and kept wiping at her eyes.

Eventually a nurse came out of one of the back rooms, sat down beside this lady and murmured softly to her. Tuned in to the changed aura of the room and respectful both of the lady's mood and of the private nature of the nurse's murmurings, the smilers instantly stopped smiling and buried their noses back in their own reading material. I remember wondering why the nurse didn't take the lady out of the waiting room to talk to her, but that was none of my business. What *was* my business was the reaction to the situation—or I should say the *non*-reaction—of my daughter.

Colleen was completely oblivious to the alteration in the room's atmosphere. Puzzled at why she no longer had an appreciative audience, she went right on reading the joke book. In fact, in an attempt to re-hook her listeners, her voice got louder and louder. Ultimately, I had to bring to her attention, in a whisper, what was going on. Only then did she subside—sulking—into silent reading, like everyone else.

Lack of ability to detect vibes is a definite hindrance to making friends. Adults are more apt to be tolerant of this disability in someone than are peers; and indeed, Colleen always had far more adult friends while growing up than friends her own age. I think most adults are experienced enough in life to have been in a few I-don't-get-it situations themselves; therefore, they empathize with someone like Colleen where peers simply can't. Many of *our* adult friends, Andy's and mine, have long tried to be good friends to Colleen and for that we will be eternally grateful. But there was another side to this I-don't-get-it coin that made it difficult for anyone to tolerate her for long.

Her brain's unawareness of sensitivity to others seemed to go hand-in-hand with an abnormally heightened sensitivity of self. Real or imagined, her own needs were always paramount in her eyes and were always urgent. Our trip to Disneyland with the girls in the summer of 1984 provides a graphic example.

In 1984 Colleen was six and Lisa ten. Both were ecstatic about the trip and it especially warmed our hearts to see Colleen looking forward to something. Ever needy by day, she was by then undergoing what the doctors termed "night terrors" and would frequently wake screaming in the middle of the night, rousing the rest of the household with her. Some children have these, we were assured at the time, and she would most likely outgrow them. In Disneyland we saw a pronounced increase in both the neediness and the terrors.

First, Colleen was unable to cope (and I've mentioned this before) with any type of delayed gratification. All children get tired of standing in long line-ups for rides and crying youngsters are, of course, a common enough occurrence in places like Disneyland. But let's face it: the staff there is expert at crowd management and does a marvellous job of moving lines along and of entertaining waiting people. Colleen, we noticed, was only very briefly consolable at the best of times. If Goofy or Pluto was actually shaking *her* hand or hugging *her*, she was temporarily diverted. But when Goofy and Pluto moved on and her needs were no longer directly met, she immediately began to fuss again about everything: the heat, the noise, some horrible smell, wanting a snack someone else had, another kid staring at her, and on and on. When she wasn't ranting about external annoyances she'd say she didn't feel well: her arm hurt, or her leg, or her stomach. If we, or the rest of the world, weren't paying her constant attention, she was dissatisfied and ill-tempered.

I remember wondering to myself even then whether Colleen's sense of discomfort and emotional upset was more vivid than that of "normal" people. Certainly I'd read articles about the heightened senses of autism sufferers, read that mundane attempts to divert autistic children might succeed only briefly and more stimulating diversions—like Disneyland rides—might be almost too intense for them to bear. Colleen had a few enjoyable experiences during that holiday but on the whole she spent it either fussing about her aches and pains or alternately laughing hysterically and sobbing with fear when she went on the rides. On one particular ride featuring animated dinosaurs she persuaded herself they were real and wanted to leap from the car that carried us. When we forcibly restrained her, she screamed incessantly until the ride was done. Histrionics? Originally, we put it down to that.

Colleen's "I-don't-get-it" syndrome, coupled with her "it's-all-about-me" syndrome were actually identifiable symptoms that Andy and I—and a good part of the psychiatric world of those days—either knew too little about to recognize for what they were, or were reluctant to diagnose in a child. As her parents, we suspected she might be emotionally delayed in some way. But look how bright she was! Such a bright person was bound to learn, sooner or later, to "pull herself together".

Today, despite a total lack of hard evidence detailing Colleen's specific brain structure, I know differently.

7. Harried Holidays

If there's one impression I *don't* want to give in this book, it's that I regret not having pitied and pandered to Colleen more than I did. I don't regret that at all. I still believe that pitying her and pandering to her would not have helped her in the slightest. But there are ways I *could* have tried to help her, had I only known about them. More of that later.

People with major handicaps such as deafness and blindness can and do make it in this demanding world of ours—as, indeed, do people with various forms of mental impairments. So I told myself. What about Helen Keller? Keller was both deaf *and* blind and yet, once she mastered sign language, went on to lead a productive and distinguished life. Whatever mild impairment our daughter might have, she—with our encouragement—would undoubtedly make it as well, perhaps even with a distinction equivalent to Keller's.

Andy and I both sympathized with the struggle Colleen seemed to be having with her emotions. *We* were neither deaf nor blind, and because we'd always coped with life fairly competently, we knew that people like us can have no real idea what it must be like to live life hampered by impairment. Nevertheless, we told ourselves, Colleen's reasoning processes were working just fine. She ought to know better than to behave the way she did. No doubt she *did* know better. We just had to keep reminding her of that.

The phrase "you ought to know better" is a guilt trip, pure and simple. Parents *intend* it to be a guilt trip. On the average kid, it has the desired effect; it induces shame and the determination to improve next time. On Lisa it always had that effect. On me, as a child, it always had that effect. On Colleen—to my tremendous astonishment—it had, if anything, the *opposite* effect.

In the last chapter, I spoke of our first holiday to Disneyland. That chapter has spawned, almost of its own accord, the title for this one: a chapter unto itself about vacations spent with Colleen. Deserting chronology for the moment, I'm opting to describe just how tense our supposedly relaxing times were when in her constant company for any length of time. *Harried* is the adjective that best applies.

Both of us worked hard at our respective careers and knew that "R and R", when we took it, was well deserved. Andy, as a geologist, rode the wave of the eighties oil-industry boom; I, as a teacher, had a steady, reliable income. So we were well enough off to be able to show our children some of the rest of the world and the opportunity to do so was a delightful prospect.

Three years after Disneyland, we did a two-week Hawaiian holiday to the islands of Oahu and Maui. During our week in Oahu, we made one morning excursion up the Diamondhead volcano. The trail was not excessively steep; it was a tourist's, not a hiker's trail. Children Colleen's age and younger happily tramped along with their parents, enjoying the crisp morning air. Many children, in fact, were far more energetic and enthusiastic climbers than were the adults.

Colleen was the exception. She had stubbornly refused to wear runners, claiming another flimsier pair of her shoes was more comfortable. I'm sure they were hurting her feet, though she refused to admit it. "You ought to have known better than to think those shoes would be suitable for walking," I remember saying to her. My remark had the effect of a fuse setting off a firework.

From that point until the end of the climb she ranted and railed nonstop: it was too hot; it was too steep; she was dizzy; she felt faint; her legs were so sore there was no way she'd make it back down. Once we'd reached the top, gloried in the view out over Oahu and the other islands, and purchased a bottle each of pop from an enterprising local with a stand up there, she subsided into more sullen misery. Declaring the effort hadn't been worth it just for a view, she adopted an irritating "I-told-you-so" attitude about how well she had coped with the climb! Andy and I shook our heads and sighed. I mean, she was still only nine and had a lot of growing up left to do. Kids will be kids.

To say we often found Colleen an embarrassment and an irritation on holidays is understating it. When she made a scene, other parents glared at us as if in condemnation of our ineptitude at parenting 101. More than once, people made suggestions about approaches we should take that would yield better results for both her and us. How frequently those with easier-to-handle children tend to assume that this is exclusively to their own credit and thus count themselves authorities on the way it should be done! Colleen, though, was our beloved daughter whose constant distress was *our* constant distress, and in those days we were ready to listen to anyone and try anything.

Shortly after the Diamondhead excursion, we flew to Maui and stayed at a rental condo in Kihei. One morning, we took the kids snorkelling off the island of Molokini. We were on a hired boat with several other passengers and, before donning masks and flippers to hit the water, we were given a talk on the underwater life we would see. Small whitetip or blacktip reef sharks, the skipper said, were fairly common in these waters and were harmless to humans, so don't panic if one appears. On that day the ocean was crystal-clear, and what all of us *did* see was an abundance of fascinating marine life with a couple of reef sharks off in the distance. In those days they were still allowing people to feed the fish, and awareness of our food brought the reef sharks in a little closer. Everyone else stayed focussed on the colourful yellow tang, parrotfish, raccoon butterfly-fish, and other such fascinating species swimming all around us. Colleen focussed on the reef sharks.

We put it down to histrionics again, rather than true panic. She'd heard the skipper's talk and she was anything but stupid. For several minutes she floated face down, breathing through her hose and watching fish calmly enough; then she started screaming. The boat crew was instantly concerned, then annoyed. She received a lecture about "crying wolf" without cause. "You're old enough to know better," reproved the skipper. His words escalated Colleen's mood, evoking temper and scorn as she continued to insist unrepentantly, as she had about the dinosaurs in Disneyland, that the sharks were "real".

Easter 1988 found us in Mazatlan Mexico during the kids' and my school break. Immersed for the first time in a very different culture, both our girls were fascinated by street markets displaying whole animal carcasses skinned and fly-ridden, intrigued by cobbled streets where mangy and emaciated half-wild dogs foraged for discarded scraps, and moved to tears by the sight of ragged shoeless beggars (some of them children) loudly clamouring for alms. Lisa, a shy fourteen-year-old, was understandably reticent about becoming part of this scene in any more than an observer's capacity; Colleen, a precocious ten-year-old, threw herself into it with gusto. She wanted to see the skinned carcasses close up, pet the mangy dogs, and talk to the entreating beggars. She was a consummate haggler over prices, better than any of the rest of us. And—in a world not subject to the same liquor laws as ours—she also turned out to be a consummate tequila consumer.

Andy and I have often referred to ourselves as "cheap drunks". It doesn't take much alcohol to make either of us lightheaded. I have a higher tolerance than he, but neither one of us has ever been more than a glass-of-wine-with supper or a couple-of-Spanish-coffees-with-a-friend type of drinker. In our Mazatlan hotel in 1988, tequila flowed as freely as hospitality, so we sometimes even had *two* with the evening meal. We probably had two each on one festive evening when the hotel hosted a buffet style piñata party for its guests.

At that party, a generously-laced tequila cocktail in a large punchbowl occupied one end of the buffet table. The local hooch was inexpensive, so guests were free to serve themselves and the staff kept re-filling the bowl. Lisa, with no objection from us, tried a sip, made a face, and opted for pop. (I don't doubt Lisa has had a few too many once or twice during her university life, but today she professes herself to be the same cheap drunk as her parents!) Colleen, as usual, was a whole other story.

Almost immediately she ladled a liberal amount into a glass, drank it all down at once, and began to help herself to more. We intervened. "Colleen, you know better than that," Andy warned. "You've had quite enough." Responding with a pasted-on grin, Colleen returned to our table, only to slip back later—on the pretext of needing to use the bathroom—to slurp on the sly. Suddenly, she was very drunk and flirting with one of the waiters. Though only ten, she had already begun to develop breasts and a woman's figure, so I'm sure the waiter thought she was much older. "Come, *querida*," he smiled, putting an arm around her shoulders and twirling her onto the dance floor. In my naiveté I said to Andy, "Well, at least she's having a good time for once. Let's just hope she isn't sick as a dog tonight." Despite what she had consumed, she wasn't. That in itself should have sounded an alarm bell inside my head.

By the summer of that same year, Colleen's body and her "party girl" personality had developed further. We had a short vacation in Clearwater Florida where we visited Disney World. No vestige of childish wonder remained now; her attitude was prevalently scorn and boredom, except toward the thrill-seeker type rides which simultaneously lured and terrified her. When we opted to stop at an exhibit documenting the lives of the U.S. presidents and she objected, I again trotted out the "you-know-better-than-to-act-this-way" speech. Instead of stepping down the complaining, she stepped it *up*, loudly jeering to all around us, "Oh, goody! A *President!* A *President!* OH, GOODY!" (Lisa, too, had the teenager's detached aloofness, but Lisa would rather have died than create the kind of embarrassing public scenes Colleen delighted in.) It was on that same holiday that, after talking flirtatiously to some southerners, Colleen suddenly and surprisingly adopted an exaggerated Dixie accent, claiming not to know the rest of us at all.

At this stage Andy and I still nursed the expectation that someday the grownup Colleen would look back on all this and wonder, *"What was I thinking?"* We adored the colourful character our daughter was and, in the interim, we steeled ourselves to put up with a certain amount of public humiliation.

A year later, when we made our second Hawaii trip to the Big Island, she was only lukewarm about coming, and she took very little interest in the active lava flows all over the place. Geological history was literally being made under her feet and she wanted nothing to do with it. Truth to tell, the aloof teenage Lisa wasn't crazy about it either, proclaiming at one point, "It's hot here and it stinks. Let's go." But Lisa got enthused about other things during that holiday (like shave ices, acquiring a tan to show off, and buying T-shirts for all her friends). The only real interest I remember from Colleen was at the Hulihee Palace on the Kona coast, where—after being warned by Andy that she "should know better"—she demonstratively and repeatedly lifted the grass skirts of various statues on a quest for cement genitalia.

In the summer of 1990, we did a more modest holiday at Pinehurst Lodge in northern Ontario. At twelve Colleen was now blatantly interested in the opposite sex and she attached herself to a boy of about the same age while denying, as she had at Disney World, any connection with us. Still the stubborn optimists, we made light of it when we watched them both in the distance, the boy pointing at us and obviously asking if we were her parents and Colleen vigorously shaking her head. Well, we joked, she was now on the brink of those teen years. What could one expect?

Our last vacation of any self-delusion at all was another one at Kihei, Maui. It was Easter of 1991. This time Colleen wasn't even lukewarm about coming. She claimed to have renewed her friendship with Sandra, whether we liked it or not. (Sandra denied this and we had no way of ascertaining who was telling the truth and who was lying.) We were the meanest parents alive for making her leave Sandra; she adored Sandra and *hated* us. We told her she should be grateful for our taking her to such nice places—thereby guaranteeing us a huge scene all the way to the airport, complete with incessant sobbing and ranting. Throughout the holiday she sulked. The only time she perked up at all was on the flight home, when she informed us nastily that it was because we were headed back to Sandra.

Finally, I cannot close this chapter without mentioning the seasonal holidays. Except during her youngest years, Christmas, New Year's and Easter were a dreaded trial with Colleen. Usually we got together with our dear friends Grant and Dorothy Dawson and their two sons Shawn and Scott. Andy and I have known the Dawsons since university days when we were all single and belonged to the Ryerson United Church Young Adults Group in Hamilton Ontario where we grew up. Grant became a minister and, shortly into his career, assumed a pastoral charge at Knox United Church in Calgary. Dorothy became a nurse and, like me with my teaching, was able to find job opportunities wherever she and her husband chose to live. Predictably, Andy and I located in Calgary due to Andy's involvement in the oil industry. So we were delighted to hear of Grant's acceptance of the post at Knox that brought them to the same city as we.

Dorothy is an outstanding cook and she'd regularly have Christmas turkey dinner at their place; then I'd have New Year's Day dinner at ours—or vice-versa. As a toddler Colleen enjoyed playing at the Dawsons', although—like any parents of a very active child—we had to keep careful watch on where she went and what she did. As an older youngster she'd try to join the conversation, often blurting out inappropriate things which we all thought priceless. As an adolescent she'd either vie for attention at the dinner table by recounting exploits involving rebellious escapades or she'd fall asleep and dip her forehead in the gravy or spill her coffee all over her lap.

If conversation shifted to a topic that didn't interest her she'd ask to use the phone to call up "friends" and then chat for hours—sometimes loudly, sometimes in a whisper—while ignoring the rest of us. (I have said Colleen could never maintain friendships; yet she was unfailingly good at charming people upon first acquaintance, and it is to these I refer when I mention her "friends".) Sometimes, to our chagrin, she'd ask those "friends" to come and pick her up so she could leave and go out on the town with them! My telling her this was very rude and she ought to know better never stopped her from doing it. I think it *increased* her tendency to do it.

As an adult in her own apartment but unable to afford a car, she'd sometimes get "friends" to drop her off, either at the Dawsons' or at our place, for Christmas, New Year's, or Easter dinner. Upon arrival she'd want the meal right away and would sigh or turn sulky if it wasn't ready. Then she'd telephone other "friends" and chat with them while ignoring us, until such time as she could liberally help herself to the eats. The moment she'd had her fill, she'd promptly ask me or her dad to drive her elsewhere, expecting us to drop everything and leave our guests in order to comply with her wishes. The extent of her nerve never ceased to amaze us.

In all fairness, I can't leave out the one occasion on which she decided to have us all over to *her* place for Christmas turkey dinner. She had just moved to a charming little townhouse in High River, south of Okotoks, and Andy and I were pleased that she seemed proud of her new abode and eager to show it off. She assured us *she* would buy and cook the turkey, so we gave her precise instructions on how to go about it. We also offered to bring along various veggie side dishes. Lisa brought a cheesy potato dish and Dorothy contributed a delicious pie for dessert.

That is one of the few times I remember Colleen being gracious and hospitable to all. What a lovely person she could be when gracious and hospitable was the attitude she chose to portray! Her dad and I made sure we called to thank her afterwards for putting on such a thoroughly enjoyable Christmas celebration.

"It was a whole lot more work than I thought it would be," she replied disgustedly. "It'll be a cold day in hell before I ever do *that* again!"

8. "Company, Villainous Company..."

With the reader's permission I resume chronology, returning to Colleen's turbulent formative years. Falstaff's claim in *Henry IV Part I* about villainous company being the spoil of him is one I was often inclined to make about our pre-pubescent younger daughter. I guess many mothers rationalize that way; they want to blame their child's errant conduct on external influences and temptations. But then some children are not at all subject to those influences and temptations while others cave at the least instigation. And of course there's everything in between. That has to be due to something basic about the coping mechanism one inherits.

Colleen's pre-pubescence was accompanied by a significant weight gain. Quite intentionally she overate. More than the normal pre-teen she eschewed the healthy foods and wanted only the junk-type snacks. When we took her to a weight clinic run by Alberta Children's Hospital she accompanied us defiantly to the sessions, wouldn't participate in the exercises, and sneaked candy packages into her pockets that she noisily dug out, opened, and chewed while the instructor talked about healthy eating. The instructor told her, "If you aren't serious about this, then don't come." She replied, "This sucks. It was my parents' idea, not mine." Ultimately we gave up taking her to the weight clinic. Getting her to go became such an energy-draining fight, for little or no return, that nothing productive was being achieved.

Yet back then, we still saw glimmers of an incipient kindness to her nature that struggled to emerge. When a teaching colleague of mine, Ed Bagyinka, informed us his wife Lorraine was very ill in hospital, Andy, Lisa and I went to visit, bearing a card and a basket of fruit. Colleen came with us bringing "Good-Luck Bunny", one of her stuffed toys. What she said at Lorraine's bedside moved me to tears.

"Here." She thrust Bunny into Lorraine's arms. "I had him when *I* was in the hospital and he helped *me* to get better. I thought maybe he could do the same for you." As moved as I, Lorraine thanked her profoundly—at which point Colleen instantly morphed into the comedian clown we all knew. "Besides," she added, "he's the only one of my stuffed animals that isn't too mangled to give to anybody." (Lorraine was diagnosed with lupus, put on medication, and soon felt much better. I like to think non-mangled Bunny, and Colleen's kindness, had something to do with it!)

On another occasion that same kindness was directed at *me*. Colleen overheard my kitchen conversation with Andy one morning about some teaching problems weighing upon me. Next thing I knew she appeared in the doorway clutching a furry monkey (one of her *mangled* stuffed toys) with a hand-scrawled sign hung around his neck. *When you're feeling tired and sad*, the sign said, *just hug me*. The sign has long since disintegrated but I have that monkey to this day. He is one of the treasures I'll never give up while I am still in this life.

I realize I'll never give him up because he represents a side of my younger daughter that I saw more and more rarely as time went on. At the weight clinic she rejected not only the rules but any social contact (the *other* reason for the clinic) with the rest of the overweight pre-teens there who were sincerely trying to overcome their problems. The opportunity to form bonds, share input on how to deal with cruel teasing at school, and simply *make friends* she spurned outright. "I don't want anything to do with those losers," she jeered. "They're all freaks."

Instead she attached herself first to "Sandra"—until I put an end to that—and then to a girl I will call "Twyla" who lived around the corner. Twyla was Colleen's own age which pleased us until we discovered Twyla led a largely unsupervised life. Colleen would go over there to play and return with tales that Twyla's mother was a slut who'd run out on Twyla and the dad, and that the dad was a drunk with a bad temper. Here's where my "villainous company" rationalizations come into play: that poor girl, I told Andy—much as I pitied her—was a negative influence on our Colleen. Colleen might be going through a difficult phase right now, but Twyla was obviously headed down the same thorny path as her mother. Neighbourhood scuttlebutt had it that, at twelve, the girl was already sexually promiscuous and would sleep with much older men for money. The same scuttlebutt proclaimed (seemingly verified by police cars at the house several times) that the girl had regularly been caught shoplifting. I felt we had to try and steer Colleen toward other better-quality friendships.

"Why don't you hang out with Allison instead?" I suggested. Allison lived right across the street and was a sweet, rather shy girl whose parents were both teachers. "You used to play with Allison when you were little. Maybe the two of you could re-connect."

"She's a goody two-shoes just like Lisa." Colleen's voice dripped with scorn. She'd picked up that expression from me when very young and had often applied it to her older sister. If Colleen now placed Allison in the same lower-form-of-life category where she placed Lisa, then in her eyes Allison was a write-off.

Back in happier childhood times Allison had sometimes come over to play. She and Colleen would go downstairs to the family room, and the sounds issuing from there seemed to spell fun. When I'd check on them, they'd be immersed in giggle-punctuated girlish whispering. But then Allison came over less and less and finally ceased coming altogether. Lisa, not at all a snitch unless perceiving something grave that might warrant it, informed us Colleen played cruelly with timid girls like Allison and had once bragged of shutting Allison in a large homemade toy chest we kept downstairs and then sitting down on the lid to prevent the poor terrified girl from escaping—only letting her out after Allison *begged*. How had we not known this before? And what had Allison gone home and reported to her mother of the incident?

When we asked Colleen about it she denied the whole thing and accused Lisa of making it up. She also said—which almost distracted us from our original angst—that she and Twyla were on the outs now and she hated Twyla. They weren't going to see each other any more. One of the reasons she gave for her so-called hatred was that, as well as being a slut, Twyla smoked—something she, Colleen, would never dream of doing.

It was that year (her grade 6 year) that Colleen had the third surgery on her weak leg: a screw was inserted into the left big toe to strengthen it. Temporarily she couldn't see Twyla anyway because she was in the hospital. She also had a legitimate reason for not attending school, which suited her just fine. The day she was released from hospital she threw a terrible tantrum and said she wanted to stay there. When we got her home, she lay down on the couch demanding to be waited on hand and foot. She had a headache; she was in too much pain to walk (although she didn't seem to have any trouble when she needed to use the bathroom) and she was sure she wouldn't be able to return to school for quite a while. The surgeon, on the other hand, told us she could walk on the cast in just a couple of days as well as resume her normal activities.

So for a couple of days we were lenient about letting her be an invalid. But then we began to urge her to follow the doctor's advice. It was obvious to us she wasn't sick: her appetite was robust as ever and, when she didn't think we were watching, she got around just fine on the walking cast. Braced for a huge fuss, we told her she'd missed enough school and it was time to go back. She didn't disappoint us in the fuss category: going back was impossible, she screamed, trotting out a whole litany of symptoms to justify still being an invalid. What we were beginning to realize is that Colleen *liked* being an invalid; it was one of her favourite roles. It made people sorry for her and it gave her an excuse for opting out of the world.

Still, we stuck to our guns and dropped her off on the following Monday at her "Before-and-After-School-Care" Centre. They had their own shuttle-bus into which they loaded all the school-age kids to give them supervised transportation to Deer Run Elementary. They would ensure she got there. Alas, there was nothing whatever they could do about ensuring she *stayed* there once she arrived.

As I've mentioned before, we could see the playground of Deer Run Elementary across the green space from our back yard. When, in her kindergarten year, Andy had got up at the obscene hour of four-thirty and waited in line to enrol her there, we'd thought it would be a *good* thing for Colleen to go to school in her own neighbourhood. Now, it became a distinct disadvantage. If she'd been a bus student at Fairview, Colleen wouldn't have been able simply to leave and walk home. At Deer Run Elementary, she could and did.

Lisa's best friend Kristin, a lovely girl who lived a short way down our street, remembers catching movement on our roof one afternoon as she herself was heading home from school. To her amazement and concern, she realized it was Colleen up there, stumping around in the walking cast and seemingly oblivious to the danger of falling. Colleen had climbed out the master-bedroom window after removing its screen.

Naturally, Kristin reported this to Lisa and Lisa told us. When we questioned Colleen about it, she originally accused both Lisa and Kristin of being liars and just trying to get her in trouble; then, when other neighbours reported seeing it as well, she admitted she'd taken off the screen to let more air into the house and the *cat* had jumped out onto the roof. So she'd had no choice but to go out onto the roof herself to save the cat. What was she doing at home playing with the cat during school hours? She'd felt unwell, she claimed, and had come home to rest. But she felt better now; it wouldn't happen again.

Of course only a fool would have believed such a story. (I think Lisa spent much of her teenagery convinced we *were* fools and wondering why we didn't have a better handle on Colleen's deviousness. I also think Lisa was conflicted herself: as Colleen's big sister, she was often torn between "ratting" to us and the urge to protect her younger sibling from our disapproval.) Andy and I never bought the fresh-air argument as Colleen's reason for removing the screen. And we strongly suspected what the *real* reason was.

"It's that Twyla," I said to my husband. "We know she's a smoker. I'll bet she's got Colleen smoking now too." By then Twyla and Colleen had made up their initial tiff and both of us had noticed a couple of times that Colleen smelled of cigarette smoke.

"The more we advise her against being friends with Twyla, the more she'll gravitate to the girl," Andy said. "And if her best friend is a smoker, of course *she* smells of cigarette smoke as well. So there's no proof that the smell isn't just from Twyla's second-hand smoke."

No, there was no proof. And Colleen, at that age, was canny enough to know it. Asked point-blank if she too had become a smoker, she stared straight back into our eyes and stormed, "I *told* you I hate it that Twyla smokes. You just don't trust me about anything!" So well did she lie that she actually made a person feel guilty for not believing her.

Freda Nagy, Principal of Deer Run Elementary at the time, described in colourful terms both her canniness and her brightness when we, as concerned parents, went to the school to discuss her lack of attendance. "'She'll invent any number of creative reasons for needing to leave the classroom," Freda related. "And then she doesn't return. She's unhappy because she's bright, has a large vocabulary, and also has a way of making herself incomprehensible to her peers." With a laugh the Principal added, "The other day she was here in my office telling me she had as much right to an extension on an assignment deadline as did a learning-disabled girl in the same class. Colleen said the term "integration" means including the girl with the rest of the group and treating her just like the rest of the group; therefore the same rules on assignment deadlines ought to apply to the rest of the group as to the girl. I was stymied. I honestly didn't know what to respond. I mean, she was right, wasn't she? That's amazing reasoning *and* arguing ability for a student in grade six! Someday, at the university level, Colleen will stand out as the brilliant person she is. Maybe she's even headed for a career as a celebrated courtroom lawyer."

Andy and I thanked her, went home and had a good talk with Colleen about what Mrs. Nagy had said. We emphasized, as she had, that becoming that lawyer—or becoming anything successful—was contingent upon at least a basic level of school attendance. Colleen agreed with us and blithely continued to skip school.

Our rule for both our daughters while they were growing up was that they weren't to have anyone else in the house when we weren't home. Under ideal circumstances (that is, when they were at *school* during school hours) there was very little time they were in the house without supervision; *their* school hours were *my* school hours. However, Colleen flouted all the rules: she came home whenever she felt like it during the school day. And she brought Twyla with her.

We didn't immediately discover what they were up to because, as I've pointed out, our alcohol consumption is sporadic at best. But one evening when Andy and I had friends over and offered them something from the liquor cabinet, we both noticed that the levels in two or three of the bottles seemed lower than they had been.

"It's that Twyla," I grumped again. And so it was, no doubt. But it wasn't *just* Twyla and maybe it wasn't even *mainly* Twyla. Confronted about it, Colleen threw her customary tantrum and said it must be Lisa because she, Colleen, knew nothing. We were always blaming *her* for the things Lisa did. When we told her she was grounded as punishment she said, "That won't do any good; I'll just sneak out as soon as you're not looking!" When we forbade her to have Twyla in the house ever again she just snorted with disdain. No question she intended to ignore us.

Another neighbourhood girl named Tracy (who moved away before Colleen reached grade six) told us Colleen had talked her into stealing some ripe tomatoes from the deck of a house down the street. Again, Colleen stoutly insisted the plan was all Tracy's idea and said she hated Tracy anyway because Tracy was always trying to get people into trouble.

Villainous company..? I had no choice but to revise my original contention. The truth was becoming increasingly apparent. When it came to nefarious schemes, Colleen was instigator far more often than follower.

Once so impishly cute, our precious daughter was not the one being spoiled by villainous company. She *was* the villainous company.

9. I Hate You! Don't Leave Me!

When I first conceived the title for this chapter, I was completely unaware that a *book* by that name already exists—a book written by Jerold J. Kreisman, M.D. and Hal Straus (a respected writer about health issues). I have since read the book, and I'm sure these gentlemen won't mind that my chapter and their book share a title. If anything, the content of my chapter clearly reinforces some of what they describe in their book.

In Colleen's case, two separate incidents of this profoundly puzzling behaviour—professing to hate us, yet seemingly terrified we were abandoning her—stand out clearly in my mind. The first took place one or two years before the second, but both belong in this chapter.

Marking Alberta grade-twelve English diploma exams was something I had done almost from the start of my teaching career. It happened at the end of each semester, in January and July. Teachers hired to do this job travelled to Edmonton where they were put up in hotels for a few days while they marked together in a downtown government annex building. When the girls were young, Andy typically drove with them up to Edmonton during the July marking, and the three would join me in my hotel room for a weekend. The girls loved it. During the day they got to swim in the hotel pool and go with their dad to Storyland Valley Zoo and in the evening they got to have a restaurant supper with both of us.

Colleen was thoroughly familiar with the routine of my marking sessions in Edmonton. She knew I flew between Edmonton and Calgary on the "Air Bus", and she knew I stayed away no longer than a few days. But the first incident I refer to involves one particular occasion when, instead of sharing a taxi to the airport and a flight to Edmonton with colleagues, Andy—with the girls in the car—drove me to the airport to see me off.

Colleen was an unwilling passenger on that ride. She complained about everything, including how she'd rather be with Sandra or Twyla than going to the stupid airport. When I told her to stop whining she rudely responded, "One good thing about this trip is we'll be getting rid of *you*." That brought on a threat from Andy that another such crack would mean she wouldn't get the treat she'd been promised while we awaited the plane.

The rest of the way she was sullen and taciturn. At the airport she ordered a large slice of blueberry pie and wolfed it down. When departure time for my plane approached, she, along with her dad and sister, came with me to the security gate. Andy and Lisa gave me a good-bye hug and kiss each.

And that was when Colleen suddenly threw her arms about my shoulders, clinging as though her very life depended upon it. "Don't go!" she screamed. "Something bad will happen! Don't go! Don't go!"

As inured to these public scenes as we were getting to be, Andy, Lisa, and I found this most upsetting. Forcibly detaching her arms, Andy gestured at me to proceed through the gate. I did so, feeling the familiar lump of unshed tears in my throat. That evening when I called home from my hotel room, Andy reassured me she'd settled down in bed at last after vomiting her blueberry pie. "I'm still washing blueberry-stained sheets," he said cheerfully. "But at least the histrionics are over."

Bless him! A man with less backbone and more selfishness might have flown the coop by that time. Andy never had the slightest inclination to cut and run. His devotion to our family has always been unwavering.

The second incident, every bit as extreme as the first, occurred when Andy left for a week to attend a geological conference in Hamilton, Ontario. He combined the trip with a visit to his widowed mother. This time the roles were reversed: *I* was the one who stayed behind with the girls and *I* was the one who did the driving to and from the airport.

Lisa was over at a friend's house and did not accompany us that time. By herself in the back seat of the car, Colleen grumbled all the way there, as before. The previous evening when she'd taken too large a helping at supper, her dad had made her put some back, and I think she was still annoyed with him about that. But she was even more annoyed with him for going on this trip, seeming to regard it as a personal desertion.

"Dad will be back in a week," I assured her as we stood at the security gate giving him farewell hugs and kisses. Andy added, "Be good while I'm gone." She clung to him hard for a moment and I feared a repetition of the scene we'd had when I'd left for Edmonton. To my relief it didn't happen—not right then. Instead she suddenly pushed away from him and said to me, "Okay, let's go."

We'd left the airport and were in the middle of heavy traffic on Deerfoot Trail before she began the screaming. "Turn the car around *right now!*" she yelled. "Go back to the airport! We have to stop Dad's plane! It's going to crash!"

I took a deep breath and forced myself to stay calm—though what she'd said made my heart hammer. "Colleen, I *can't* turn the car around right now," I told her. "Don't you see the traffic is bumper-to-bumper? You're feeling some separation anxiety, that's all. That feeling will go away soon and you'll be fine. Just try to relax." I later congratulated myself because I believe my reaction—or lack thereof—*did* help her to get through the panic attack on that occasion. I shall never know for sure. However, I drove all the way home talking softly to myself with a sobbing, screaming child in the front seat beside me paying no visible attention at all to what I said. And that night she woke several times with her "night terrors", which both Lisa and I did our best to allay.

The thing that almost reduced me to hysterical laughter by the next morning is that Colleen seemed to have snapped out of her anxiety as abruptly as she had succumbed to it on the previous day. "Why," she asked me at breakfast, "did you make such a big deal yesterday with all that lecturing on the way home from the airport?" I nearly choked on my orange juice.

It was hard to stem my irritation when she made such remarks—and just as hard, when we went to meet Andy's incoming flight at the end of that week, to avoid becoming irked by her insistence that I was waiting in the wrong area of the airport. Ignoring my protests, she approached a uniformed security person whom she engaged in conversation before returning to me and loudly declaring, "See, Mom? I *told* you we were in the right place."

"Where did we *get* her?" Andy wondered that evening when I recounted these incidents to him. "It's like she belongs to some alien world whose language we don't speak and can't learn."

He was far closer to the truth than either of us then realized.

10. "Tormented Motherhood"

The day Colleen announced her intent to get into the flyer delivery business in her spare time I dared to hope that gainful employment might be our younger daughter's way to salvation. For one thing, she'd be too busy to contemplate villainy, fears of abandonment, or self-centredness. For another, delivering flyers involved plenty of walking, which would contribute to her emotional well-being as well as helping her shed those extra pounds.

Colleen did not approach her father or me for permission to take on the job; she simply presented the concept as a *fait accompli*. A few days prior she had struck up a conversation with the local flyer lady and this lady had promised to stop by and have a chat with us.

True to her word, the lady rang our doorbell a short time later. A cheerful moon-faced soul of ample proportions whom we'd frequently seen going door-to-door in the neighbourhood, she outlined a plan that sounded ideal.

"First she'll fill out the required application form and then one or both of you will sign saying you approve of her doing this. I'll sign the part where I agree to supervise her. She'll report directly to me and I'll be her contact if she has any problems. Provided you're okay with this, I'm quite prepared to help her get started. I see in her a little bit of myself when I was a kid; she's having a few growing pains, the way I did. But I'm fine now and she will be too."

What a sweet lady! I don't remember her name but I made a point of thanking her. We were touched by her kindness and willingness to give a leg up to someone she viewed as worth helping.

"Having my own spending money and knowing I had earned it fair and square did my self-image the world of good," she declared. "And that helped me out at school too. I ended up not feeling such a misfit there." She gave a disarming shrug, a pert grin lighting her moon features. "Guess I still love to eat, so I still weigh more than I should. But even my weight isn't the issue it once was."

Naturally we gave wholehearted permission. Colleen was, after all, showing a certain entrepreneurial streak in wanting to tackle this. Maybe it was in the world of business enterprise that she would excel. Who were we to stand in her way?

The first bundle of flyers appeared in our driveway a few days after this conversation. They appeared there and they stayed there. "Aren't you planning on delivering these?" we asked Colleen. "You said you wanted to do this." "I'll get to it," she said. A second bundle appeared, then a third. When she finally *did* get to it she didn't deliver to more than a few nearby houses before calling her dad and announcing she wasn't feeling well. She'd do the rest when she felt better. For now she needed a ride home.

Of course her dad went to get her. The line about not feeling well works every time on parents; Colleen learned early of its effectiveness as a blackmail tactic. She knew we could never be sure whether or not she was lying, and that was good enough for her. She next decided that if we could just deliver *this* load for her she'd be okay to deliver the next load herself.

Andy and I were in adamant agreement that rescuing her—tempting as it might be—would be doing her no favours in the long run. "You created this situation by procrastinating and you're the one who needs to get yourself out of it," I told her.

She responded with one of her usual tirades: I was an awful mother and she hated me. This time she ranted on further: if it weren't for me, her life would be just fine. Dad was a nice person and she knew *he* would have helped her if *I* hadn't talked him out of it. Several months ago she'd made the same statement when the girls had asked us if they could have a tank of pet goldfish. Andy had replied, "Maybe. We'll see." *I* had replied, "Keep your bedrooms tidier and *then* we'll talk about goldfish." At that time Colleen had accused me of dissuading Dad from ever letting them have any fun; this time she dredged up the fish incident once again as proof of how mean I was.

I wish I could say I always remained calm in the face of such conflict but if I said that I'd be lying. Colleen brought out the fiery side to my nature that I get from my own mother (whom I adored). When she railed against me and cursed me I would try to remain composed despite hurt and anger but all too often I lost my temper and lashed back. Once, having just read an article about how girls these days are more rebellious and less responsible than boys, I said something I've berated myself for ever since: "They say girls your age are sassy and hard to control. If you'd been a boy, maybe you wouldn't be giving us this trouble!" About the flyers I shouted, "You think it's *our* problem you can't get it together? If you're looking for someone to blame, look in the mirror!"

Andy, my gallant husband, is the one who remained calm. Because of that Colleen regarded him as a wimp, totally subjugated by me. I believe she realized differently as time went on—as did Scout in *To Kill a Mockingbird*—and eventually came to admire her father a great deal. English teacher that I am, I could certainly sum Andy up by calling him the Atticus Finch of fatherhood: quiet and peace-loving, yet a courageous force to be reckoned with when it comes to standing up for his principles and beliefs. If there was one thing Colleen *did* learn, no matter how she chose to perceive it, it is that we were always a united front. Her efforts to play one off against the other never met with any success.

When she saw no possibility of our bailing her out, she turned to other kids in the neighbourhood. Next thing we knew, Allison, Twyla, and several more were sorting through the flyer bundles. So…she was *delegating!* In the business world that's a common enough practice. Could she pull it off? We hoped so. But our hopes were soon dashed. A few got delivered because Colleen had promised to pay the kids but the task was already far too enormous to be completed in one, or even two, out-ings. When payment wasn't forthcoming the kids quit. Colleen and Twyla put their heads together and suddenly some of the remaining bundles disappeared. We knew the flyer-delivery fairy hadn't whisked them to their assigned destinations.

"The company makes calls to households to confirm delivery," the supervisor lady informed us. "I'm thinking Colleen didn't realize she'd be checked up on because she, or whoever was helping her, has been dumping whole piles of flyers in back alleys. That won't do of course." I'm sure the lady was on the point of firing her but Colleen announced she was quitting anyway. She refused to do any more deliveries; it was too strenuous. The following day, a truck came by to retrieve the remaining bundles.

Sadly, Colleen blamed everyone but herself for the back-alley dumping caper. It had been Twyla's idea and the other kids went along with it like sheep. Andy pointed out that the job belonged neither to Twyla nor to the other kids; *Colleen's* was the responsibility to ensure the flyers were delivered. "If you hadn't quit they would have let you go," he told her. "And you would have deserved it."

"I hate the job anyway—*and* that stupid lady with her stupid rules," was the defiant response. With those words, she dismissed flyer delivery from her life.

Despite her hostility I made repeated attempts to have mother-daughter talks with Colleen. Sometimes I felt we were moving towards some kind of tentative truce; other times our exchanges ended only in mutual frustration. Her school attendance at Deer Run Elementary was still a big problem, as was her acceptance amongst her peers. Attempts to resolve these issues never met with more than temporary success.

Briefly she joined the local Brownies troop run by neighbour Beryl ("Dots") Peppar, whose classmate daughter Samantha ("Sam") tried hard to be Colleen's friend. But Brownie troops too have their rules. Furthermore, Dots told me on the phone, Colleen was openly scornful of many of the planned activities. On one fall outing to look at leaves in Fish Creek Park (a beautiful provincial park of some three-thousand acres that we are lucky enough to have—almost literally—in our own back yard) she kept shouting sarcastically, "Leaves. Oh, goody. OH GOODY!" It was a repeat of the Disney World experience at the Presidents' pavilion. "Sam and I love Colleen and her individuality," smiled gentle Dots, "but I don't think she really wants to be a Brownie."

"I *hate* Brownies," was Colleen's pronouncement on the subject. "I'm not going any more." (We had already bought the uniform and various other not inexpensive accoutrements.) Thus she dismissed Brownies from her life as summarily as she'd dismissed flyer delivery.

For a while—again at some expense—we tried giving her private piano lessons. She liked the piano and enjoyed composing her own tunes so the *idea* of formal lessons appealed to her. The reality did not. Once she realized the lessons themselves involved both rules and regular practice, her enthusiasm vanished.

"I'm going to work at a dog grooming place instead," she announced. "The piano teacher says if I quit I can't come back because others are waiting for the spot. Good! I've quit." The owner of the dog grooming facility tried out Colleen exactly once and then let her go. Colleen had intimated she possessed some experience at washing and grooming dogs; her lie became evident the moment she arrived to start the job.

A request for horseback riding lessons came next, and in that we saw a healthy (if expensive!) pastime with the potential to teach her discipline, coordination, and respect for working in partnership with animals. On and off for about three years, from ages twelve to fifteen, she went to the lessons and got to know and love the horses. Good friend and expert horsewoman Jill Stephenson invited her to ride on the Stephenson farm, just south of Okotoks where I taught, and offered to spend time giving her pointers. We, her parents, had a semi-effective carrot we could use to get her to attend school, and she, in her own right, experienced success at honing a new skill.

Success, though, seemed something that a perverse part of Colleen's psychological makeup was determined to undermine whenever it threatened to come her way. The moment she won a few ribbons in a jumping class, she would cut school and incur the penalty of having to miss a lesson, or she'd get into some disagreement with another rider, profess her hatred of that person, and say she wasn't going to go any more. As a bribery tool horse lessons worked for us intermittently but by no means consistently.

Getting her involved with the church Youth Group was another ploy on our part to encourage her to mingle with nicer kids amongst her peers. "But she just didn't fit in," says Paul Isaak, the Youth Group leader of those days. "She didn't seem to *want* to fit in. And she was always after Scott, the other leader."

Scott was a number of years older than Colleen and she developed a crush on him every bit as intense as the one she'd once had on Michael Jackson. Worried that the fixation was unhealthy, Paul spoke to us about it and we asked the advice of Rev. Linda Hunter.

As I've mentioned Linda is an "above-and-beyond-the-call-of-duty" person if there ever was one. Her husband Gordon, Colleen's Assistant Principal at the time, is the same. That they are *both* United Church ministers today is the result, not the cause. I have boundless admiration for these people. While Gordon tried to help Colleen with her school problems, Linda would come to pick her up and take her out to McDonald's for a milkshake and a heart-to-heart. Their heart-to-hearts covered everything, says Linda, from how much God interferes with our daily affairs, to the best books to read, to how to handle it when you have a crush on somebody.

Those were very distressing times for me. I so pitied Colleen and her rejection by her peers—though, from all accounts and from everything we observed, she went out of her way to invite that rejection by being flamboyantly *different*: the one thing children won't tolerate. Linda had more success at getting her to open up and reveal confidences. As I'd envied Sandra the close relationship she'd had with my daughter, so I envied Linda—all the while desperately wanting Linda to help her, the way we, her own parents, could not.

When *I'd* had crushes as a child, the first person I'd confided in had been Mum. Mum had been my best friend. Colleen sought a best friend in everyone *but* her mother: Linda, various other adults, and her big sister Lisa. Lisa's sensible and level-headed brand of advice was something Colleen sometimes appreciated but wasn't always in the mood for. Often enough, the two of *them* fought, as well. In fact Colleen always called me *mom* and spelled it with an "o" just because Lisa called me *mum* and spelled it with a "u".

That was a bad period in Lisa's life as well as in mine. At fifteen she was a normal teenager in all ways except for having a troubled sister. She and I had our share of go-rounds about all the typical teen things: her untidy room, her loud music, too much time spent on the phone, her curfew for school nights and for weekends. I recall us having a few meaningful talks but not as many as I would have liked and certainly not as many as I'd had with my own mum at her age.

On one occasion during summer holidays I made a pot of tea and decided to call Lisa downstairs from her bedroom to share it with me. Andy was at work and I longed for the companionable times Mum and I used to share so lovingly. Standing at the foot of the staircase I called out, "Lisa, would you…?." I got no further. "I *will!*" she yelled back in a furious tone. She'd thought I was going to ask her to turn her music down. I drank the tea alone and cried.

On another occasion Lisa fired at me this furious volley: "How can you expect us to be close when the only person you and Dad pay any attention to is Colleen—the *bad* one in the family? My reward for being the *good* one is that I get ignored."

She had a legitimate point. Colleen drained all our energy, leaving us with none for anything or any*one* else. Lisa's words reduced me to despair. What a far cry this was from what I'd envisioned when I'd given birth to two beautiful daughters! In contrast to the warm and emotionally intimate relationship I'd imagined having with both, I had almost no relationship with either.

Ironically, my sanctuary and my validation became Foothills Composite High School, located in the town of Okotoks just south of Calgary. The Composite was the school where I taught and where I was frequently a confidante for troubled kids who asked for—and *heeded*—my advice on all manner of personal as well as academic problems. Jo Anne Morris, a colleague and friend, used to say, "You might as well have 'Guidance Counsellor' stamped on your forehead." Terry Storch, my Vice Principal—for whose praise I remember being disproportionately grateful—called me an excellent communicator both with kids and with staff. On the home front my solid marriage with Andy never faltered, though many of our conversations caused us stress because they were about Colleen's stormy life.

English teacher and literature devotee that I am, I couldn't help identifying with the phrase "tormented motherhood" from D.H. Lawrence's famous story *The Rocking Horse Winner*. Like me, that pathetic, albeit money-grubbing woman in the story had a disturbed child. Me, I had *two* children from whom I felt alienated: one angry with me and the other regularly reiterating, with bone-chilling coldness, how much she hated me. I spent many nights sobbing myself to sleep in Andy's arms. He cried too. In those days I detested my life and wondered whether things would ever get any better.

And those were only my first steps down the road to hell.

11. Smoke Screens

"When hormones kick in, brains kick out," I remember hearing a colleague state. My job gave me daily verification of that. One boy who spent the better part of his days in my class stoned out of his gourd—when he came at all—once made a single contribution to a class discussion in the entire semester. "Do you smell onions?" he inquired with a bewildered frown. Naturally his peers had a field day jibing him and suggesting he return to the planet he'd been on before he decided to join us. Today that same fellow avoids drugs like the plague and has become, of all things, a grief counsellor.

There was the kid in the school play who downed a generous swig of dish detergent during intermission (mistaking it for pink lemonade) and blew bubbles all through the second act, much to the glee of both staff and peers. There was the kid with the bad case of acne who called all fat girls cows and yet was so hurt the day I angrily called *him* "pizza face" that he told me he'd never do it again. There was the imaginative pyramidal structure a class built out of the desks in my classroom one April fool's day. And when I wasn't laughing myself silly at their antics or shaking my head in wonder at their ingenuity, I was in tears.

There was the sweet girl with cystic fibrosis, still courageously raising money for the cause the day she passed away. There was the boy who came to school very depressed, gave none of us any signals about how bad he was feeling, then went home and hanged himself. I could go on and on, but of course that's a whole separate book. The point I make here is that I was living in an environment of extremes and rampant melodrama: the teenage world. Yet Colleen was an extreme in a world of extremes.

What I dealt with at school was magnified tenfold by what I was dealing with at home. I remember one poor grade-ten boy I taught who was small for his age and who was mercilessly teased and bullied on the school bus. With tormented eyes he one day turned around and bent over to show me his backside, covered with dusty heel marks where the kids had kicked him. I spent time with that boy, trying to give him help and advice about how to handle this situation—which *did i*mprove for him eventually. And yet with my own daughter I was helpless to bring about any improvement whatever.

Deer Run Elementary was one of the feeder schools for Wilma Hansen Junior High, located in the neighbouring community of Queensland. At the end of her grade six year, at age twelve, Colleen was conditionally passed—despite her sporadic attendance--and transferred there. Like that poor unfortunate boy, she had to ride the school bus, and also like him, she was mercilessly kicked by the other kids. Worse still, I knew nothing about this until a few weeks later.

One might ask why the school bus drivers didn't address the issue but I have been teaching far too long to ask that. Of course the drivers address the issue if they *see* an issue but they often don't. It happens surreptitiously while the driver is watching the road rather than his passengers. Furthermore, a victim of such bullying is well aware that ratting to the driver on his peers will only make matters much worse for him in the long run. What a horribly feral and savage place high school can be for certain kids who seem to exude an aura of inability to cope—an aura that, like true wild savages, certain other predatory kids can *sense*! And sensing it, those predators act just like the pack of wolves they are and move in for the kill.

Colleen's first few weeks at Wilma Hansen were somewhat of a honeymoon period: new kids, new teachers and new surroundings. But by mid-October she had stopped attending. She and Twyla would leave school together shortly after arriving, and return to our place where they drank our liquor, hung out, and cooked things on the stove. The two of them burned a saucepan once and hid it in the bushes behind the backyard fence. Colleen claimed (originally leaving Twyla out of it of course because Twyla wasn't supposed to be in our house at all when we weren't there) that she'd been trying to make rice-crispy squares *after* school and had had to throw the pan away. I'd like to think the "rice-crispy squares" part, at least, was the truth and that they weren't cooking up anything more sinister but I'll never know for sure.

Furthermore, Colleen also claimed to have found at a garage sale another pan much like ours so she'd bought it for us—she said—to replace the one she'd ruined. *That* was too uncharacteristic for either of us to believe. (Some time afterwards, we found out that Twyla's dad was coincidentally missing one of *his* saucepans.)

She had been playing hooky for only a very short time before the jig was up. I received a phone call at *my* school from a counsellor at Wilma Hansen regarding Colleen's non-attendance and I immediately got a colleague to cover the rest of my day's classes and drove back to Calgary to investigate. Arriving home in the middle of the day I caught the girls red-handed. When I told Twyla I'd have to inform her father she said defiantly, "Go ahead. He won't care." I shall always feel sorry for Twyla but at the time I couldn't handle making *her* my problem as well. My own daughter was problem enough.

Intense grilling of Colleen after Twyla had left initially produced a lot of bluster and rage but she finally broke down and sobbed that she couldn't attend Wilma Hansen because no one there would be friends with her. She told me about being kicked on the school bus and she said that no one would sit anywhere near her in class or in the cafeteria. She had thought she could start over in a new school but there were too many students at Wilma Hansen who already knew her from her old school. Starting over was impossible.

I bought the story hook line and sinker. My heart torn apart for my baby, I hugged her to me and assured her that her dad and I would find some way to help her. Even today I don't doubt that she *was* kicked on the school bus and I'm quite sure that peer rejection was something the poor girl experienced daily. It's just that the way *she* told it that day and the way the Wilma Hansen guidance counsellor told it a few days later weren't quite in line.

"Colleen often causes her own misery," the counsellor related. "She's not some meek little mouse that everybody picks on. Some kids are horrible to her, yes, but she has usually been just as horrible to *them*. And other kids have definitely tried to befriend her and *stop* the bullies from preying on her. She won't have anything to do with those. It's as though she doesn't *want* to belong, here or anywhere."

"Do you think a new start somewhere else might be the answer?" I queried. "I mean, all of us want to belong *somewhere*. She just needs to find out where that is for her. Perhaps if we were to put her in a different school where nobody knows her and she were to begin again with a clean slate…"

The counsellor shrugged. "I'd like to think it's that simple but I'm afraid it isn't. I've had several conversations with her and, to be honest, I think more intensive help is called for than a mere school change. For example, she's very obsessed with the dark side of life and with death. We had a student die in gym class not long ago—a defective heart, apparently. Colleen couldn't stop talking about it and was even convinced that, with her last breath, the girl had gasped out, 'Tammy'. *Tammy,* by the way, is the name Colleen goes by here. She obviously dislikes herself enough to try and shed her real identity completely."

Stunned, I felt my eyes smart. Quite frankly I was *still* putting some of Colleen's past behaviour—like pretending on a holiday to be someone else or loving to wallow in the morbid and the macabre—down to having too much intelligence and not enough emotional control: a situation that would right itself with time. As Colleen had professed to me about her own hopes, I'd been counting on a fresh start in a new school to turn things around for her. I'd been counting on that hormone influx my colleague mentioned to make her old concerns kick out and a more mature (even if boy-crazy!) new self kick in. Instead the issues were as serious as they'd been at Deer Run Elementary, perhaps more so.

In the next few months Andy and I saw ample evidence that Colleen's emotional instability was escalating. When Buttons, our pet cat of many years, became ill, both girls accompanied us to the vet, but it was Colleen who, as we were leaving, caught sight of several heavy-duty polyethylene bags at the side of the building waiting to be picked up. All were tied up at the mouths except one. "There's a paw sticking out of that one!" she called excitedly. "I'm going to go look!"

"No way!" we chorused in unison, but already it was too late; she had darted toward the bag and peered inside. It was full of euthanized animals, obviously on their way to the dead-stock disposal plant. The sight brought from Colleen a torrent of loud sobs that lasted through the next several hours despite all our attempts to comfort her. And yet—in the words of that Wilma Hansen guidance counsellor—*she* had definitely been the active if not eager author of her own misery.

Visions of that bag haunted her dreams for weeks afterwards, as did visions of Buttons the cat, who passed away of kidney failure a short time later. Already used to being woken by Colleen's night terrors, we grimly endured an increase in their frequency and became an even more sleep-deprived family than we already were. And it was during that time that our troubled daughter announced one day—to our chagrin and horror—that she wanted to die and had already made one unsuccessful attempt on her own life.

Until this point Colleen had seen counsellors at school and had also been examined and talked to quite extensively by our family doctor at UCMC Michael Tarrant, as well as by other psychologists and psychiatrists to whom Dr. Tarrant had referred her. Now we were advised to seek more regular counselling for her, this time through Alberta Mental Health. We made her an initial appointment with a male counsellor at an AMH office in the northeast end of town. This counsellor recommended weekly sessions aimed at helping her see the positive side of life in general and of school in particular.

At first Colleen liked the male counsellor. Even more she liked having to miss an afternoon of school once a week in order to see him. Andy and I took turns picking her up from school (when she wasn't professing to be too sick to go) and transporting her there and back. Sometimes we both went, setting out from our individual workplaces, meeting at the AMH office, having a cup of tea at the restaurant next door while Colleen saw the counsellor alone, and then talking to the counsellor together at the end of Colleen's appointment. But it wasn't long before this particular counsellor sat us down and said he didn't think he should see Colleen any more.

"She's asking for a female counsellor now," he explained. "She says she doesn't feel comfortable talking to a man. So we'll honour her wishes. One of my colleagues, Janet Wilson, will be taking over the file."

"She seemed comfortable enough originally," Andy couldn't help commenting. "What has suddenly changed?"

The counsellor looked sober. "I'm no longer letting her chat about all her gripes while I do most of the listening. I'm starting to get more involved in an advisory capacity, telling her things she doesn't want to hear—like that staying home from school isn't an option and neither is expecting the rest of the world to change just to accommodate *her* wishes. Telling her things she doesn't want to hear has made me the enemy. It's not unusual."

"And do you think Ms. Wilson is likely to have more success?" I asked.

He gave a patient smile. "We can only find out by trying. Like many troubled teens—especially the bright ones—Colleen puts up one smoke screen after another. To get to the root of the problem we have to get through all those smoke screens. And ultimately we can only do that if she decides she wants to help herself as much as we want to help her."

"We'll work on convincing her," I vowed fervently.

Janet Wilson lasted longer than had the male counsellor, but eventually she, too, came up against an impassable barricade erected by her client. Less blunt and more soft-spoken than her predecessor, Ms. Wilson treated Colleen with gentleness yet firmness at the same time. I have since heard colleagues and friends speak highly of her and credit her with helping many. At the time I heard only one opinion of her: Colleen's.

"She expects *me* to tell *her* how I should get out of what she calls my *predicament*. What use is that? I don't want to see her any more." Our daughter's voice held the customary scorn. In vain did we emphasize to her that Janet was trying to teach her strategies for finding her own solutions to life's difficulties; our statements fell on deaf ears.

"She's all smoke screens and defensiveness," Ms. Wilson told us. "And she's quite ingenious at going off on tangents and evading the real issues. My attempts to probe into those issues have been met with nothing but stonewalling on her part. She says she doesn't want to see me any more and I can't force her."

Smarting with disappointment, we asked Janet about Woods Christian Homes. I'd heard about the wonderful work they do from a friend who'd had two troubled children, both of whom had spent a brief time there in a seven-day intensive counselling program. Janet Wilson was as praising of Woods Homes as my friend had been but emphasized there was never a shortage of children needing these services and Colleen would only find help there if she decided to cooperate. Once again, I vowed fervently that we would work on convincing her.

As it turned out Colleen didn't take much convincing. She was now refusing to attend either her weekly counselling appointments *or* school and the prospect of being away from us and our "constant harassment" obviously appealed to her. She agreed to go.

Woods Christian Homes (which dropped the more exclusive-sounding "Christian" from its name in 2007) is a community owned and operated children's mental health facility with centres in Calgary and several outlying towns. Based on the principles of reaching out to all troubled children and staffed by trained crisis counsellors and social workers, they have a reputation for persistence and for not turning anyone away. Their various programs provide a timeout period for families having difficulty coping. Rebellious or otherwise stressed children get a break from their parents and vice versa. Andy and I admitted to ourselves and to each other that the "vice versa" part would do us, as a couple, a world of good!

There are some longer-term (up to thirty days) Stabilization Programs offered at Woods Homes but what was immediately available to us was a bed for the seven-day program at the centre in Parkdale, close to the Foothills Hospital. We helped Colleen pack a small suitcase and we drove her there. The staff welcomed her with kindness but it was made clear to Colleen as soon as she arrived that she wasn't there for a vacation. She'd be up early and she'd be expected to adhere to the structure of the day. She'd also be expected to make an open and earnest effort to work with the counsellors on addressing her problems. Before they'd finished talking to her I saw the hostility in her expression and my heart sank.

Every day of the residence period we went there for an hour's visit. From the counsellors we heard, once again, about smoke screens and lack of cooperation; from Colleen we heard about how terrible it was there and how much she hated it. Their rules sucked and were unfair. One night she and another teen decided to run away. Woods is not a lock-down facility, so the two of them walked out the door and were gone for a couple of hours before deciding there was no alternative but to return.

I came to dread our visitation hour with her, which was mostly a litany of how miserable she was, interspersed with threats to run away again and sobbing pleas to be allowed to return home. By the end of the fifth day I could stand it no longer. Our baby was suffering and when she promised to improve her behaviour if we allowed her to come back, we caved.

"This is yet another smoke screen," a Woods counsellor told us. "She muddies the waters by finding objections to the most minor of issues—like whose turn it is to do the dishes or how much bigger her room is at home—in order to evade plumbing the depths of her real feelings. She hasn't the remotest intention of being honest with us and we can't even begin to help her until she is."

Thanking them, we gathered up her stuff and left. Perhaps *we* could persist with her and ultimately batter our way through those smoke screens she was creating. Maybe her gratitude at being home again—in her larger room—would now be enough to initiate in her some effort of her own...

Who was I kidding? I have a lot of respect for psychologists and counsellors and I didn't for one moment doubt the accuracy of their statements. Our daughter seemed bent on ducking down hidey-holes rather than revealing anything about what was really going on inside her head.

But I think my biggest dread by then was that perhaps she *dared* not tell the rest of the world—dared not even tell *herself*—what was going on inside her head.

12. Escalating

Using the horse-riding lessons as both carrot and stick, we limped Colleen through the rest of her grade seven year. Once again she was conditionally passed despite sporadic attendance. Two occurrences caused her to suffer enormous setbacks: the death of Marmite, our old Sheltie dog, and my running over the neighbour's cat with my car.

Marmite was in liver failure and had to be euthanized. Andy, Lisa and I all spent tremendous effort consoling Colleen, who went off the rails. "You killed my dog!" she kept screaming over and over. "I hate you, I hate you!"

"Marmite belonged to the whole family and we're *all* sad," Lisa countered crossly. "It's not just you. Why is everything always about *you*?" But statements like Lisa's, accurate as they might be, never cut any ice with Colleen. Just as she was unable to read vibes, so she was unable to see beyond her own suffering to take into account what others might be feeling. That part of her brain simply didn't seem to function.

As for the cat I ran over, I felt terrible enough about it without Colleen's help, even knowing I wasn't to blame. I'd been driving slowly when the silly kitty literally chased a butterfly out into the street and under my wheels. I braked at once, but too late. When I went to tell the neighbour we exchanged hugs, both a bit teary; then the neighbour said, "I've nearly hit the little dummy several times myself. We loved her dearly but she's never had any traffic sense. I should have kept her indoors. It was my fault, not yours." The one who *did* hold me responsible was Colleen.

"You're a murderer and I hate you!" More than ever lately she couldn't stop screeching at me these declarations of her hatred. "Why did you have to be my mother? I wish Dad had married someone else." And despite knowing she was a troubled child, I couldn't seem to get over the hurt. Those hatred statements never failed to make me cry.

Nevertheless, she was our baby. Fiercely protective parental instincts made us want to make everything better that was upsetting her. Andy took her to the SPCA (I was marking grade twelve provincial exams in Edmonton at the time) and let her choose another dog, a lovely-tempered blue heeler whom she and Lisa named Smokey. Smokey had been rescued from a life of abuse and soon became as ardently protective toward all of us as we felt toward Colleen. Smokey also hit it off with

Spunky cat (another SPCA rescue we'd adopted to replace Buttons) and it wasn't long before dog and cat were sleeping snuggled up against one another. Colleen adored them both obsessively and spent far more time with them than did Lisa—but that was a good thing. Along with the horses she rode, they provided a substitute for peer rejection and their unconditional love gave her a source of comfort. Lisa, who had always got on well with her peers, loved the dog and cat in a normal way but never needed them as substitutes.

Besides, Lisa now had Shawn Patapoff, a young fellow who'd come up through school with her and who was becoming increasingly sweet on her as she was on him. From the moment he started coming over and hanging out with Lisa, Andy and I liked Shawn. He was shy but polite, and he was very devoted to our elder daughter. Colleen despised him for the same reason: he was stealing her sister's time *and* love to which Colleen felt *she* had exclusive rights. Particularly as she had trouble making friends of her own, Colleen wanted Lisa all to herself.

Her pain was our pain. Now fourteen and heading into her grade eight year, she was more terrified than ever by the prospect of returning to Wilma Hansen. Totally sympathetic, I felt the way I'd felt sitting with her in the Alberta Children's Hospital when, as a toddler of three, she'd had her heel-cord surgery. Then I'd soothed her pain by rocking her on my lap until she fell asleep; now I soothed her pain by transferring her out of Wilma Hansen and into the Foothills School Division where I taught. In those days teachers could do that as long as there was room, and I knew of several colleagues who had done it in the past. It enabled them to keep closer tabs on their children as well as have a positive bonding experience while they and their children drove together to school and back. I admit I found major reassurance in the thought that my taking Colleen there would guarantee beyond doubt that she went. Going to school in Okotoks would also get her away—at least during the day—from Twyla's bad influence. And yes, this truly *would* give her the fresh start she craved.

Ecstatic about the plan, Colleen hugged me, told me how grateful she was and how much she loved me, and swore she would do better. Fervently hoping that was true, I enrolled her in Okotoks Junior High School just up the hill from where *I* taught at Foothills Composite. Every morning we would set off together heading south down the highway and watching the sun rise to our left, silhouetting herds of grazing horses and cattle against an orange sky as we passed picturesque farms. For my entire career with Foothills School Division I have loved that drive, looking upon it more as meditation than commute. My teenage passenger didn't share my reverence for the view, but then that wasn't unexpected. I think teens regard the mere act of getting up before sunrise as vaguely obscene.

In other respects, however, the drive with Colleen at first proved gratifying. She liked the town and relished the fresh-baked muffin I usually bought her at the Hi-Ho Gas Bar on the way into town (a spot of bribery but well worth it if it gave her positive associations). We bonded over a joke jingle two Calgary DJs sometimes sang over the radio after a weekend. *Monday, it bites the big one,* went the lyrics. Laughing, we would chime in together and for the first time in many years I saw a more relaxed, happier Colleen. "The kids are way nicer than in Calgary," she claimed. "They're not mean at all."

Gladdened as I was by this pronouncement, I couldn't help being wary. My past experiences with school and my girl of extremes were that she couldn't say enough good things during the "honeymoon" period of the first few weeks; then shortly thereafter she couldn't say enough *bad* things. I found myself on edge, braced for her attitude to sour.

Colleen's homeroom teacher was Gerry Thomas whom I'd known as a friend and colleague for several years. Gerry was a kind and caring man but not a parent. He tried to develop more of an "older adult" relationship with Colleen, and I would often pick up Colleen at OJ at the end of my own school day and find the two of them engaged in an after-school chat. Like many of her teachers before him, Gerry praised Colleen's intelligence but he also mentioned her ability to be manipulative and cagey, always looking for excuses to get out of class. Jolan Yuha, another colleague and friend who taught her Language Arts, echoed Gerry's sentiments and added, "Colleen needs to learn her place. She talks back to teachers in a very disrespectful way. At times she treats kids disrespectfully as well." It was disappointing and upsetting news.

When Colleen announced she'd formed a friendship with a girl in her class named Heather, I worried that Heather might be another Twyla but was pleasantly surprised. Like Allison on our street, Heather was shy but definitely one of the "nice kids". Colleen asked if she could invite Heather for a sleepover that coming Saturday and I gave my blessing. I talked to Heather's mother and arranged a time for us to drive Heather back home to Okotoks on Sunday.

We rented some Disney movies for the girls to watch and set up beds for them in the downstairs family room. In the early evening they whispered together and watched the movies. Heather appeared to be having a good time. By Sunday morning that had changed. What took place Saturday night rendered their friendship a thing of the past. Heather never wanted to come for a sleepover with Colleen again.

"Heather's an idiot," Colleen scoffed when we asked. "Her mom said she can't watch horror movies because they give her nightmares, so she wanted to watch lame stuff all night and she cried when I made her watch some better scary stuff on TV. What a baby!" It was the Allison thing all over again. And Colleen had waited until *we* were asleep and oblivious to impose her domineering will on poor shy Heather.

Naturally I apologized to Heather's mom and didn't blame the lady in the slightest for telling her daughter to stay completely away from Colleen. We were now several weeks into the school year and Colleen began to talk about other kids making fun of her in Phys. Ed. because of her weak left side. Angry about the way she'd treated Heather and knowing better than to accept at face value Colleen's take on the situation, I still *did* pity her. Remembering my own un-athletic school days, I ruefully acknowledged that at least *I'd* belonged to the "nerd herd". Colleen had no niche at all.

Native intelligence aside, my daughter had already missed so much school that there were huge gaps in her academic knowledge. She compensated by resorting to bluff and bluster—which used to work in her younger years because of her brightness and ability with words. But kids, as any teacher knows, are not fools, especially as they get older. I have seen beginning teachers doom themselves by trying to bluff knowing the answer to something instead of simply saying, "I'm not sure. I'll have to look that up." (Or better yet, "Why don't *you* look that up for us?") In a similar way Colleen doomed herself with the kids at OJ.

One special young man named Dennis (whom I later taught at the senior-high level) made an outstanding effort with our daughter, encouraging her to see the good things about herself and to persist with school. He also *dis*couraged her from seeking out "the wrong crowd"—without success. Not fitting anywhere else, that was the group Colleen gravitated towards, claiming those kids alone were "cool".

I must also mention at this point another friend and colleague, Rob

Irvine, then Principal of Okotoks Junior High. Colleen spent the inevitable disciplinary hours in Rob's office glowering and being defiant. Recognizing her as the troubled child she was, Rob attempted to help her develop coping strategies and he was as persistent and dedicated in that attempt as had been her elementary school Assistant Principal Gordon Hunter. Even Colleen herself once said, "Mr. Irvine never gives up." Sadly, Rob has since passed away, and I know his dear wife Lorraine (also a good friend) would be proud to consider those words an epitaph to her much-respected late husband.

A combination of last-ditch hope and plain desperation had caused me to bring Colleen into my sanctuary world—the world in which I'd previously sought solace when things with my daughter became too intense. Now that sanctuary world had become synonymous with the stressful life I led outside it. I got constant calls about Colleen at work from my OJ colleagues who needed to discuss with me her bad attitude, her failure to turn in assignments, her clashes with other kids—and yes, her truancy: the one thing I'd counted on this plan to curtail.

More and more often, Colleen began claiming she was sick and refusing to ride with me. When I forced her to go she would scream all the way there. When I dropped her off at the school she'd go in the front door and straight out the back. On the infrequent occasions she *was* there, she was unfailingly in trouble. Finally I conceded that we may as well deep-six the plan. Andy and I withdrew her.

And what were we to do now? No way were we going to allow her to hang out at home—particularly unsupervised—while the rest of us went off to our daily occupations. On the advice of Dr. Tarrant who helped us make appropriate contacts, we enrolled her in the Young Adult Program at the Foothills Hospital, a live-in program designed to help troubled teens like her.

Protocol for length of stay in the Young Adult Program was four to six weeks. When teens were there for two to four months, says social worker Peter O'Brien (family therapist for the program at that time and also coordinator and facilitator of its affiliated Parent Support Group), it meant that in the concerted opinion of professional staff, there were considerable challenges with sorting out diagnosis and/or an effective treatment plan—or that more time was needed to see the benefits of therapy "take". Colleen ended up spending four months there.

Peter O'Brien was a sympathetic yet practical and down-to-earth man. He told Colleen they'd work with her on relationships both within the family and outside it. Our entire family would be expected to attend regular counselling sessions and the Parent Support Group. The doctors there would explore medication possibilities for her that might help "soften the sharp edges" of her emotions. Colleen scowled and snarled, "I like my edges!" It was a remark that boded ill for the success of this venture also.

While she was there we visited Colleen several times. She startled us during these visits by saying how much she missed two people she'd met only a short time before: a lady who belonged to a very fundamentalist independent church and the pastor of that same church. The lady had driven Colleen to a few church meetings, warning her that this church insisted upon women wearing skirts long enough to cover their knees. Colleen had described the church—and its pastor—as boring. She'd even sneeringly dubbed it "the No-Knees Church", saying she probably wouldn't bother attending any more services there. Then, upon her admission to the Young Adult Program, "No-Knees" suddenly became the most wonderful group in the world and her nightstand prominently featured a framed photo, not of any of us or of anyone else she knew, but of its pastor!

Our forebodings did not take long to prove correct. Shortly into her stay we got a telephone call from Foothills Hospital. Colleen and another teen had simply walked out the hospital's main doors and run away to the streets.

13. Upping the Ante

Like Woods Homes, the Young Adult Program was not a lockdown facility. Colleen had been told that from the start. "No one can force you to stay here or to work on changing your life for the better," Peter O'Brien said to her. "That desire must come from you and you alone." Dr. Phil on his television show has made precisely the same point. If you won't own it, he says, you can't fix it. That stands to reason. But Colleen was not interested in reason.

What brought her and the other teen back to the hospital was that they had nowhere else to go. They hadn't the experience to know how to find help on the streets. They got cold and hungry so back they came—hostile as ever to the prospect of getting any *real* help.

Colleen adamantly declared it was we, not she, who were crazy. She hated it there and if we were decent caring parents we would just let her come home. That Peter O'Brien chose to back *us* up was only further proof that all adults are allied in one vast conspiracy against kids.

Andy and I requested and received time off work to attend the family counselling sessions. Throughout most of them Colleen was sullen and contributed very little. Lisa too was a reluctant contributor at that time; I think she found the whole thing most embarrassing and resented our being treated as though *we* were the dysfunctional ones. As well, Andy and I attended Peter O'Brien's evening Parent Support Group at Foothills Hospital. This bonded us to those whose family situations were like ours and it also reinforced that—despite our kids' frequent resistance—we were doing the right thing insisting they get professional help.

Schoolwork was part of the deal at the Young Adult Program; no sleeping-in or skipping was tolerated. Kids were woken early, told to get up and get dressed, given breakfast, and then assembled for morning classes. Only because of this unrelenting regimen did a protesting Colleen end up passing her grade eight. Against her will she completed the four months and then, with one of her coy unreadable grins, she told us she was ready to come home and be better behaved from now on.

That grin made us super uneasy. Neither of us believed her and I'm sure Lisa didn't either. At the same time we felt guilt for not believing her. And of course the Young Adult Program's staff members could make no guarantees that their efforts had "taken". "Keep coming to the Parent Support Group," Peter O'Brien advised. "It can only be beneficial."

Our skepticism, as it turned out, was well founded. Colleen had another scheme up her sleeve. Someone had told her about AARC, the Calgary based Alberta Adolescent Recovery Centre, and she wanted in. Her informant, whom she vaguely identified as "a counsellor I saw" but later confessed was a school dropout from the Okotoks drug scene, had described the program as one in which you get to live away from home in a setting where people *understand* you. Parents had only to be willing to offer their support. When we drove Colleen to a follow-up psychiatric assessment at Foothills Hospital upon her completion of the Young Adult Program, all she could talk about to the doctor there was her need to get into AARC.

That appointment day was memorable even before the psychiatrist spoke to us. Sitting with her in the waiting area, we watched in a kind of intermingled fascination and horror as she hailed an unkempt-looking fellow in a chair across the room, then went over beside him to begin a conversation. His response was to gaze back at her blankly, pupils enormous, body twitching in spastic motions. Like an automaton he kept raising one hand above his head, lowering it slowly towards the floor, and fixedly watching its downward, then its upward movement. "Before he fried his brains on heroin he used to be a nice guy," Colleen commented in an offhand manner, returning to us moments later. True to form, she basked in our discomfiture.

"AARC, in my opinion, is yet another hidey-hole Colleen wants to use as an escape hatch," the psychiatrist theorized. "What seems to appeal to her the most is that it involves a year-long period during which she would be out of the regular school system. Yes, she tends to substance abuse but I don't think she has the slightest intention of actually addressing that issue—which is the primary mandate of AARC. She wants in there because, and only because, it would keep her out of school. Nevertheless I encourage you to follow it up yourselves and see how *you* feel about it. They do good work and they'll certainly be willing to give Colleen a thorough assessment as a potential candidate."

We complied with his advice, making an appointment to see an AARC counsellor. It was a good thing to do anyway; Andy and I knew little about AARC other than that we had heard of it as a long-term treatment program aimed at curing the "disease" of chemical dependency in adolescents. Our session with the counsellor told us more.

AARC uses the same twelve-step recovery system employed by Alcoholics Anonymous (AA) and Narcotics Anonymous (NA). The client resides in a Recovery Home during the first phase of treatment which may last six months. Recovery Homes are the parental or family homes of clients further along in the recovery process—which would mean that *we*, as the family of such a client, would eventually be expected to house and to supervise other, less advanced clients. I'll fully admit that even contemplating that prospect made me bone-weary.

And what about schooling? Yes, clients were not sent to regular school but attended a year-round on-site Learning Centre staffed by two certified Calgary-Board-of-Education teachers. In this smaller setting they had the chance to work more intensively on their problems *and* their education. That part certainly sounded ideal.

The inevitable discussion about money ensued. Provided assessment tagged Colleen a suitable candidate, treatment fees were based on the family's ability to pay. Average treatment length was about a year, with follow-up after-care encouraged. AARC's policy today is the same as it was then: not to turn anyone away for lack of ability to pay. However, a family like ours with two professional incomes could realistically expect little help offsetting what would probably amount to at least ten thousand dollars by the time the treatment was done.

We gulped but were not deterred from requesting an assessment for our daughter. If AARC could help her, then we would find a way to pay. Colleen spent three days in exhaustive analysis by their trained staff, at the end of which we received a verdict identical to that of the Foothills Hospital psychiatrist: she sought entry into the AARC program for the wrong reasons. Her statements about wanting to stop substance abuse seemed insincere. Her agenda, they felt, was to use AARC as a way out of having to cope with real life, and her issues were much more with mental health than with drugs. She was denied admission.

The denial sent her into meltdown mode. Convinced she'd been turned down on account of our refusal to pay, she ranted at us about our stinginess and our selfishness. *Good* parents, like the mother of her Okotoks dropout friend (who, she now confessed, had given her the idea) were willing to do *anything* for their children. What was the matter with us?

The same question was asked of me a few days later by that very mother, whose child *had* been admitted to AARC, and who had bought entirely Colleen's story about our putting our pocketbooks above our daughter's welfare. She came to see me at the end of my teaching day, her mission being to talk me out of my hard-heartedness. Worthy motives or not I felt tremendous impatience with the lady, who knew squat about us *or* about Colleen's situation, yet presumed to make judgments upon both. Quite summarily I sent her packing, no doubt confirming in her mind what a terrible parent I was.

Psychiatrists and psychologists are hesitant to put specific mental-illness labels on teens and that is understandable. As I knew from my own experiences with kids at school, raging hormones send a significant number off the rails, at least temporarily. "It's a tumultuous period of life at best," O'Brien had often reminded us. "Even extreme cases like Colleen can sometimes calm right down after the hormone-influx phase is over." And I had seen for myself the truth of what he said.

One of my female students, during her off-the-rails phase, stole a large number of her mother's anti-depressant pills and took them all at once because a boy she loved no longer wanted to go out with her. Fortunately she vomited them all up before they had the chance to do her any harm. A few years ago I ran into that same former student in the supermarket. In place of the maladjusted teen was a cheerful vibrant woman, enthusing about a successful career in management and about the doings of offspring she obviously adored. (Okay, one encounter doesn't prove she was no longer troubled. But her large smile, confident manner, and happy chatter are good indicators of a now-fulfilled, well-adjusted person.) Such turnarounds do happen. If we could find the right school setting for Colleen, it was just possible we could eventually bring about such a turnaround in her.

There are kids whom the public school system fails. That is evidenced by the springing up of charter schools and private schools. The public system tries to be all things to all people and the danger is that, taken to its ultimate, such a philosophy is at risk of producing schools that end up being nothing to anybody. My years with the Foothills School Division and at Foothills Composite High School in particular did not disillusion me with the public system: the Composite turned out numerous graduates who were—and are—model citizens, hard workers, and dedicated achievers. Some of them remain my friends to this day. Standards amongst staff were high. Teachers were dedicated and caring people, many of whom went above and beyond with the kids. Today, as then, I'm proud to have served with these people as my colleagues. But I've also seen other students fall through the cracks, others whose needs simply weren't met. Like Colleen, they stopped coming. And like us, some of their parents sought alternatives.

For Colleen we looked at Calgary Academy, a school dedicated to kids who—for whatever reason—could not function in the regular system. Class sizes were small, typically twelve or fewer students per instructor. It was the same kind of smaller-group setting that Colleen had found attractive at AARC. Teachers focussed intensively on building kids' self-esteem and making them feel successful. Maureen and John Pysclywec, a couple from church who'd taken an interest in Colleen, had enrolled their son there and they told us they'd been pleased with his progress. Tuition was hefty—that same ten thousand per year discussed at AARC—with only a small tax break if you could produce medical evidence of your child's need for such measures. (An FSD colleague of mine who was Colleen's guidance counsellor at OJ helped us out with that.) But Andy and I agreed totally: we could manage it even if it meant tightening our belts. We'd been willing to do it if AARC had deemed it a good idea and we were willing to do it now. If it worked, it was well worth the financial outlay.

As with OJ, Colleen was initially grateful. Realizing Calgary Academy had the same sort of classroom conditions she'd coveted at AARC, her anger with us over that rejection dissipated. It was a new school year and this would give her another fresh start. As with OJ, there was the typical honeymoon period to begin with: the school was great, the teachers were wonderful and the other kids were nice. But that honeymoon period was shorter than at OJ. Only weeks into the year she had a butting of heads with the Phys. Ed. teacher who tapped her on the shoulder and told her to hurry up and get out on the gym floor. Refusing to budge, Colleen threatened to sue the man for daring to touch her. They discussed it and established a quasi-truce but then we began to hear again that she was cutting classes and hanging out with "the wrong crowd". One day she turned up drunk which earned her a month's suspension.

To add to our problems, Andy got the news at the same time that he'd been laid off. So prone to vicissitude is the oil business that many geologists have experienced layoffs once or twice in their careers. True to his stoic temperament, Andy reacted with aplomb and even saw an advantage: he'd be home to supervise Colleen's schooling and conduct during her suspension. Indeed, he did just that. *Both* of us were teachers for that month and Andy was the one with the more challenging task. Colleen attended the one-pupil "school of Porter", a far more rigorous school than Calgary Academy. She was woken before seven each day and taken out for an hour's walk with her dad and the dog: the Phys. Ed. component. A packet of academic materials with which we had been supplied occupied the rest of her day. Colleen found a far less lenient instructor in Andy than in the Calgary Academy faculty: when she lipped him off or refused to do as he said he didn't hesitate to punish her by sending her to her room and/or withdrawing privileges. This interaction took a large toll on my beloved husband. His Crohn's disease is aggravated by stress and he is such a peace-loving man by nature that his clashes with Colleen often gave him bad stomach pains.

And Colleen didn't take this rigorous regimen lying down. As she'd done with the Phys. Ed. teacher, she threatened to make trouble for her dad if he didn't stop badgering her. To our shock, she made good on the threat by calling a children's help line. Still angry with Lisa as well (who continued to insist on having a boyfriend) she accused her sister of sexual molestation, intimated her dad had touched her inappropriately, and claimed *I* beat her on a regular basis. Next thing we knew two social workers showed up on our doorstep.

We gasped and asked them in. Seated on the couch in our family room, they interviewed us all. They had to check it out, they said; any call for help must be investigated. And so it must. I can't argue with that. What I couldn't believe is that our daughter would do such a thing to us, to our family. It never occurred to me that she would go so far—because I, in her place, would never have considered going so far, no matter how mad I was at my family. But I was not Colleen.

Lisa looked stricken throughout the interview. She woodenly answered questions directed at her. Andy and I maintained our equanimity but felt deeply agonized. When they'd finished questioning us and making their notes, the social workers left—with apologies for having disturbed our evening! Nothing beyond that interview was ever pursued. They had evidently assessed the situation as a false alarm.

But that event marred forever our relationship with Colleen. A place in our hearts began to harden out of pure self-preservation. We had discovered our younger daughter to be not above hurting us, even ruining us, to achieve her own ends, and that injected wariness into our dealings with her from that point on.

This didn't mean Andy and I ceased to parent her or to try and make her feel loved. It *did* mean we started to divorce a part of ourselves to keep from going over an emotional cliff. The psychologists conducting the Parent Support Group we still attended endorsed such a strategy. "People of a sociopathic disposition are entirely self-absorbed," one of the discussion-group members said. "They remove obstacles in the way of what they want without a second glance." I gagged to hear my child lumped with "people of a sociopathic disposition". I mean, sociopaths were psychos, whack jobs, nut cases—even serial killers! No. That description of our daughter I was *not* ready to accept!

At heart, Colleen was a good person. She was simply in too much pain for that side of her to show very often. She was too busy lashing out in retaliation at real or supposed insults. She was rarely happy. Her perception of the world had become one in which everyone was out to cause her grief. Inside and out, I wept torrents of tears for the poor tormented soul my beautiful baby had become.

Still defiant and defensive, Colleen returned to Calgary Academy after her suspension. For the rest of that year she was frequently "sick" and unable to go to classes. We forced her to continue family counselling sessions with us and Lisa but she persisted in being surly and taciturn. Once she said to Peter O'Brien, "I wish everyone would just leave me alone." He replied, "Be careful what you wish for."

One glimmer of hope arose when she said she'd go back to regularly attending Youth Group at church. We soon found out, however, that she was only doing that so she could try and get closer to her beloved Scott, the older mentor on whom she still retained an obsessive crush. As well she re-established her liaison with Twyla and cultivated a new one with a girl named Kim. Kim, like Twyla, had a reputation for being in trouble and already had a baby daughter whose teenage father had run for the hills. When not at Youth Group or forced to go to school, Colleen would sneak off at every opportunity to hang out with the one girl or the other. It was Kim who one day convinced Colleen to call up Scott and to confess frankly her feelings for him (the *last* thing I would ever have done myself in her place, or advised her to do). When she did call him, Scott tried to be kind but levelled with her about not returning her feelings and about how she should be pursuing other interests and hobbies at her age. Forced into a corner as he was, how could he have done otherwise?

Colleen reacted to what she perceived as the cruelest of rejections by going to her greatest extreme yet. She bought a bottle of sleeping pills at a nearby drugstore and downed the lot.

14. People of a Sociopathic Disposition

Almost at once, and with a remarkably blasé attitude, our daughter disclosed to her dad what she had done. Of course Andy called 911 and then whipped her to the hospital to have her stomach pumped. Physically there were no lasting effects from her second suicide attempt and emotionally she adopted an astonishing devil-may-care stance about the whole thing. She hadn't really meant anything by it, she told Peter O'Brien—as though *we* were the ones making a huge fuss over nothing. No, she didn't like Scott any more and Youth Group was a waste of time.

She won't even be honest with *herself*," O'Brien stated. "More diagnostic testing might be a good idea. But she won't hear of any help at all, medical, psychiatric or otherwise. And since she's fifteen, we can't force her."

The helplessness Andy and I felt was demoralizing. Thank goodness Andy got hired by another oil company and ended up better off than he'd been before his layoff. Thank goodness *I* had my teaching career and the knowledge that I was helping other people's kids even if I couldn't help my own. We plodded on doggedly during those months, sadly taking refuge in the workplace as diversion.

When weather permitted, I also started jogging in the early mornings before leaving for work. Regularly I'd don my runners at five a.m. and take off into Fish Creek Park with Smokey by my side to do eight to ten kilometers. It was a habit born of desperation but one I came to cherish due to the health benefits and one I've never given up to this day (though on account of a hip replacement I've had to slow it to a fast walk or, in icy conditions, to a session on my elliptical machine). Without the exercise regimen I think I might have turned to alcohol or drugs myself!

Colleen "graduated" Calgary Academy after being dragged by us to write her final exams. At the graduation ceremony our family sat with the Pysklywecs. Maureen asked whether we planned to enrol her there again for high school—something *they* planned on doing with their shy son, who seemed a very nice young fellow. Maureen had faith that Calgary Academy would eventually help Colleen but by then we didn't share her opinion. She and John had seen a great improvement in their son; we had seen nothing in return for our ten thousand dollars except the identical rebellious misconduct Colleen had exhibited in the public system. We answered no; we *didn't* plan on continuing Colleen at Calgary Academy. I could tell Maureen was upset with us.

Interestingly Colleen—notorious for *not* picking up on vibes in most social situations—observed Maureen's displeasure right away and milked it to the max. Suddenly Calgary Academy was back to being the best school on earth as she tearfully wailed how much she'd miss the great staff and all her good friends there. It was an awkward moment. To Maureen (as to the mother of that Okotoks school dropout who'd touted AARC as the fix-it-all panacea) we came off as hard-hearted parents with no regard at all for their child's happiness. Colleen knew how it appeared and she revelled in it. Dear kind Maureen was more upset than ever about our decision. Who can blame her?

Lord Beaverbrook is the public high school that serves the Deer Run area, a large school accommodating some fifteen hundred students. Colleen spent that summer chafing against being enrolled at Beaverbrook. She threatened to cut classes and refuse to go. Andy said, "So what else is new? We gave you the chance at a private school and you blew it. Why should we throw our hard-earned money down the drain? Beaverbrook it is!"

Both of us spent considerable time and energy that summer pep-talking Colleen and trying to allay her fears. But one night just a few weeks before the September start-up, I heard her sobbing in her room and entered to find her in a panic. "I just *can't* go to Beaverbrook," she wept. And I gave in, gathered my baby into my arms and promised I'd see what I could do.

It was the only move I've ever made not in concert with Andy. He seemed so set on his position—a logical one—that it was time to stop shielding our daughter and force her to adapt to the world. Without telling him, I made some phone calls and arranged for Colleen to have an interview at Alternative High School, a tax-supported school with the mandate of helping kids who can't adjust to the regular system. I even got a colleague in on the plot because I needed a second signature on the initial application form. Yes, they told me, they *could* find room at Alternative—as long as Colleen passed the interview to which each candidate was subjected. I made her the appointment.

Then, of course, I could no longer avoid telling Andy. Bless his heart, he was immediately onside! Together we broke the news to Colleen and she hugged us both in gratitude, swearing as always that she'd do better this time. Her nostalgic memories of staff and friends at Calgary Academy evaporated in a trice. She'd never liked it there and had only said she did because she was so scared about Beaverbrook. *This* would truly be a fresh start.

My husband and I were jaded enough by now that we always maintained our emotions in self-preservation mode. But who knew? There was a chance Alternative would be the answer for our daughter whereas the dreaded Beaverbrook (where Lisa, by the way, did wonderfully and received all too little recognition from us for it) was definitely not.

Alternative High School was housed in a former elementary school building in the southwest end of the city. Like Calgary Academy, its class sizes were small—twelve or fewer to a class. Its approach was unique in that student council members served along with teachers on the Admissions-or-Expulsions Interview Board and their votes counted as heavily as faculty votes in making decisions. Dress code was more liberal than in a regular school. Alcohol and drug use were strictly forbidden and, if proved, were punishable by expulsion. The faculty conducted classes informally and went by first names. A large black canine mascot wandered freely up and down the halls and through the classrooms, accepting stroking and tummy rubs from any and all comers. It seemed like a great environment. What was not to *love* about being here?

Colleen, of course, charmed the proverbial pants off the Interview Board and had no trouble being accepted for admission. We forked over some money for a few new outfits and Lisa took her shopping. She came home with a wild black number she planned to wear on her first day: a low-cut blouse and matching flare-leg pants. "It's loud for my taste but well put-together," Lisa said. We agreed. We also agreed to pay for an Afro-type hair perm at a then-expensive cost of fifty dollars. Our ready agreement to the fifty caused Colleen to agitate for a jet-black colour treatment as well which pushed it up to seventy-five. Wanting her to feel good about her first day of school, we conceded.

Grade ten at Alternative began well enough for her. The school was a fabulous place, heaven on earth. She bucked going to family counselling sessions with us, saying there was a much better counsellor at Alternative. Our dear friend Linda Hunter (who was still a neighbour but by then minister at a different church) continued to take her out for coffee or milkshakes and try to help her sort through her problems. Incoming minister Jennifer Ferguson made similar efforts with her, as did devoted congregant Jean Nash. Maureen Pysklywec was a fourth sympathetic ear, several times asking Colleen over to her house.

On one such occasion Lisa, who was driving by then, went to the Pysklywecs to pick up Colleen in the car and bring her home for supper. "I was invited in," Lisa recounted when they returned, "and treated by Maureen as though she was *sorry* for me having to live with such abusive people! Colleen, what have you been telling her about our family?"

Colleen had a characteristic bout of bluster and rage, accusing Lisa of trying to get her in trouble but not really denying the charges. Andy and I hadn't a doubt in our minds that she *was* telling all kinds of melodramatic stories to anyone who would listen about the terrible life she led under our parental tyranny. But we were just as frustrated and just as powerless to do anything about it as we were to do anything about forcing her to get more intensive medical and psychiatric help.

The need for *money* arose in Colleen's life quite abruptly. The miserly allowance we gave her and Lisa (which we knew to be about mid-range in comparison to what other parents gave their children) she declared unfairly inadequate. Lisa, she complained, always had lots of money. "Lisa babysits," we pointed out. It was true enough: a couple of years previously Lisa had taken a babysitting course offered at our community centre and since then—having proved herself reliable—she'd had a steady clientele and therefore more available cash for "cool" clothes and outings with her friends.

Colleen coveted Lisa's cash situation and announced she too was going to start babysitting. It was the first time she'd expressed interest in having a job since the flyer-delivery fiasco.

"Take the course," Lisa urged her. "They give you a certificate at the end and that will help you get more customers." Colleen resented the idea of the course but it was only a few evening sessions on basic child care, so she followed her sister's advice. Considering her history, Andy and I weren't at all sure how we felt about her babysitting, but at Parent Support Group we were urged to let her try it. Sometimes a little responsibility brings out the best in problem teens.

Once certificated, Colleen set about seeking clients. She soon spotted an ad taped to a nearby mailbox: a working mother wanted someone to escort her young children via LRT to the local recreation centre once a week after school. It sounded an ideal way for Colleen to "get her feet wet": not a late-night job and not a job involving the care of infants. These were elementary school-aged children whose mom said were quite trustworthy but simply not yet old enough to ride the LRT by themselves.

Colleen phoned the number on the strip she tore off the ad, spoke to the mother, was invited over to meet the children and returned home to say she was hired. We congratulated her.

The first time she reported for duty, the mother gave Colleen enough money to cover the cost of entry fees, snacks, and ride tickets there and back. Upon her return from the job Colleen claimed all had gone well and the kids had enjoyed themselves.

A few minutes later the mother called to explain why Colleen was fired. As in many cities, payment for using Calgary's Light Rail Transit is done on an honour system with sporadic unannounced monitoring. Instead of buying tickets, Colleen had pocketed the money and warned the children to mention nothing about it. The moment their mother had paid Colleen and seen her out the door, the children had sung like canaries.

"Those aren't the values I want my kids to see modelled," the mother reproved. Flooded with anger and embarrassment, I said I didn't blame her; those weren't *our* values either. I'm not sure she believed me.

Naturally we confronted Colleen about it, saying she owed the woman an apology *and* the LRT money back. Without repentance she grinned and said, "Those kids are liars! And that woman won't be able to find anyone else. When I tore the strip of paper off her ad, I tore off all the other strips too so I wouldn't have any competition." I found her attitude—and that grin—terrifying.

And I began to wonder whether "people of a sociopathic disposition" was an aptly descriptive phrase for my daughter after all.

15. If You Only Knew Half the Story

Colleen got very few calls for babysitting and she couldn't comprehend why. She claimed what she'd done wasn't such a big deal. Andy, Lisa and I were dumbfounded.

More dumbfounding still was the fact that she began rifling freely through our possessions while we were gone from the house. That she'd stolen that box of chocolates as a little girl and eaten them over at Sandra's I'd dismissed back then as a childish misdemeanour. After all, Lisa too had gone through a period of sneaking clothes out of my drawers to try on and sneaking a package of chocolate chips or a can of pie filling out of my baking cupboard as a snack. These antics had annoyed me at the time but they hadn't *frightened* me in the same way this did.

I realize now that Lisa's sneaky behaviours were those of a normal if resentful kid—a kid who was always a lousy liar and who was profoundly embarrassed when caught in a lie or misdeed: the sure sign of future honesty. I also realize that *Colleen's* stealing, which I shrugged off, was as serious as was her deliberate childhood tracking of mud all over my just-cleaned floors, her clumsy attempt to shock and sadden my newly-divorced colleague Ralph, and her tendency to seek out and befriend dysfunctional adults. Hindsight, as they say, is twenty-twenty.

A few months into Colleen's year at Alternative, a grave occurrence set both Andy and me back on our heels. One day, as my husband was about to go through the monthly bank statement, our younger daughter revealed to him (knowing discovery was imminent) that she had taken some money from the account. She had forged her dad's signature—which she'd practised over and over—on a cheque and the bank had cashed it without question. Okay, she'd known it was wrong, but she'd got tired of not having money to buy stuff other kids had. It wouldn't happen again. The fact she'd confessed it of her own accord was worth *something*, wasn't it?

Staggered by the larcenous nature of the act, we were yet more staggered that she'd had the smarts, and also the sneakiness, to delay discovery by not tearing off the *top* blank cheque in the book. She knew her dad recorded all expenditures as well as sequence numbers of pertinent cheques, and so would notice immediately if the next number in the cheque sequence was missing. It was a calculated, a *criminal* act! What should we do?

"You're darn right this won't happen again," Andy told her sternly. "If it does, we press charges. Is that understood?" Mutely she nodded, looking very contrite. But if she *was* contrite, the contrition didn't last.

A short time later, I began to notice two disturbing things. First, the smell of cigarette smoke was often present in the house when I got home from work. Second, small amounts of money went missing from my purse. In those days I carried more cash than I do in today's relatively cashless society. If I planned on doing any shopping on my way back, I might have anywhere from fifty to seventy-five dollars in my wallet. Initially, because of how small they were and because of an almost dogged reluctance to believe otherwise, I chose to think I'd spent the missing amounts on incidentals. But then Andy and I began to notice bills missing from a hiding place in a drawer where we kept a "cash stash" in the event of emergencies.

At the same time we also began to notice the pupil dilation in Colleen's eyes. I haven't been a high school teacher for twenty-five years and not seen that dilation before. Our daughter was into drugs. A call from Alternative's guidance counsellor, almost simultaneous to our discovery, told us Colleen's attendance had plummeted and she'd been seen with "the drug-and-alcohol crowd". Since she hadn't been caught red-handed, she could consider this a warning. Had *we* seen any indications in her behaviour at home? Was there money missing? Were there signs of other people having been in the house while we were at work? And had we checked the liquor cabinet lately? *Not again!*

I was in a daze when I hung up. Andy and I had done less and less entertaining since our problems with Colleen began escalating and at the best of times—as I've said before—I'm fairly clueless about the contents of the liquor cabinet. After the time we'd found the one or two bottles with levels lower than they should have been, we'd been spot-monitoring the levels and had always been relieved to see they were fine. A cursory inspection now *still* showed them to be fine. A closer examination revealed the bottles to contain not liquor but water.

Faced with this evidence as well as what the guidance counsellor had said, Colleen flew into a rage. She denied everything. That counsellor—whose praises she had recently sung to the skies—was a fool. *Lisa* was the one who'd drunk the liquor and *Lisa* was the one who had friends in the house when we weren't there. No, she *wasn't* stealing money and no, she *didn't* use drugs. That was Lisa as well, and maybe Shawn. What awful parents we were not to have more faith in her!

When confronted about any issue, Colleen would put on such an act of righteous indignation that she could make a person feel guilty for doubting her. But then, as she did this time, she often took it a step too far. When she blustered that we had no *proof* of anything, we decided the only way to be absolutely certain was to set a trap and get the proof we needed.

We chose Sunday afternoon, just a couple of days later, when we knew her to be in her room with the door ajar. Lisa was out with friends and would be gone for a while. In a voice loud enough to carry down the hallway I said to Andy, "We can't use the same hiding place any more. So I'm putting this fifty on the closet shelf under my handbags. She won't find it there."

"Shush or she'll hear you," Andy replied in a stage whisper. We felt like actors in a B grade movie.

Having baited the trap, we informed Colleen we were going out for a short walk in Fish Creek Park. She was used to our doing that and used to our telling her where we were going before we left. She didn't reply, though we knew she'd heard us. We made sure to stay away for at least an hour. When we returned to check out the closet shelf the money had sure enough disappeared.

Both of us had half expected Colleen to leave the money where it was until later when she could perhaps claim we'd mislaid it or used it ourselves and forgotten—or that Lisa had found and taken it. But no, she stole it on the spot. The degree of her brashness amazed us, as did her continued blustering denials. "Lisa came back while you were gone and stole it," she stormed. "But of course you don't think Goody Two-Shoes *ever* does anything wrong! I can't *believe* how you distrust me!"

"*You* are the only one who knew where the money was!" I stormed back. For a bright girl, you've done something very dumb!"

"You've also committed a second crime," Andy grimly added. "We gave you one chance when you forged that cheque. Now I think we're going to have to call the police and press charges."

"Go ahead," she sneered. "I'm leaving and not coming back ever!" Ignoring our telling her to stay put and for her own good discuss returning the money right away, she slammed out of the house and was gone for the next two days. We were frantic with worry.

"She's with her druggy friends," one mother said when we attended our Parent Support Group meeting the following evening. "That's where my daughter always goes whenever she runs away. She'll be back."

"And when she does come back you *should* press charges with the police," a father commented. "If you ignore the stealing you're giving her tacit permission to do it again and again. You have to make it clear with kids like this that you won't stand for it." Andy and I agreed with his opinion. One harried-looking woman named Bertha—a single mom—did not. "*My* daughter always says she'll kill herself when I threaten to go to the police," Bertha sobbed. "I couldn't live with knowing I caused my own child's death. I'd rather she steals from me or does anything she wants."

"Then she'll hold you hostage that way for the rest of your life," several of us protested, to no avail. That mother stopped attending meetings and I have no idea today what happened to her *or* her daughter. I only know that, at the time, my heart went out to the poor lady. I couldn't imagine trying to parent a child like Colleen all on my own.

When Colleen showed up two days after running away, she was still defiant and unrepentant. In response to our telling her how worried we'd been she replied, "So?" and flounced off to her room. There was no getting through to her. Andy and I made the painful decision to contact the police and proceed with pressing charges.

If I'd cried torrents of tears in earlier years I shed *rivers* of them now. Pressing criminal charges against our own child—the precious baby we'd been so proud of—was something I still couldn't believe we were doing. But it happened. If there's one thing psychologists, psychiatrists and counsellors repeatedly emphasized, it was that defiant kids must *never* be led to believe their parents don't mean what they say.

One police officer interviewed us; the other interviewed Colleen in a separate room. Andy had had to force her to get into the car with us and drive to the station and she lost no time telling her interviewer all about her dad's strong-arm tactics. We filled out forms to make the procedure official. One of the officers told us we'd be contacted when the court date came up. The other said, "You really shouldn't be using the court system to do your parental disciplining." And I replied inwardly—as I've done so many times since, *"You wouldn't be saying that if you only knew half the story..."*

Meanwhile, Colleen continued to flout all our rules: coming and going as she pleased at all hours of the day and night, playing hooky from school, being dropped off from cars driven by strangers and (we were positive) bringing members of her unsavoury drug crowd into our house while we weren't there. The place reeked of cigarette smoke and possibly a sweeter-smelling smoke as well. Her pupils were hugely dilated and she refused to talk to us even at meals—which she still expected to be served up regularly. On the advice of counsellors and members of our support group, we told her she couldn't live with us under those conditions and we were taking her to the Avenue 15 Youth Shelter.

Avenue 15 is a safe house for youth in trouble. It offers young people an alternative to a home situation that, for whatever reason, is untenable. Colleen was fifteen years eleven months old when we drove her there in mid-February of 1994; she wouldn't turn sixteen until mid-March of that year. We emphasized to her that this place was safe and social workers would help her deal with issues troubling her so that hopefully she could come back and live with us again. She smirked and said, "I hate you both. I hate our family and all your idiotic rules! I *want* to go there." But she changed her tune when we arrived.

"Yes, there are rules here," were the first words out of a tough-looking female social worker's mouth after greeting her. "You *will* go to school. We don't tolerate truancy. You'll be expected to take your turn with the chores like washing dishes or scrubbing toilets. If you don't like your parents' rules, then you better get used to ours because life is full of rules. You're welcome to stay and we'll try to help you if you want our help. But this isn't a holiday. If you don't choose to be here, then you choose the streets. We have others waiting for this space, so make up your mind."

Colleen unleashed a stream of obscenities upon all of us, followed by, "I choose the streets!" And she walked out the door without a backward glance. I remember two staff members holding onto my arms to keep me from going after her as I sobbed, "But she'll die out there!"

"That's possible," the tough-looking worker agreed. "More likely she'll end up coming back to us or you because she'll see that *we* are preferable to brutal reality. Until then no one can *force* her to do anything. Our society doesn't imprison children or anyone unless they're deemed a danger to themselves or others."

Utterly defeated, Andy and I returned home. For a week we had no idea where Colleen was, whether she was alive or dead. Like robots we continued going to work and Lisa continued going to school. (She was at University of Calgary by then, but still living at home.) We didn't know what else to do. I suppose I could have asked for stress leave and been granted it, and the same goes for Andy and Lisa. But where would that get us except sitting home biting our fingernails? I remember exchanging occasional hugs and words of commiseration with Lisa during that time—*occasional* being the operative word. Lisa still struggled very much with her own resentments against living in a family situation that can only be described as ugly.

At the end of her week on the streets Colleen got in touch with our minister, Jennifer Ferguson, saying she had no place to go; her parents had thrown her out. Jennifer called to let us know Colleen was safe and to propose a plan: a very nice lady named Kathleen Roberts, a congregant who lived alone, had offered to put Colleen up for a couple of months while Colleen "got her act together". Kathleen would be glad of the company and could maybe offer some objective help and advice. Were we agreeable? What a question! We would have agreed to let *anyone* try to help. Again though, I said inwardly, *"You wouldn't be making such an offer, dear Kathleen, if you only knew half the story…"*

For two months, from February to April of 1994, Colleen lived with Kathleen Roberts and we saw her periodically. She would not attend school, saying she needed a break because she was "in a bad head space". Apparently she behaved well for a short while but couldn't keep it up. She'd go off to spend time with "Judy", an adult friend of the same ilk as Sandra, whose address and last name we never knew. She once told us she and Judy were two people who knew better than anyone else how much life sucked. She even went for a brief "campout" at Judy's, sleeping on a bedroll in the basement in order to be near a woman she proclaimed to be as wonderful as Sandra, practically a saint. But then Judy must have done something to lose favour because one day Colleen simply announced that Judy was dead.

And just as suddenly Judy made a miraculous recovery! "I met her on the LRT today," Colleen stated matter-of-factly—as if she'd never dropped the bomb about the lady dying. "I'm calling her new boyfriend *Dad* now, and I'm calling Judy *Mom*." It was a taunt. Andy and I read rejection of our parenting efforts and we were hurt regardless of knowing how troubled she was.

Colleen also prevailed regularly upon the kindness of Maureen Pysk-lywec and spent time there conveying (whether by statement or implication I don't know) that we, her hard-hearted parents, deprived her of many things other kids' parents freely gave them and that she longed to come home but we had forbidden it. Maureen believed her and became increasingly angry with us. Once, Maureen called and begged us to let the poor child return to the family where she belonged. I tried explaining our position but how can you convey what you're being put through in a mere few minutes on the telephone?

I ended up telling her inside my head what I knew would be useless to tell her aloud: *"Maureen, you wouldn't be saying this if you only knew half the story…"*

16. Getting a Diagnosis

Even before her stay with Kathleen Roberts ended in April of 1994, Colleen and another girl she'd somehow hooked up with found a place (through a social worker the other girl knew) where they could room together. Colleen remained adamant she wanted nothing more to do with us and our dumb rules; she wanted to be free and in charge of her own life. The other girl had already received approval to live there. If we would agree to pay her half of the rent, Colleen would agree to go to school. Of course she knew "where we lived" in terms of bargaining with us.

The landlord's name was Lorraine, whose small but modern townhouse was in the far northeast end of town. Lorraine had fostered several young teens and felt she'd done them some good. She would keep an eye on the girls, she said, and would do her best to make this work. We decided to pay the rent and give the situation a try. At least we'd know where Colleen was and know also that she had some supervision.

Meanwhile, Colleen continued her visits to Maureen Pysklywec and when she moved prevailed upon Maureen to drive her over to Lorraine's place. On returning from that trip Maureen phoned us, said she needed to speak with us, and invited us to meet with her and her husband John at their house. Andy and I went over there bearing flowers as a thank-you for all Maureen's efforts in Colleen's behalf. Maureen answered the door looking like a thundercloud.

"I'm *very* angry," she confirmed. "How could you refuse to take your own daughter back? The place she's in now isn't that nice and the poor girl is most upset!"

Boiling with frustration and anger of my own at being judged like this by someone I'd considered a friend, I remember bursting into tears. Over tea we compared stories, specifically the stories Colleen was telling *Maureen* as opposed to those she was telling *us*—which in no way matched. John said to his wife, "There's obviously a lot more going on here than we are seeing." The evening ended on a strained note because Andy and I still weren't certain the Pysklywecs believed us. We felt the way we'd felt the day those social workers interviewed us: while trying everything we knew in order to help this girl, she was out there portraying us to the world as monsters.

Colleen did not last long with Lorraine—though she did attend school sporadically while there and actually wrote her final grade ten exams which resulted in a conditional pass from Alternative. Lorraine called to tell us it wasn't going well. Both Colleen and her roommate made hurtful fun of their landlord because the lady was heavy. They'd also used Lorraine's phone to make several calls to a "psychic" purporting to foretell their futures and they had run up a phone bill of over eighty dollars. We wrote Lorraine a cheque for Colleen's half of the amount which Lorraine never cashed. Instead Lorraine served notice: the girls had to find other accommodation by the end of June.

In the intervening period Colleen's court date came up—and yes, we dragged her to face the music. She was found guilty of stealing and "sentenced" to do community service. Throughout the proceeding she smirked. When told by the judge that *she* was to come up with an acceptable proposition for that community service, her smirk got wider. She treated the whole thing as a huge joke.

I must say we were originally surprised, even pleased, by the proposition she presented. An adult friend of hers knew of a nursing home where she could do volunteer hours as a nurse's assistant. It sounded like the sort of experience that could prove beneficial and gratifying. Indeed her proposal *was* accepted, and indeed she *did* report to the nursing home and complete the community service hours. She then told us, with a triumphant glare, that all she'd done at the nursing home was duck out the back door into the courtyard and take smoke breaks. "They couldn't *make* me do anything there," she added, "because I was a volunteer. See? You can do what you want to me but you're *never* going to see me broken!"

Were those the words of a sociopath? More and more, my fear was growing that a sociopath is what Colleen was. If we could only *force* her to submit to a brain scan…!

However, there was a second part to her "sentence" that was maybe the next-best thing: ten obligatory sessions with a qualified psychotherapist. Yes, of course we'd already taken her to numerous sessions with counsellors and psychologists but as a teen she'd rebelled against all such help. This gave her—and us—no choice. Legally we'd been *ordered* to get her there and see that she stayed for the sessions. The therapist she saw would have to sign documents verifying she had made ten visits. So we had our justification for doing what we wanted to do anyway.

Rev. Jennifer Ferguson, our minister, told us about a psychotherapist friend of hers who was very good, a Ms. Maureen Kitchur. Colleen liked Jennifer and was instantly more amenable to the idea of going to a friend of hers. Ms. Kitchur was in private practice but paying the price of the ten sessions without Health Care offsetting the expense would be well worth it if Maureen was as good as Jennifer said.

Throughout our ten drives to the sessions, Colleen made disparaging comments about the *judge* being the one who needed the shrink. As was typical, she initially seemed cooperative but soon became resentful towards the whole thing. Nevertheless we took her to the full ten sessions and upon their completion Ms. Kitchur had a talk with us.

And that was the first time someone made a tentative diagnosis: *borderline personality disorder.* We had never even heard the term. Ms. Kitchur elaborated.

"Since I've only seen her ten times I can't be sure. But she has a number of classic borderline characteristics. Borderline sufferers don't always see things the way we do. For example if I were to show her a painting of a farmer's field on a sunny day, she'd be more likely to focus on the one dark cloud in the sky and that would colour her opinion of the whole painting. In life this translates to 'black-and-white thinking' as well as mood swings of a far greater magnitude than non-borderline people have. Colleen also has quite a fixation on the darker side of life. There are ways she can be helped but only if *she* decides she wants to take the help—which she's unwilling to do."

"As her parents, how can *we* help her?" we wanted to know. My ignorance about this disorder caused my English teacher's mind to jump on the word "borderline", which I assumed meant "just barely". So—thank God!—she wasn't so mentally ill after all! She was teetering on the edge of normality. If we could only rescue her quickly, we could pull her back to safety from the ugly clutches of this disease and everything would be all right.

But that isn't what "borderline" means at all.

17. Borderline Personality Disorder

Colleen was sixteen when she received her diagnosis. There was not a doubt in my mind that she'd had this affliction since birth. Why had someone not put a label on it before? Was this the cause of all her troubles at school?

"From what I've read on the subject, lower-functioning borderlines may lack the ability to sift important information to the forefront of their brains and separate it from background disturbances," one psychologist colleague told me. "What you and I take for granted they just can't do. Therefore they have difficulty making decisions and they find it a tremendous chore to concentrate in a classroom situation. The effort literally exhausts them. Not surprisingly, they can't handle school and they drop out." The same colleague then added, "Not a lot is known about BPD. Some mental health experts disagree about its definition and others dispute its very existence."

So where did that leave us? In 1994 there were relatively few published works on the subject. A number of psychologists and psychiatrists were referring to BPD as a "wastebasket diagnosis" because it didn't neatly fit any of the descriptive criteria then set out in the *Diagnostic and Statistical Manual of Mental Disorders*, published by the American Psychiatric Association and considered the world-wide bible for diagnosing mental illness. (The manual was revised that very same year and has been re-revised since.) At the time we had to grope for whatever information we could find wherever we could find it.

On our bookshelf at home we had the *Canadian Medical Association Home Medical Encyclopedia,* published in 1992. It contained exactly one paragraph, calling the condition a form of personality disorder falling between neurotic and psychotic levels and characterized by rapid inappropriate mood changes, impulsivity and difficulty maintaining stable relationships. That was a start. We needed to learn more.

The Internet led us to several articles, one on the Mayo Clinic website. These provided additional detail. At this point I don't remember which author said what, but here in a nutshell is a conglomerate of what our first few information forays yielded.

BPD was so named in 1938 by American psychoanalyst Adolf Stern because he deemed its symptoms to fall on the border between *neurosis* and *psychosis*. Neurosis is a mental disorder in which the sufferer remains in touch with reality and is therefore distressed by his/her behaviour, recognizing it as "abnormal". By contrast, people suffering from psychotic illnesses usually do not recognize that they are ill. Psychotic illness so disturbs the ability to think, perceive and judge clearly that sufferers often do not realize they are unwell. They blame the rest of the world for things that go wrong with their lives.

Neurotics may appear to be normal, particularly to casual acquaintances, though neurosis can severely limit work and social activities. Symptoms tend to fluctuate in intensity, often in response to social and personal stresses. Those symptoms can include depression, extreme anxiety, phobia, hypochondriasis (thinking one is sick all the time) and dissociative behaviour (such as memory lapse or multiple personalities). Psychotics can be delusional, schizophrenic, and can also react to extreme emotional situations with almost no emotion at all—as though they just "don't get it".

And what did our available information cite as the cause of BPD? That was not yet fully understood. It was speculated to be several factors in conjunction with one another but was thought to relate primarily to some disorder of brain function originating in the *limbic* system, which regulates the emotions. The role of *neurotransmitters* (chemicals released by nerve endings) was suspected to play a vital part. If such a brain function disorder existed in a baby, then that baby had the predisposition to develop the disease. Parental abuse or childhood trauma might then contribute to a full-blown case—though therapists were unsure since borderlines often saw as "trauma" and "abuse" that which "normal" people did not view that way at all. Research was still ongoing.

As for how sufferers could be helped, most of what we read back then can be summarized thus: various forms of psychotherapy had had mixed results. Provided a patient was willing to undergo therapy, there was some chance of a remission in the symptoms. But a number of patients outright refused treatment—and furthermore, a number of therapists outright refused to treat BPD patients, finding them manipulative, combative, and likely to threaten to sue if they perceived their treatment not to be going successfully. Or the opposite might occur: the patient may develop a romantic fixation on the therapist, regarding him as a saint and badgering him at all hours of the day and night demanding one-on-one attention. Either way, successful treatment was not deemed a very hopeful prospect.

It was a bleak scenario. Based on these readings we had little doubt in our minds that Ms. Kitchur's diagnosis was an accurate one, and possibly other mental disorders co-existed with the BPD. ADHD (attention deficit hyperactivity disorder) with its symptoms of impulsivity and inability to concentrate certainly fitted Colleen and—as several articles we read claimed—was a common partner of BPD.

The more I've read since, the more certain I've become of Ms. Kitchur's conclusions. Ironically, the majority of what I've read since was not yet published when we—and Colleen—needed it most. Today, experts Paul T. Mason and Randi Kreger, authors of the book *Stop Walking on Eggshells: taking your life back when someone you care about has borderline personality disorder*, point out that BPD is not only recognized as a diagnosable disorder, it has lately become one of the most researched of all the personality disorders.

Here (according to *the Diagnostic and Statistical Manual of Mental Disorders*, Fourth Edition, Text Revision 2004) are the diagnostic criteria for BPD:

1. Frantic efforts to avoid real or imagined abandonment

2. A pattern of unstable and intense interpersonal relationships characterized by alternating between extremes of idealization and devaluation (also known as "splitting" or "black-and-white thinking")

3. Identity disturbance. Markedly and persistently unstable self-image or sense of self

4. Impulsivity in at least two areas that are potentially self-damaging (e.g., spending, sex, substance abuse, shoplifting, reckless driving, binge eating)

5. Recurrent suicidal behaviour, gestures or threats, or self-mutilating behaviour

6. Affective instability due to a marked reactivity of mood (e.g., intense episodic dysphoria [mixture of rage and despair, opposite of euphoria], irritability, or anxiety usually lasting a few hours and only rarely more than a few days)

7. Chronic feelings of emptiness

8. Inappropriate intense anger or difficulty controlling anger (e.g., frequent displays of temper, constant anger, recurrent physical fights)

9. Transient, stress-related paranoid ideation or severe dissociative symptoms

We had seen evidence of *all* these criteria in our daughter. Furthermore, as I've already stated, I'm certain she displayed incipient signs of them from the moment she was born. In the crib she often started violently at sounds or at our touch and then began to scream. Clinician Shari Manning, PhD, is the former President/CEO of Behavioural Tech and Behavioural Tech Research, organizations founded by Marsha M. Linehan (of whom I'll speak more later) to provide training in the therapy Linehan herself has developed for BPD sufferers. In a book she authored in 2011, Manning describes an experiment in which babies' noses were tickled with a feather. Some babies demonstrated no reaction at all; others moved around in "mild emotional response" and still others began crying and were hard to console. From birth, suggests Manning, we apparently have an encryption for how we experience emotion.[1] Mental health educator Valerie Porr (who believes BPD is a true neurobiological disorder and who cites cutting-edge science to back up her beliefs) refers to a "high startle response" in certain infants which might well indicate super-sensitivity to stimuli from external sources, and which may be a precursor of future mental disorder.[2]

As for "chronic feelings of emptiness", from the time Colleen was able to talk she would frequently wail, "I'm lonely!" She couldn't pronounce the letter "*l*" properly as a toddler so it came out, "I'm yoneyee!" We thought it was adorable and tried to comfort her with stuffed toys, treats, and various other diversions which only worked temporarily. Another thing we noticed when she was small—besides the behaviour extremes, the night terrors, and the constant claims of not feeling well—is that when she laughed, the laughter somehow had a *forced* quality to it, as though it didn't quite reach the depths of her soul. Maybe I'm not describing that very well but those who interact with borderline sufferers might know what I mean.

Mason and Kreger's book, referred to above, describes BPD sufferers as "walking contradictions" who struggle daily with the issues of engulfment and abandonment. Torn between the urge to merge and the desire

1   Manning, Shari Y., PhD. 2011 *Loving Someone with Borderline Personality Disorder: how to keep out-of-control emotions from destroying your relationship*. New York, NY: The Guildford Press: 28

2   Porr, Valerie, M.A. 2010 *Overcoming Borderline Personality Disorder: A Family Guide for Healing and Change*. New York, N.Y.: Oxford University Press: 54

for independence, their actions may not make sense because at times they seek closeness and nurturing and at other times they seem compelled to drive you away.[3] It is a description that fits the tot Colleen exactly: excessively clingy one moment, avidly resistant to touch the next.

Another characteristic of Colleen's childhood is how difficult she found it to make decisions when we, as a family, went out to a restaurant. She would scan the menu, change her mind half a dozen times, and then complain that surrounding bustle and noise interfered with her concentration. Once, at a KFC takeout, she actually burst into tears because the place was being renovated. "I can't *think* with all that drilling going on!" she screamed. Invariably, when the food arrived, she would be displeased with her choice and would want to trade with one of the rest of us. The scenes she created often made our restaurant meals miserable. Yet my colleague's comment about the BPD brain's inability to sift important information to the forefront and block out background interference offers a plausible explanation for those scenes.

Reluctance on the part of therapists who saw Colleen in her early years to declare a child mentally ill is understandable—even granting they *were* BPD savvy, which many weren't. Children's personalities are still developing and hesitation to put such a label on a young child was the norm. As for teenagers and their raging hormones, the same colleague I've quoted above quipped, "*All* teenagers are mentally unstable. That goes with the territory." It seems logical, though, to deduce that at least *some* of the children and teens we tag with the adjective "troubled"—or in my British dad's terminology "bloody-minded"—are, in fact, sufferers of BPD.

My readings disclose an estimated *six million* North Americans, or two percent of its total population, to be victims of the affliction. According to the DSM-IV-TR quoted above, eight to ten percent of all people with BPD (that is, 480,000 to 600,000, or one in twelve) will die by their own hands. That is mind-boggling. Mason and Kreger call it "equivalent to a Titanic sinking every day for between four months and a year."[4]

---

3   Mason Paul T. and Randi Kreger. 2010 *Stop Walking on Eggshells: Taking your life back when someone you care about has borderline personality disorder.* Oakland, CA: New Harbinger Publications

4   Ibid. 170

Because of her refusal to accept help, I can only theorize about what was going on inside my poor dear daughter's impaired brain. At a United Church Men's Conference held in Banff in 2009, Andy had a conversation with Dr. Rod Densmore, who runs the Primary Care Social Medicine Clinic for Complex Neurodevelopmental Conditions in Salmon Arm B.C. About twenty years ago Dr. Densmore, a family physician, adopted a child with fetal alcohol syndrome and ended up making an intensive study of brain disorders and publishing, in 2011, a book/DVD series on the subject: *FASD Relationships: What I have learned about Fetal Alcohol Spectrum Disorder*. In 2009 he was a presenter on the subject at the Banff Conference.

BPD, Densmore told my husband, causes some similar brain-function abnormalities to fetal alcohol syndrome. Today's sophisticated brain imaging techniques—such as fMRI (functional magnetic resonance imaging), CT (computerized tomography), PET (positron emission tomography), and SPECT (single photon emission computed tomography)—have elucidated some of the anatomical and physiological differences between the BPD brain and the "normal" or typical brain. These studies seem to imply *overactivity* of those parts of the brain involved with impulse or emotional response (the limbic system) while demonstrating *underactivity* in such areas as the prefrontal cortex—the part of the brain involved with executive thinking and the "reining in" of impulses.[5]

What this translates into, in Densmore's words, is severely reduced communication between brain areas where impulsive urges arise and brain areas that consider possible consequences of those urges. For example, the BPD sufferer may want to take drugs in order to gratify an immediate urge to feel better. Rationally, he knows this could lead to addiction but his "immediate urge" area is often not adequately inhibited by his "consequences" area. What he wants he wants *now*. At the moment of awareness of the urge, he has only a dim awareness of consequences.

Immediate urges totally override consideration of the result or effect of an unwise action.

By contrast, the typical brain possesses more robust communication pathways between the "urge" and the "consider the consequences" areas,

---

5   Eric Lis, Brian Greenfield, Melissa Henry, et al., "Neuroimaging and Genetics of Borderline Personality Disorder: A Review", *Journal of Psychiatry and Neuroscience* 32 (2007): 162-173

and therefore a typical person, even if he experiments with drugs a few times, will be wary of taking up the practice regularly. By the same token, if a typical person sees in a store an item he wants and cannot afford, he will "override" the urge to shoplift because his "consequence awareness" area tells him resulting criminal charges could cause him long-term damage. Far less powerful "consider the consequences" brakes exist in the person affected by BPD.

What I am saying here (and Dr. Densmore told Andy he agrees with this) is that criminal prosecution of a person who has such brain damage probably has minimal rehabilitative effect. As sorry as he might be for what he has done and as bad as he might feel about it *after the fact*, he will go right ahead and repeat the criminal act the next time temptation presents itself. Then he will be sorry again, and so on, and so on *ad infinitum*. An impaired ability to apply enough restraint *at the exact moment of temptation* is the issue. People with BPD can suffer perpetual cycles of highs and lows: the elation of acting upon an appealing urge followed by feelings of remorse, self-condemnation and misery about the results.

Knowing this helps me understand—as I and many others didn't at the time—that the condition's cause (disturbance in the brain's pathways that regulate emotion and impulse) renders it a true medical disorder and no more under the person's control than is diabetes or hypertension. Colleen's brightness made all of us feel she should be able to figure out how to "pull herself up by her own bootstraps". But, say Kreisman and Straus, "a borderline suffers a kind of emotional hemophilia; she lacks the clotting mechanism needed to moderate her spurts of feeling. Prick the delicate 'skin' of a borderline and she will emotionally bleed to death."[6] "The borderline lacks the boots, much less the bootstraps"[7] with which to pull herself up.

In light of these descriptions, one can't help wondering if a severe case of this disorder isn't worse than being born with a mental handicap that affects the prefrontal cortex. After all, that kind of handicap makes for blissful ignorance about one's own limitations and about being kept at arm's length by others. Others, in fact, tend to be *kinder* to a truly mentally-handicapped person, not expecting as much of him and making

---

6   Jerold J. Kreisman, M.D. and Hal Straus, *I Hate You—Don't Leave Me: understanding the borderline personality* (New York, N.Y.: Penguin Group, 2010): 12

7   Ibid, 127

far more allowances for his behaviour. BPD sufferers, on the other hand, live their lives in full knowledge of their alienation from others and, worst of all, their alienation from themselves. Small wonder a good percentage of them either consciously or unconsciously make repeated attempts on their own lives.

At *www.BPDCentral.com* Randi Kreger has set up an online support community for BPD sufferers and their families known as *Welcome to Oz*. (How Andy, Lisa and I could have used that!) This online site has resulted in sufferers themselves speaking out about what they endure. How does BPD look from the *inside*? Say Kreger and Mason, "Imagine the worst you have ever felt, and then triple it."[8]

Kathy Rouleau, an intelligent and charming lady who attends our church and who is a diagnosed "mild" BPD sufferer, consented to try and describe her feelings to me. Interestingly she began by saying, "When I'm down, I probably feel six times worse than the worst *you've* ever felt. I lash out at people and call them names. I want to over-medicate myself to make the pain go away. I don't want to live. After I've calmed down somewhat, I hate myself for acting the way I did. At times I struggle with feeling unworthy. I take my prescribed meds faithfully and continue to hope that, if I make the effort, I will get better and better. But to tell you the truth, I would rather have been born without arms or legs than have this disorder. The mind is *everything*. If your reasoning processes aren't working right, then your whole world isn't working right."

Kathy is forty-seven years old. Her prognosis, she feels, is relatively hopeful. She has articulated what my poor darling daughter could never bring herself to articulate. Most likely Colleen, being a more severe case, could not stand far enough back from the chaos wrought by her emotions on her thought processes to achieve Kathy's more detached view *or* Kathy's willingness to seek help.

As I've said before, Colleen always declared that *we* were the ones who needed the help. That was her reality.

In his book *Dancing Wu Li Masters: An Overview of the New Physics* (New York, NY: Perennial Classics, 2001), Gary Zukav, an American

---

8   Paul T. Mason and Randi Kreger, *Stop Walking on Eggshells: Taking your life back when someone you care about has borderline personality disorder* (Oakland, CA: New Harbinger Publications, 2010) 168

self-empowerment guru, expresses better than I ever could—in a word pattern that reads like a continuous loop—the impossibility of *any* of us achieving an objective, non-mind-filtered reality:

Reality is what we take to be true.

What we take to be true is what we believe.

What we believe is based on our perception.

What we perceive depends upon what we look for.

What we look for depends upon what we think.

What we think depends upon what we perceive.

What we perceive determines what we believe.

What we believe determines what we take to be true.

What we take to be true is our reality.

Kathy's reference to being born without arms and legs hits the nail on the head. Severe borderline sufferers lack *emotional* arms and legs. Much of the time, their version of reality is one that totally incapacitates and cripples them.

18. Without Arms or Legs

It is important to remember that much of the information I have just given about BPD comes from material not yet published while Colleen was growing up. It is relatively recently that I have attained the level of understanding I now have about the condition. Yet I knew then as I know now that as much as you might pity a person without arms or legs, you cannot allow that person to manhandle you or to walk all over you. (How glad I am that I've retained enough of my funny bone to see the humour in what I've just written!) In truth there's nothing remotely funny about BPD or its effects on those living with BPD sufferers.

And yet possessing a sense of humour is so essential for coping with any aspect of life! It is part of one's stabilizing emotional mechanism—the mechanism I'm sure Colleen was born without. Like the stabilizers on a huge cruise ship that keep the ship from being tossed and pitched about by every oceanic rise and fall, humour provides a buffer against those emotional ups and downs created by stressful situations. As does physical exercise, the very act of laughing floods the brain with endorphins, those desirable "well-being" hormones. And laughing has surely de-fused many a potentially hostile clash since the beginning of time.

In her Introduction to the book she co-wrote with Paul T. Mason, Randi Kreger estimates that at least eighteen million North American family members, partners and friends of BPD sufferers regularly blame themselves for behaviour that has little to do with them. About the self-blame she's absolutely right. Andy, Lisa and I have all given in to that at times. What could we have done for Colleen that we didn't do? Or what *did* we do that we shouldn't have done? Despite all reassurances from counsellors I have consulted, I know these questions will haunt the emotional part of me until the day I die.

At the United Church Men's Conference in Banff, Dr. Densmore told Andy that no parent of "normal" children can possibly comprehend the hell of trying to parent sufferers of BPD and related disorders—which is why our Parent Support Group (led by Peter O'Brien alternatively with other mental health professionals and often observed by those studying to *become* mental health professionals) was essential to helping us cope. Those mental health professionals and other parents were our stabilizers, giving us the "sea legs" to weather storms Colleen wrought upon us. And

I believe we reciprocated. As well-meaning as all our church friends were, they could not possibly understand what we were experiencing.

And yet, God bless them, their efforts were unremitting. Rev. Jennifer Ferguson chuckled, "Maybe we should all raise each other's teenagers! It might make for a lot less stress all around." Jennifer talked to Diana Badenduck, a congregant with abundant compassion and a spare basement room to offer. Colleen moved in with Diana on June 23, 1994.

As always, there was the "honeymoon period" at first. Diana found Colleen charming and sweet. Colleen got on well with Diana's young children and the whole family. She attended Alternative frequently enough to write and to conditionally *pass* her grade ten exams. I'm sure Diana, like Maureen, began to wonder whether the problem was with *us* and I don't doubt Colleen at least intimated to her that it was.

Every time Andy and I talked to Diana during that period we figuratively held our breath. When was the other shoe going to drop? At first Diana reported all was going quite well: Colleen's room was messy but otherwise things were okay. Yes, Colleen had mood swings but then what teenager doesn't? The laid-back routine of summer holidays made for reasonably smooth sailing. Then holidays ended and it was time for Colleen to begin her grade eleven year.

Being over sixteen now, Colleen's status at Alternative was that of "adult living outside the parental home". The staff there didn't legally owe us any information at all about how she was faring. But they were teaching colleagues, so we *did* learn she'd started the year off well enough but was again slipping. She'd developed an obsessive crush on a boy named Seamus who was the most wonderful fellow in the world. If she were not so clingy Seamus might have liked her back. But as things were, the boy was always gently trying to extricate himself from her clutches. The staff feared Colleen was riding for a fall.

We saw exactly what they meant the evening Colleen asked us to give her a ride to a school dance. (It blew our minds how she simultaneously wanted us out of her life and yet never hesitated to ask for favours as though totally entitled to them—and as though *she* had a monopoly on being hurt when people mistreated her.) Provided her requests were not unreasonable, we *did* do our best to accommodate them whenever possible. It was our only link, however tenuous, to any kind of a relationship at all with our daughter.

The moment she got to the dance Colleen deserted us completely, calling out "Seamus!" and flinging herself upon a boy sitting close by. She climbed into his lap, straddling him as though he were a horse. We could see how uncomfortable the boy was and were mortified in her behalf. One of the staff supervisors suggested we leave and said someone on staff would look after giving her a ride back to Diana's.

Not long after that evening, Colleen was expelled from Alternative. She'd shown up high for class, using up the last of her warnings. The Admissions-and-Expulsions Board consisting of students and staff together had held a meeting and had unanimously agreed she'd been given several chances and deserved no more. She was sixteen—beyond the legal age of *having* to be in school—and yes, there was a waiting list for her spot. She was gone.

It was close to the end of October. Colleen's expulsion apparently corresponded to what had been the inevitable rejection by Seamus. Out for one of our "getaway walks" (as we'd come to call them) in Fish Creek Park, Andy and I arrived home to a message from Diana on our answering machine. "Call me," Diana said, sounding on the verge of tears. "It's extremely urgent."

Diana had found Colleen passed out in her room and had been unable to rouse her. Colleen had been taken by ambulance to Emergency at Rockyview Hospital. Immediately we drove there, leaving a scribbled note for Lisa as to our whereabouts. By the time we arrived Colleen was awake enough to be screaming obscenities at the attending physician—obscenities she heaped equally liberally upon us.

"She won't tell me what she's taken," the physician said. "I've called a psychiatrist. When I leaned on her to tell me, she gave me a list that would have killed a horse. I've had to order her stomach pumped. Has she got a history of doing this?" Too choked to speak, I nodded.

To Colleen he said, "You may not *want* your stomach pumped but it's happening whether you like it or not. So it's up to you whether it happens the easy way or the hard way. Either you calm yourself and let us do it or I call security to hold you down. Which is it to be?"

Colleen responded by unleashing another stream of obscenities. As two uniformed security people entered, the attending physician motioned us to leave and ushered us out. But just before he did, he flung one final remark at Colleen that appalled me. I shall never forget those words. He said, "Why don't you kill yourself and get it over with, and stop torturing these nice people?"

I'm sure I gasped aloud. Andy was equally shocked. What this doctor said next however, when the three of us had left the room, possibly offered some justification for the approach. "Nice hasn't worked so far. Let's try hitting her over the head with a ton of bricks. These drama queens are so self-absorbed they have no idea what they're doing to others."

Despite my distaste at hearing my daughter described as *these drama queens*, I had to admit to myself he was right. Nice had *never* worked with Colleen. Nice meant you were weak and could be used. I don't think Colleen consciously thought of it like that but that's the way it always turned out. Her "nice" friends like Allison and Heather were the ones she took advantage of and bullied. The "cool" people in her eyes—the drug crowd as well as the ones who bullied *her*—were the ones she sought after. As for boys, those who rebuffed her or were most likely to rebuff her were those she unfailingly admired and chased. Wasn't it Groucho Marx who said, "I'd never join a club that would have me as a member"? Marx made us laugh when he said it, but as a self-destructive life pattern for Colleen and those like her, it's anything but comedy.

Was the doctor's strategy a valid one to try on Colleen or was it a gross error on his part? That I can't say. We who *don't* have BPD can see beyond our own pain to the effect it has on others around us. I think those with milder cases of BPD, like Kathy, are also capable of that empathy—which necessarily involves a distancing of oneself from one's own emotions, a deployment of those inner stabilizers. The doctor put himself in Colleen's place, reasoning that if *he* had just made a suicide attempt he might be "guilted" out of ever trying it again if reminded of what he was putting his loved ones through. And yes, such a strategy probably *would* have worked on him—because he doesn't have BPD and in the world of *his* reality, that would be a feasible strategy to try. I have never blamed him for trying it, though I *do* think it was the wrong strategy with Colleen.

In any event, that didn't matter. Other than the unrequited ache for her beloved Seamus, Colleen had no memory at all of that day's happenings. Andy and I, on the other hand, will remember them always. We spent several hours at Rockyview Hospital talking to different psychiatrists and doctors about how our daughter was doing and whether she'd caused herself any lasting damage. The answer to the last part was no; they'd pumped her stomach in time to save her life and to keep her physically unharmed. And for that she was letting them know, through constant cursing, that she was *not* thankful.

Of course they admitted her to make sure she remained stable. Andy and I were sent home; we could be of no further use there. It was late enough into the night by then that it wasn't worth going to bed and we decided we'd just stop off at the house to brush our teeth (and talk to dear neglected Lisa!) and then go straight to work.

As we walked hand-in-hand down the hall toward the exit, I felt a soft touch on my shoulder. When I turned in its direction I was looking into the face of a beautiful young woman named Carrie whom I recognized as a former student. Carrie, with her rosy pink complexion and cloud of blonde hair, was now a member of the hospital staff. But to my grief-clouded perception she looked like nothing less than an angel sent down from heaven.

"Don't worry Mrs. Porter," Carrie soothed. "I promise we'll take good care of her." And having held it together reasonably well up to this point, I remember melting into Carrie's arms and giving way to sobs.

At the moment of my most intense need for comfort, the embodiment of that comfort had appeared. I felt as though God himself had given me a nudge and whispered into my ear, "You're not alone."

19. Avoiding Homelessness

After the suicide attempt Diana informed us Colleen could no longer stay with the Badenducks. Again, who can blame her? She couldn't risk putting herself or her family through such an emotionally harrowing time again. "Colleen can be so loveable," she said tearfully. "There's a whole lot in that girl that's worth saving! I'm really sorry I couldn't help her."

Like us, Diana felt absolutely lost for answers. In former times, as my dad once pointed out, individuals whose chaotic behaviour wreaked havoc on family or society could be declared incompetent by parents or relatives and locked away against their will in institutions. (In fact, this is the very subject of the bestselling book *Girl, Interrupted*, in which author Susanna Kaysen is labelled a borderline sufferer at age sixteen in the nineteen-sixties and spends eighteen months at McLean Hospital, a Massachusetts psychiatric facility.) In centuries past, patients in a psychiatric facility could be *forced* to conform to certain routines through use of straitjackets, medications, and shock treatments. Maybe that protected them somewhat, but to what end? Their problems were not sufficiently understood to be treated with much effectiveness and they spent their lives in the company of similarly afflicted people, reinforcing their own mental turbulence. Even if (as Dad also pointed out) such measures today might prevent death by their own hands, would not that very death be infinitely preferable to spending a life shut up like a caged animal?

Moral and ethical questions aside, there's no point to such a debate. *Our* society tries to assist the mentally ill in coping with the world as it is. If their mental illness prevents them from *seeing* the world as it is to "normal" people, then medications and therapies exist that can help them address that. The task is convincing resistant ones to *want* those therapies and medications. Resistance poses an insurmountable obstacle to treatment. If this book persuades even *one* BPD sufferer to seek treatment, it will not have been written in vain.

Andy and I annually sponsor a meal for the homeless served at the Calgary Drop-In and Rehab Centre located in the heart of downtown Calgary—an amazing facility dealing daily and admirably with prevention of hunger on the streets. Any Calgarian who has not visited it should make a point of doing so. There is an education to be had there in terms of seeing how reduction in available mental-health care has swelled the ranks of the needy and the indigent who otherwise have very few help options available to them. "They should just stop being so lazy, find work, and start making useful contributions to society!" a colleague who didn't last long in teaching once commented. That may apply to a limited number of Drop-In Centre habitués but it doesn't to the majority. And most people Andy and I call our friends would never harbour such a narrow view.

The money we contribute is donated in the form of a cheque to the Outreach Committee at our present church, Red Deer Lake United. (We changed churches after we retired and had a bungalow built in the south-west community of Evergreen, overlooking our beloved Fish Creek Park. I'll speak more of that later.) Since we began making this donation five years ago, approximately thirty volunteers, mainly from the church, have regularly accompanied us to the Centre where our group serves between nine-hundred and eleven-hundred suppers to clientele especially numerous in very cold winter weather. Why have we felt moved to do this?

"Why not?" might be the simplest reply and indeed I wish I could say it's just all-round selfless altruism with no gain reaped in return. But that's not strictly true. I believe our reasons are much the same as the ones driving me to write this book: that is, attempting to identify with and help those who daily contend with crippling torment such as that endured by our daughter—whom we could *not* help. Were it not for our financial assistance Colleen would have been on the streets right along with these Drop-In Centre clients. At times she was on the streets anyway.

So when Diana said she could no longer live with the Badenduck family, that threat of homelessness hung over Colleen's head like the proverbial sword of Damocles. We knew she'd never come back to us and live by our rules—and quite honestly we weren't sure by then that we could survive having her under our roof—but neither, as long as we could prevent it, would we *ever* see her homeless.

The immediate problem was solved by the fact that, for five days after her suicide attempt, she was transferred for assessment to the Psychiatric Unit of the Holy Cross Hospital. From there she called us, refusing to speak to me when I answered and tersely asking for her dad. She wanted him to bring her cosmetics, another pair of pyjamas and a dressing gown. She wanted no interaction with me at all. So Andy drove there alone, taking with him the items requested. He tried to talk to her but she sent him away. She was expecting friends to visit and didn't want him there when they arrived. When my dear husband recounted this upon his return home, I could see how deeply hurt he was. I had thought I was wrung dry of tears but for his hurt I cried again. We both did. Yes, teenagers can sometimes be ashamed of their parents but this was rejection of one of the few supportive people left in her life! How could she behave that way: biting the very hand that reached out to help her? Ill or not, her conduct was abominable.

As for the homeless issue, fate stepped in just before she was discharged five days later—having been deemed "not a danger to herself or others". The United Appeal was conducting a campaign amongst Calgary's oil companies and a representative showed up at Andy's office to give a talk on various services in town that such donations went to support. One of the services he mentioned happened to be finding housing for youth who could not live at home. Andy connected with him after the talk and was advised to contact the person in charge of housing at McMan Youth, Family, and Community Services.

McMan, located in northwest Calgary, opened its first program in 1975 in an inner-city area of Edmonton and has since grown to the point where branch offices exist across the province. By the time Colleen was discharged from hospital we had given her this contact information and she had acted upon it. That was how she first met and formed a bond with Darlene Petrie, then a Youth Worker there and now Program Manager. Recently Darlene consented to speak with me about the bond she'd formed with Colleen.

"She was such a bright girl! We had many long conversations and she often called me when she was in trouble—usually, but not always, about a place to stay. Some she found on her own; some I found for her. Today I'm not sure which is which but I was always impressed by her resourcefulness when up against a wall. What I regretted was that crisis seemed to be the key ingredient in calling forth her best efforts on her own behalf. Then as soon as she'd resolved one particular crisis, she immediately set about creating another! Nevertheless I and others on our staff couldn't help seeing what a talented and engaging person she could be."

Another thing Darlene says she couldn't help seeing is that Colleen loved both of us very much despite having perspective issues brought on by mental illness that prevented her expressing that love and possibly prevented her admitting it, even to herself. (In light of present ongoing BPD research I would venture to say our daughter felt *invalidated* by our "let's get on with it" attitude about life. From her standpoint, getting on with it was frequently impossible, so paralyzed was she by her own inner turbulence. And she was as helpless to make us understand her position as we were to make her understand ours.)

When Diana couldn't take Colleen back, Darlene found her temporary seven-day lodging with a lady in North Hill named Rose. Before that week was up Darlene had found two other places for her to choose from: one in Millrise, a community just south of us, and the other in Shaganappi, not far from the old Children's Hospital. Colleen chose the second, though we picked her up and drove her to the first where she was informed smoking was forbidden in the house. "Stupid rules!" Colleen muttered, rejecting the house. "It's close to *you*," she added as though that confirmed her decision. "I don't like these rich neighbourhoods. I don't belong here."

I have never thought of Millrise as a particularly *rich* neighbourhood but I think I know what Colleen meant. Upper-middle class values, which were more likely to involve "no smoking" dictates as well as stipulations about tidiness and noise, were not her cup of tea. Unfailingly she chose to cohabit with people less uptight about those things—which is why she ended up with Edna.

Edna herself smoked and she and Colleen had frequent chats over cigarettes. "I'm a tough old bird," Edna told us over the phone. "I've crashed and burned myself a few times in my life. And I've had lots of experience with teenagers. If there are any problems I'll know how to handle them."

Edna spoke the truth. Her approach to problem solving was kind but firm. "Get used to it," she told her tenant. "There are *rules* here, just as there are rules everywhere. Did you think you'd be escaping that by coming to live with me? No such luck! On week nights the curfew is ten o'clock. No reason you should need to be out past that. It's a ten minute leeway; then I lock the door."

Colleen had lived with Edna six months before Edna drew that line in the sand about the curfew. In the course of the six-month period Edna had done her best to bond with Colleen but with typical perversity Colleen began to do the Groucho Marx thing: disdaining the club that would tolerate her as a member. She pushed the limits further and further, finally forcing Edna to take a stand. And the moment Edna delineated a boundary and Colleen heard the hated word *rule*, she purposely disobeyed, staying out well past the ten-minute leeway.

Edna stuck to her guns and locked the door. Colleen called the police on Edna, belligerently declaring that as a rent-paying lodger (which she wasn't; *we* were) she had the right to her own key. After the police forced Edna to let Colleen in, Edna told Colleen she had to be out as of mid-April.

Again Darlene from McMan stepped into the breach, finding her a basement suite in a house with a lady named Theresa in the north central part of the city. It was a comfortable enough place but Colleen had to go upstairs to make telephone calls. Deprived of Edna's company she reacted with characteristic BPD perversity and now craved nothing more than Edna's company: a number of those calls were made to her former landlady!

One weekend Theresa had the nerve to go away on a family camping trip, locking the upstairs part of the house—along with the telephone—away from Colleen. Colleen went ballistic. No doubt the phone was, in her view, a literal lifeline without which she felt isolated, cast adrift, and friendless. Rose-coloured glasses aside, it is also entirely possible she'd been about to score a hit on some street drugs when her communication line was cut off. In any event she broke down the door leading to the upstairs in order to get in and use the phone. Theresa served notice. That was July 1995; she had lasted no longer than three months there.

"I don't get along with landlords," she told Darlene. "I want my own place. And I want independence from my parents. Then I can really start to do something with my life." At seventeen and still a student, she legally qualified to have those things. Darlene helped her fill out forms to get on social assistance and found her a tiny but very comfortable and bright apartment in the Inglewood area near the Bird Sanctuary. We helped her move in. Having made such an issue about her independence, Colleen did an abrupt about-face and began calling us almost every evening. "I don't like being on my own, Mom," she wailed. "It's too lonely. I want someone to come and tuck me in at night. It was the "I hate you; don't leave me" thing all over again. She lasted only *two* months there, moving out at the end of September.

"They often don't know what they want at that age," my psychologist colleague ruminated. As you and I both know, sometimes they drift around for a while and then just suddenly get it together. Something as fortuitous as meeting the right boy can do the world of good."

I remember smiling and nodding doubtfully at that comment, having no faith at all that "the right boy" (as in someone who would love her and treat her well) would have any appeal whatsoever for Colleen. Quite honestly, what I was beginning to dread more and more by then was the appearance on the scene of "the wrong boy": someone who would treat her like dirt, hurt her even more than life had already hurt her, and then discard her like trash. Her self-image was fragile enough that an encounter with such a fellow might be all it took to send her over the edge.

As it turned out, my vision of "the wrong boy" in no way measured up in nightmarish quality to the real thing.

20. The Nightmare

Chronic feelings of emptiness brought on by BPD cause many sufferers to compensate by engaging in promiscuous sexual behaviour as soon as they enter puberty. BPD girls typically go for the "bad boys", those who flout convention and skirt the edges of the law when not breaking it altogether. The cause I didn't understand in the way I now do when Colleen was in her teens, but the behaviour I had no doubt about despite being the last person she'd ever confide in. That she'd told Lisa of several pregnancy scares was proof she already had a sexual history.

At risk of generalizing, romantic liaisons entered into by BPD sufferers tend—as do all their relationships—to storminess and are often short-lived. It's the Groucho Marx thing yet again: the moment the "club" accepts them, it becomes inferior. They feel themselves unworthy of being in any way valued by others and especially by those who treat them well. Predictably, therefore, the partners they choose tend to be society's abusers. This I instinctively knew about my daughter even at a time when far less published material existed on the subject of her disorder.

Her next stay, upon moving out of the Inglewood apartment, was at a house in the Marlborough area with a landlady I'll call Jan. Again there were rules she refused to abide by, and again she lasted no longer than two months. The difference, however, is that Jan had a relative—nephew, cousin, I don't recall—whom I'll call Brad. Several years older than Colleen, Brad was handsome in a roguish sort of way with a lean rangy build, a swagger to his step, and an easygoing charm. Colleen fell hard. And with that perversity—and nerve—that never ceased to amaze, she phoned us one day at the end of November 1995 first to say she and Brad were now together for good, and second to ask if we'd invite the two of them over for supper so we could meet our future son-in-law.

Yes, we were taken aback by the announcement; yes, we were very leery of the prospect—and yes, we *did* issue an invitation to them to come over a few days later and share our evening meal. Both Andy and I made a conscious decision *not* to be predisposed to dislike this boyfriend. I remember I cooked up a beef roast with potatoes, vegetables, and gravy, followed by pie for dessert. One never knew. It was barely possible this fellow would turn out to be the answer to our prayers. Stranger things have happened.

He had the snide smile I recognized as belonging to certain types of students I taught—the ones regularly in trouble who counted upon being able to sweet-talk their way out. The moment I thought this I sternly berated myself. *No*, I said inwardly. *I won't be unfair!* Colleen was clearly very much in love, the way she kept devouring him with her eyes, the way she took his hand and squeezed it from time to time, and the way she danced attendance upon him at table. His response to her eager ministrations was laconic if not mildly annoyed. He made lighthearted reference to a recent stint in jail, having "taken the rap" for a couple of his buds who now owed him one. (How noble of him!) Enormous pupils—evidence of heavy drug use—lent a seedy vacancy to his fatuous grin. And this was when he was on his *best* behaviour! My heart sank.

Relatives of Brad's had said the two could stay there for the next few weeks, Colleen claimed, and after that their plan was to move to *Ontario* and live with Colleen's Uncle Stephen, Andy's brother. This news made me gulp because I had grave doubts Steve knew anything at all about it. My brother-in-law teaches learning-and-behaviour-challenged children at the elementary school level and has his own place in Toronto. From childhood when her uncle visited us, Colleen had reacted to Steve's affable easygoing manner by assuming he lived a life much like hers: without responsibility or rules. Ergo (in terms of her logic) he wouldn't mind in the slightest if she and a boyfriend simply showed up unannounced at his bachelor pad and declared they intended to stay a while.

"Steve won't go for that," Andy told her. "Even if he doesn't mind you moving in with him, he *will* mind your attitude of entitlement to his hospitality. And how will you support yourselves? You can't expect *him* to support you."

"Uncle Steve is cool," Colleen countered. "He's not a nerd like you. He'll be fine with it. If he isn't, we'll go to Grandma and Grandpa or to Nana."

Grandma and Grandpa—my parents—lived in a condo in Hamilton. Mum was terminally ill with pancreatic cancer and Dad had bladder cancer plus congestive heart failure. They were able to stay in their own place only because my brother Brian lived with them and looked after them. Nana—Andy's mother—had her own apartment, also in Hamilton, but was a widow with the beginnings of dementia whose days of living independently were numbered. Colleen was aware of all this and yet, as always, her own needs took precedence.

"Our parents aren't an option," I told Colleen. "They're too ill. That would be unfair. If you move to Hamilton, get yourselves jobs and settle down there, I'm sure they would love to see you. But you can't ask them, at their stage of life, to take on the burden of having you as long-term houseguests." Our daughter's glazed stoniness told us our words were falling on deaf ears. Imposition or not, she and the boyfriend meant to do exactly as they wished.

They were taking a WestJet flight there for which Colleen had already purchased one-way tickets for both of them. Where she'd got the money was a mystery. Realizing we wouldn't get an answer to that (at least, not a truthful one) we didn't bother asking. Brad's relatives would supply the ride to the airport. Everything was all set.

"So have a nice life!" Colleen gave us a brittle emotionless smile as the two of them departed—a smile we'd come to know was only a veneer. It was a mere movement of the lips unenhanced by any expression at all in the eyes. "Guess we won't be seeing you all that often, since we're moving out there."

What about the wedding? Did they have any definite plans for one? If so, those plans obviously didn't include us. Were they going to call ahead to Stephen and inform him he was to expect them? Did they have enough money to cover the taxi fare to Toronto or did they think he'd drive all the way to Hamilton to pick them up? None of these questions seemed to concern them. *We* were the concerned ones.

As soon as they'd left we made phone calls, first to Steve and then to our parents. We did not hide from Colleen our intention to make these calls. On the contrary: we told them both as they were leaving that it was the polite thing to do. Colleen gave a nonchalant shrug. She was certain Uncle Stephen would welcome them, phone call or no phone call.

Steve's reaction was the one we expected: "Sure, I'd love them to drop by but I have no room to put them up. This place is hardly big enough for me." My folks said essentially the same thing and I assured Mum and Dad they shouldn't feel bad about it; no one in their circumstances should have to be entertaining houseguests of any description, never mind guests of questionable trustworthiness. Andy's mother sounded confused, which worried us. Her confusion would make her a prime target.

"*Don't* take them in," Andy warned Nana. "They're both on drugs and I wouldn't put it past them to steal from you." Alas, Nana had zero short-term memory so when they showed up at her doorstep on January 11, 1996—shocked at being turned away by Steve—she let them in. They crashed at her place for the next seven days during which she told Andy, "I don't know what to do. I mean, she's my *granddaughter,* not some street girl, right?"

"Wrong," sighed poor Andy. "A street girl is exactly what she is. You need to give them a date by which they have to be out or they'll be mooching off you indefinitely."

Nana followed his advice, telling them they could only stay the week and must be gone by the eighteenth of that month. For that she paid a price—or more precisely *we* paid a price. Before they left, they liberated Nana's several prescription narcotic medications as well as the few hundred dollars' cash she kept in her apartment. The cash we restored. The medications she was able to renew. The tragic loss of trust by grandmother for granddaughter was irredeemable.

"Looks as though no good deed goes unpunished," was my dad's grim summation. He added that Colleen had called *them* and he'd told her she was welcome to visit but needed to find a place of her own to live. On that occasion she spoke to neither Brian nor Mum—though she later claimed, for reasons I'll never understand, that she *had* spoken to Mum who'd said she never wanted to see Colleen again. To dear Mum's dying day she remained hurt and bewildered about why Colleen would manufacture such a story. Me, I have to put it down to my daughter's low self-esteem. Perhaps a part of her felt unworthy of any further relationship with her other grandmother after what she'd done to Nana.

Ten days went by and we heard nothing. Then on January 28, Colleen telephoned in tears. She and Brad had been fighting and now Brad had beaten her up and left her. She had no money and no place to stay. Softhearted Nana, seeing her swollen face, had *again* taken her in temporarily until she got her head together. If she decided to return to Calgary, would we be willing to fly her back?

We *were* willing—on one condition. Colleen had to agree to check into Calgary's Renfrew Recovery Centre the day after she arrived and get clean of drugs. Without hesitation she made the promise. Had she the slightest intention of holding to it or did she see it simply as her only avenue to a ticket home? Motivated largely by desire to rescue Nana, we were too jaded to have any faith in her sincerity.

On the evening of February 8 we drove to the airport to meet Colleen's flight, watched other passengers disembark, and wondered what on earth had happened to her. As we were about to go and enquire whether she'd ever boarded the plane she appeared, nonchalant as ever, saying she'd had to stop for a smoke as soon as she'd landed due to the stupid rules about no smoking in transit. "*What?*" she snapped at our non-reply. "I was *stressed* having to go without a cigarette that long!"

One night was all we allowed her to spend with us. Prepared to offer sympathy and a listening ear about the relationship breakup, we were met only with complaints on her part about "this Renfrew thing". If we were any kind of parents we'd realize she didn't need Renfrew.

We drove her there the following morning. Renfrew, located in northeast Calgary, is a forty-bed, publicly-funded residential facility offering medically supported detoxification to Albertans addicted to drugs and/or alcohol. Showing up at the Centre between 8:15 and 8:30 a.m. is enough to warrant consideration for admission. Colleen was not turned away. She stayed exactly as long as it took her to contact Brad's brother-in-law, wail about how awful Brad had been to her and wangle an invitation to move in with him.

"He was having a party that night," she told us later. "I couldn't miss a *party*, right?" Her blatant scorn of us and all we stood for and her treatment of us as patsies made us chafe against having bought her the ticket back into our lives.

And yet of course we were stuck with her in our lives. She was our daughter. It was a blackmail tool she freely wielded, even though we never let ourselves become enslaved the way poor Bertha of the Parent Support Group did. "We can't allow her to draw us into her nightmare," was the way Andy once put it. "But I have to be able to look in the mirror and know the man I see there has done all he can."

It was the only philosophy that made sense any more. Even so, it was not wholly successful—especially the part about not being drawn into her nightmare.

After Brad left Colleen, he made his way back to Alberta and took up with another girl in Red Deer. That girl was a single parent with a four-year-old son. Nine months later, in that same year, I heard Brad's name (his *real* name) mentioned on the local news. He had brutally beaten the little boy. Social Services removed the child for the next nine months to the care of grandparents while Brad received anger-management therapy. At the end of a round of therapy Social Services allowed the poor frightened little boy to return to the couple's home: a mistake that will probably haunt for all time those who handled the case.

Driving home from work one day, I again heard Brad's name on the news. This time I had to pull over until I'd regained my composure. Brad was to be put on trial for beating—and *biting*—the same little boy to death. He blamed Social Services, claiming they should have known better than to consider him "cured" of his anger problem.

Brad's lawyer pleaded his case down to manslaughter. He was sentenced to ten years in prison. Andy and I had hoped the charge would be murder and they would throw away the key. We dreaded the strong possibility, at some future date, of the nightmare's re-entry into Colleen's world—and ours.

And the reason for our dread was based on far more than our daughter's romanticizing of her "bad boy" ex-lover or her several attempts to get back in touch with him once the media had made him (in her eyes) a celebrity. Now we had a personal tie—a family tie—to Brad whether we liked it or not. Three months following Colleen's return from Hamilton to Calgary, she announced she was pregnant.

21. Jaimie

I'll admit to some self-pity on learning of the pregnancy. Normally the impending arrival of a grandchild is cause for rejoicing, not dread. It wasn't fair!

But as soon as I stopped feeling sorry for myself I moved seamlessly into the "what if" stage. That was an even more angst-ridden place to be. What if Colleen's and Brad's heavy drug use had interfered with the baby's normal development? What if Colleen decided to keep the baby but was a negligent enough mother to put the baby at serious risk? What if Colleen gave the baby away and we never got to know our grandchild?

What if bad-boy Brad came back into the picture to wreak havoc on all our lives?

Colleen was eighteen years old. In view of her sexual history it was a miracle she hadn't got pregnant before now, a miracle she hadn't contracted one or more STDs. Or had she? *What if she had an STD right now that was jeopardizing the baby's health?*

Ultimately I moved on from this stage as well. Ill as she was, my mum—my best girlfriend—kept telling me over the phone in the course of our regular "coffee chats" that it was useless to worry myself over things I couldn't change. She was right and I knew it—just as we both knew how much easier it is to give advice than to take it.

After Colleen's return from Hamilton and her breach of promise to check into Renfrew (but before her knowledge of her pregnancy) our daughter's stay with Brad's brother-in-law lasted no longer than two weeks. Late one night near the end of February, she phoned us to ask for shelter. She and the brother-in-law had had a fight and he'd kicked her out. She only wanted a roof until she could find some other place to stay.

Again McMan Centre and specifically Darlene Petrie helped her out. (Andy once commented wryly that Colleen must have been a full-time job unto herself for dear dedicated Darlene!) For two weeks she stayed with a lady in Oak Ridge named Belinda; then for the next six weeks she was with a Gloria who lived in the Marlborough area. At the beginning of May she moved in for a month with a young girl named Karen who had a tiny house in Bowness. (This prompted another wry comment from my husband that there weren't many parts of town Colleen *hadn't* lived in.) It was while in Bowness that she announced to us her pregnancy.

June found her living in Lynwood Ridge with someone called Marg. Three months elapsed there before discord arose and she had to move again. In September Darlene found her a bedroom for rent in a trailer owned by a grandfatherly widower named Merv. Easygoing and genial, Merv lived in the far northeast area of Arbour Lake. Since his trailer park was an "adults only" community, Colleen would have to find other accommodation soon after the baby was born.

I haven't looked into whether there are any studies about what pregnancy hormones do to the BPD brain. But during the baby's gestation period, our daughter became introspective for the first time. "I'm not sure what I'll do," she told us one afternoon when we invited her for lunch. "If I keep the baby I might not be a good mother. I can't even take care of *myself*, never mind a baby. Would you think less of me, Mom, if I gave the baby away?"

I did a double take. (*Who are you and what have you done with my daughter?*) Colleen so rarely treated me with anything but scorn that for a moment I was stuck for a reply. That she gave a fig one way or the other about my opinion was almost never in evidence. Eyes watering I said, "No Colleen, I wouldn't think less of you. If you put the baby's best interests above your own needs, I would think *more* of you."

But shortly after that, the old Colleen reappeared. Jennifer Ferguson, our minister at Deer Park United Church, came up with an ideal-sounding plan: a young couple, congregants who couldn't have children of their own, were offering to adopt the baby and to allow Colleen and our family to be a part of the baby's life. "Snatch that offer," Andy urged. "The child would grow up in a stable home and would still be able to see you regularly and to love you." Colleen's mouth turned down at the corners, her normal perversity back.

"Legally the baby belongs to *me*," she pouted. "Why should anyone else get *my* child?"

Useless to point out (although we did) that the baby was not a piece of property but a human being. Colleen knew that, yet she couldn't bring herself to surrender, or even to share, custody with anyone else. As the time of delivery approached she became increasingly adamant that, no matter what *anyone* thought, she'd decided to keep her baby.

In her third trimester, she made me gulp once more by selecting *me* as her labour coach. We practiced breathing exercises together and I talked her through back pain as she became heavier and heavier. As the end of October neared and she still hadn't delivered, I began to be fearful something was wrong.

"The doctor said everything's fine," Colleen assured me. "This is a case of delayed fertilization. I still have a couple of weeks to go."

Delayed fertilization? I had never heard of such a thing and neither had Andy. My medical encyclopedia—and the Internet—do mention it in relation to certain animals whose offspring, if born too early into harsh winter conditions, will not survive. Therefore those animals have the ability to nurture egg and sperm separately within their bodies and hold back the fertilization process for a few weeks until the onset of milder weather. In humans its occurrence is uncommon and—because both egg and sperm deteriorate quickly in the absence of fertilization—is associated with certain birth defects, in particular Down's syndrome. *Oh, no!*

Colleen's labour began on the evening of November 23, 1996. It stopped and started three or four times, making her understandably cranky. At Foothills Hospital where she herself had been born, she finally delivered a beautiful baby girl. In accordance with her astonishing wishes, our entire family was present in the room to witness the birth. I had the honour of cutting the cord and of introducing the precious bundle to the rest of the family before placing that bundle into new mom's waiting arms. Attending doctor and nurse excepted, there wasn't a dry eye in the room. I remember reiterating my colleague's phrase—the same one I'd recalled when my own children arrived—that the world debut of a newborn is unquestionably "one of life's biggies".

"I'll take the *best* care of her," Colleen vowed. "If ever you don't see that happening, you have my permission to take her away." It was a promising pronouncement.

Lisa was in her fourth year at the University of Calgary by then, majoring in Dramatic Arts and qualifying to become a teacher. For the first three years of university she'd lived at home—but home was about as far away from U of C as you can get and still be in the same city. In fourth year, with our help and that of student loans, she'd opted to move to a downtown apartment just a brief LRT ride away from the campus. With glowing pride Andy and I had looked on while independence and burgeoning self-assurance gradually moulded our elder daughter into a lovely young woman.

Now it was that lovely young woman, weeping at having just been made an auntie, who asked her sister, "What are you going to call her?" And when Colleen claimed to really like friend Kim's suggestion of *Scarlet Rose*, Lisa visibly winced. "Then you better teach my niece to become a streetwalker because that's where she's headed with a name like that!"

Wow! Sometimes it takes a sibling to go where a parent fears to tread. From that point on we never heard another word about *Scarlet Rose*. Instead, Colleen settled on *Jaimie Elizabeth Jean*—the "Elizabeth" after Lisa and the "Jean" after Nana. (I know my darling mum felt slapped in the face yet again but I comforted her on the phone, saying, "*I'm* not in there either and I'm Colleen's mother. We can't let it matter.")

The name had a nice ring to it—a ring of success.

22. A Light in the Darkness

The day after Jaimie's birth, we visited Colleen in hospital to find her on the phone with Brad. We hadn't even realized she knew how to reach him or had maintained contact with him. By then he was with the new girlfriend in Red Deer whose son he had beaten up, though he had not yet committed the monstrous deed that sent him to prison.

"I think she may have your hair and eyes," Colleen cooed. She hung up very shortly after we got there, claiming she'd only updated Brad out of courtesy. She didn't want Brad's name on the birth certificate and she didn't want Brad to have any association at all with Jaimie.

Courtesy, however, did not describe her tone of voice on the phone before her awareness of our presence. She wanted Brad back and was using the baby to try and achieve that. Andy and I strongly suspected it was *he* who didn't want his name on the birth certificate and *he* who wanted no association at all with the baby. That was just fine with us!

Besides, we were sure Brad denied being the father. "Do the math," he must have said. "What kind of an idiot do you think I am?" Indeed, much as Colleen continued to claim she hadn't been with anyone else, Andy and I never bought the "delayed fertilization" story. Even if Colleen and Brad had had sex right before he left her on January 28 (which is not impossible but is doubtful because they were fighting) the gap between then and November 24 was simply too great for this delayed fertilization claptrap to bear any credence.

And Jaimie showed no signs of any of the aberrations delayed fertilization can cause; she was a healthy normal little girl. From day one—like Lisa—she ate well, slept well, and was content. We looked after her regularly enough during her babyhood that I am able to say that. No signs existed of the crying frenzies or excessive clinginess that had pervaded Colleen's early years. Whatever genetic pool Jaimie had dipped into had contributed its soundest and best and our gratitude for that was boundless. I don't think any of us—least of all Colleen herself—could have handled raising another Colleen.

Like any new single mother however, Colleen found parenthood challenging. All of us helped out as best we could—when she was willing to accept our help. She didn't want to return to Merv's right away and so stayed at Lisa's apartment for the first few weeks, where her sister shared the tasks of feeding and changing. I drove her and Jaimie to the doctor's office for Jaimie's six-week checkup. When she did return to Merv's, Andy and I bought her an old-style English pram that, with the limited space there, served as bed and stroller both. When she moved out of Merv's, someone from Deer Park United Church donated a crib.

One very positive outcome of Colleen's choice to keep her baby was that she suddenly saw logic in returning to school. Again Darlene Petrie assisted her in that regard and, while still pregnant, Colleen finished her grade eleven as an adult student at Viscount Bennett School. For her grade twelve she was accepted at Louise Dean School, located in northwest Calgary. Originally called "The Louise Dean School for Un-wed Mothers", this centre is named after a former Board of Education trustee and "Citizen of the Year" recipient of 1976. It is operated by the Calgary Board of Education with the assistance of Calgary Catholic Family Services. Its mandate is to provide the support of an educator, a social worker, and a health professional to each pregnant student in order to help that student upgrade academically, deal with social/emotional concerns, and achieve healthy lifestyle choices for herself and her baby. Daycare, career counselling, and medical assistance is available right on the premises. For Colleen it was ideal. All this support, along with her new burst of motivation, actually carried her through to high school completion. What a triumph!

At Louise Dean, Colleen met Charlotte, an aboriginal girl who had a baby son. Charlotte lived in a small apartment close to the school, and when Colleen left Merv's she moved in with Charlotte. The two girls minded one another's children and in various ways helped one another cope. Though this living arrangement proved temporary and Colleen moved after only one month into the basement apartment of a nearby house owned by a Tracy, the girls still met regularly and maintained their friendship. It was encouraging.

More encouraging yet was Colleen's next decision: to enrol for train-ing in "Events Management" at DeVry Institute of Technology—which would hopefully lead to being hired by the Calgary Events Management Group to manage and coordinate special events being put on in the city. As it turned out, her motivation was that she'd become enamoured of ice skater Curt Browning and planned to take a four-year qualifying course and then become a Sports Events Manager in order to work more closely with him—hardly the conventional reason for pursuing post-secondary studies. But maybe the end would not only justify but guarantee the completion of the means. We prayed so.

Colleen lived at Tracy's for seven months, from July 1997 to the end of January 1998. While there she started DeVry and said she enjoyed it. Cat, an artistically-talented drama-student friend of Lisa's, accompanied our elder daughter there several times and with the landlady's permission enhanced Colleen's bare basement walls with bright hand-painted flowers. When Andy and I would visit, Jaimie always gurgled a cheerful greeting, asking to be picked up by holding out plump little arms. She looked happy and well cared for.

How was Colleen doing during this period? She unfailingly responded that everything was just fine. We could see everything *wasn't* as fine as represented but anything amiss appeared to be minor. Tracy had asked her to vacate, she said, because Tracy wanted to reclaim the basement area. For the next two months she lived in Whitehorn, north of Forest Lawn, with someone named Gabe. Gabe's mother minded Jaimie. Once when we were over at Gabe's, Colleen quite deliberately urged Jaimie to call this lady *grandma*. The poor lady shrugged helplessly at me saying, "Don't, Colleen. You'll confuse the child. I'm *not* her grandma." Whether Colleen meant this as a slight to me I'll never know. And as I'd advised my own mum with regard to the issue of Jaimie's name, I chose not to let it matter.

In April 1998, Colleen moved from Gabe's into her own apartment in the Greenwood area. This was the first time she'd lived by herself since the tiny place in Inglewood where she'd been simultaneously assailed by the need to be alone and by intense loneliness. (Kiera Van Gelder, in her recent book *The buddha and the borderline: a memoir* describes precisely the same contradictory feelings that kept her alternately moving in with various boyfriends and then out on her own.[9]) In Colleen's case however, a fundamental change had occurred since Inglewood: no longer was she by herself. Her companion was now toddling, learning to talk, enjoying the stories Mom read, and asking for a doggie as a pet. Colleen somehow acquired a cute toy Pomeranian she called Sam and their little family of three dwelt in Greenwood for the next two-and-a-half years. Things definitely *were* stabilizing.

---

9   Van Gelder, Kiera. 2010. *The Buddha and the borderline: a memoir.* Oakland, CA: New Harbinger Publications

"Isn't it funny how life goes?" Andy grinned. "We were so worried Colleen couldn't be a fit mother and here she is, settling down and seeming happier than she's ever been. Jaimie has proved a light in the darkness for her."

No one could deny that. Colleen had sworn off drugs, saying she never wanted her baby to see her stoned. She'd sworn off cigarettes, saying she never wanted her baby breathing second-hand smoke. She'd entered DeVry, saying she wanted to qualify for a job paying a salary decent enough to support her child. How we rejoiced! *At long last* our rebellious "bloody-minded" daughter was getting it together!

Or so it seemed.

23. The Brittle Smile

Andy and I had formally made our wills some time before. We now updated them to include Jaimie. We also put in a "just in case" stipulation about Brad: that due to his desertion of Colleen and his violent behaviour he never be allowed to get his hands on any money that might come to Jaimie through inheritance. The event of his ever trying to contact Jaimie was as unlikely as the story that he was her father; yet because Colleen continued to insist he was, we put in the stipulation as a safeguard.

We also started an education fund for Jaimie in hope she would someday attend college or university. Colleen thanked us with sincere-sounding gratitude for ensuring our grandchild had the best opportunities available. I don't doubt she genuinely meant it at the time.

Towards the end of August 2001 Lisa informed us that Colleen's neighbours were threatening to cite her for leaving a barking dog in a crate all day while out at school. The neighbours were concerned about Jaimie as well because they often heard Colleen yelling loudly. *Our* enquiries of Colleen raised our own level of concern. She pasted that brittle smile on her face and denied everything. "None of that is true! Have the stupid neighbours said something to you? They ought to mind their own business! Everything's *fine*."

Shortly thereafter, she announced she was moving from Greenwood (*her* idea, or the landlord's?) to a larger apartment she'd found in the Radcliff area. One of my former students who'd just lost both parents to cancer helped her furnish it by donating some very nice couches and lamps. She and Jaimie would have more room there, Colleen said, and it was closer to DeVry. She'd have to get rid of the dog but knew someone willing to provide a good home for him. Maybe she'd look at getting a cat instead.

We felt her decision to exchange the dog for a more appropriate apartment pet signified she was at last developing the capability to exercise sounder judgment. Jaimie, at five, clapped gleeful hands upon hearing the news they'd been offered *two* kittens. And we, despite growing certainty that Colleen was reverting to some of her old "smokescreen" behaviour, still saw in her daughter a happy child whose loving parent was trying hard to do her level best.

After a promising start, DeVry did not turn out well. Colleen had taken advantage of student loan resources available to her and felt driven to succeed and land a well-paying job so that repaying it wouldn't prove a problem. But even though she'd finally got her grade twelve at Louise Dean, her huge truancy-caused knowledge gaps made post-secondary studies difficult for her.

I'm sure her difficulty was further increased by her brain's inability to filter out background interference. At the end of her first year she was short some courses which she had to repeat the following year. She blamed the instructors, her fellow students for distracting her, the career counsellor for giving her bad advice—everyone but herself. That she had a disorder for which she should seek help she simply wouldn't acknowledge.

By September 2001 when she moved to the Radcliff apartment, she was still attending DeVry but had begun to talk disparagingly about the quality of education it offered. "I wouldn't be there at all," she sneered, "if the Events Management lady hadn't *promised* me a spot. I'm going to be the Events Manager in charge of organizing ice-skating competitions for Curt." She was now referring to Browning by first name only, as though the two were intimate friends. Indeed, when she came for Christmas that year, she handed us a present: a family-photo frame purporting to be "from Curt".

Lisa eyed her narrowly. "Colleen, why on earth would Curt Browning give *us* a Christmas present?"

"Well, he stays over at my place sometimes," breezed Colleen. "In fact, Jaimie has already started to call him *dad*."

As with her insistence upon Brad being Jaimie's father, Colleen never did change her story of having more than a close friendship with Curt Browning. She intimated that they were lovers and that he stayed at her place whenever he was in town. "I'm going to be meeting his parents," she once told us. "They live in Caroline (a small farming community north of the city)." And sure enough, as Darlene Petrie has since confirmed, she *did* succeed in contacting them (upon what pretext nobody knows) and she *did* go to Caroline—driven there by Darlene—to spend a day with them.

"In the real world," my psychologist colleague theorized, "Colleen has not had much success. She compensates by diving into a make-believe world where she regularly rubs shoulders with celebrities. Sometimes sufferers of mental illness get so caught up in their own lies that they start to believe them themselves—particularly if they can intersperse grains of truth into them. It's exactly the neurosis/psychosis 'borderline' after which the disease is named."

Colleen persisted with the Curt Browning idealization and the story of the Events Management lady's promise to her about managing the skater's career through four years at DeVry. Having repeated first year, she did get through another two. "Her natural brightness took her a long way," says Darlene. "But then in the third year of her courses, when the Events Management Group was making final decisions about candidates for their program, she got turned down." This Colleen never revealed to us. Her story was that DeVry's inferior instructors were lame and that she'd talked to several DeVry graduates who claimed the institution didn't prepare its students properly for the professional world. There was no point in arguing with her when she made such derogatory statements. I'm sure she knew we didn't buy them—and something deep within her probably also knew we somewhat understood her efforts to save face.

In the third year of her courses, Colleen also met and fell for a military man named James. James crashed at her Radcliff apartment for a short while, availing himself of her sexual favours. (We suspected this at the time; it has since been confirmed by Jaimie.) We also suspected he was abusive to Colleen—which would have made him all the more desirable in her eyes. Supposition was all we had to go on because Colleen never told us about James and cautioned Jaimie never to mention him either. (Jaimie did slip up a few times, and we also noticed in Colleen a reappearance of bruises and fat lips.) James didn't last long. His departure pitched Colleen into a blue funk that totalled her DeVry studies.

Briefly she took a job at Boston Pizza, which was within walking distance of her apartment, but was fired when she decided to go on a weekend jaunt with some crowd she'd met instead of reporting for her shift. I think *we* looked after Jaimie that weekend, having been handed one of Colleen's eternal plausible-sounding stories about taking off for a couple of days in order to "get into a better head space".

Threatening to sue Boston Pizza for wrongful dismissal, she then got a job at the Olive Garden restaurant, also within walking distance of her apartment. There she met a same-sex couple I'll call Pat and Sue. This couple, to whom we've recently talked, confirmed that by then Colleen was back into substance abuse, both alcohol and drugs. Those good-hearted ladies saw in our daughter a person headed downhill, and they were especially sympathetic because they themselves had had their own such struggles in the past. They spent considerable effort both counselling Colleen and looking after Jaimie. We, her parents, got shut out as always, receiving only the brittle smile and the disquieting platitude, "Everything's fine."

That she couldn't be truthful even to herself about the demise of her career dreams or the failure of her latest relationship no doubt caused this non-communicative behaviour—which, in addition to being symptomatic of her illness, had to mean some part of her *did* love us and *did* care very much what we thought of her. If only she would allow us to reach out to that part! If only she were not absolutely averse to seeking the professional help she so desperately needed!

Lisa ended up providing us a looking-glass through which we could peer behind the smokescreen. Having graduated university in 1996 with a Master's degree in Fine Arts and a specialization in teaching drama, our elder daughter obtained her first post in the small community of Calmar just outside Edmonton. Shawn moved to Edmonton with her and took a job in a plastics factory there, owned by a relative. The two shared an apartment and, with our help, purchased their first car. How great it was for us to see them both step into the role of adulthood! And when neither of them liked their respective jobs and decided, after a year, to return to Calgary, how great it was to welcome them back and to be able to visit with them again more regularly!

Yet dear Lisa and Shawn were encountering their own hurdles along the road to "finding themselves" as a couple. Once back in Calgary and settled into an apartment in Kingsland (overlooking the rugby field!), Lisa landed a job at A. E. Cross Junior High School and Shawn—with a friend's help—worked for a while in a bank. Lisa's job panned out; Shawn's didn't. The banking business, he told us, was not his thing. Not long before, he'd gone to B.C. to re-establish a connection with his dad (who'd split up with his mom when he was very young and who was now remarried and living in Surrey) and he'd realized that career opportunities in computer graphics—the field he really wanted to break into—were more abundant there. He had already taken some qualifying courses but in Calgary, jobs fitting those courses were in short supply. Upon leaving the bank, he briefly worked as "tech support" for a computer company but found it unsatisfying and limiting. Shawn was at a crossroads. He needed to determine what path the rest of his life should follow.

It was during this period that he and Lisa decided to break up. Lisa shed tears when she told us and so did I. Shawn was like a son and the two seemed so right as a couple. Yes, Lisa *had* dated others but the two always re-gravitated to one another. From junior high days, Shawn had cutely declared himself by writing on Lisa's binder: *Shawn P. is the man for me!* I had long assumed they were just "meant to be".

That our elder daughter picked herself up and went on with her life will always be to her credit. It showed what a capable and resilient young woman she had become. On her income alone, rent for the Kingsland apartment would be too high for her to make any savings and her ultimate goal was to buy a house. She gave up the apartment, staying for a few weeks with two girlfriends; then she had a conversation with Colleen and they made an agreement.

Lisa had been working three years at A. E. Cross by 2001 when Colleen moved to Radcliff. To cut costs, she too moved into the Radcliff place with her sister and resided there for the better part of a year.

So it was through Lisa's eyes that Andy and I were finally able to peer behind the brittle smile and the platitudinous "Everything's fine". Lisa was our portal of entry into what was *really* going on in Colleen's world.

24. Behind the Smokescreen

The years following Jaimie's birth were ones of transition not only for Lisa but for us. Our decision to build a bungalow in the then-new southwest community of Evergreen, to which we moved in 1996, stemmed from several considerations. One was that we found our dream retirement lot overlooking Fish Creek Park with a westerly-facing back yard that gave spectacular mountain views and direct park access. Another was that our Deer Run home had been a place of some happiness but also of much stress and sadness. Dusting and vacuuming Colleen's prematurely empty bedroom had often produced spontaneous tears. A third was strictly practical. Mitigating circumstances aside, both our children were now out on their own and we were a couple again. The new view from the windows of our brand new residence symbolized for me the fresh start to a brand new stage of our lives.

I retired in 2001 and Andy in 2004. We both worked contract jobs in our respective fields for a few years after our formal retirement; then we quit gainful employment altogether and gave ourselves to hobbies, recreational park activities, and various voluntary tasks at our church—which by then had become Red Deer Lake United, just west of world-class riding facility Spruce Meadows.

Why did we change churches? I think the "fresh new start" feeling had a lot to do with it. Deer Park was going through a bit of upheaval around then, and upheaval was the last thing we wished to deal with. Much as we love the Deer Park people and will always regard them as treasured friends, Red Deer Lake offered a small-country-church atmosphere we found alluring. Our first winter in the Evergreen house, I nearly went off icy roads twice while driving to choir practice at Deer Park. I looked upon that as a sort of omen, an indication it was time to move ahead and put our Colleen problems behind us. At Red Deer Lake no one even knew we *had* Colleen problems. From the very first Sunday we attended there, the warmth of our welcome overwhelmed us. And at coffee time after the service, not a single soul asked about Colleen's latest escapades because not a single soul knew me as the heartsick parent of Deer Run notoriety.

Being able to talk about other things besides Colleen was an undreamt-of respite. Of course we continued contact with our closer Deer Run friends, all of whom understood absolutely and all of whom remained supportive of our troubled daughter. Some, like the lovely lady named

136

Jean Nash whom I've mentioned before, went out of their way to maintain liaison with Colleen and to keep track of her growing toddler's progress. I cannot say enough about how wonderful these people have been.

In 1997, we transferred our membership to Red Deer Lake and began playing an active role in events there. Andy joined the Worship Committee; I joined the choir. Upon our retirements, more participation on our part followed: Outreach Committee, Prayer Ministry (of which I am the coordinator), Healing Ministry, Pastoral Care, even being sometime lay service leaders when the regular minister was away. Pat and Martin Claydon and Pat's sister Eileen Tillett are three outstanding folks who were especially welcoming and with whom we soon formed a close bond. They are all pillars of the church in terms of the support they regularly offer to others. Yet even with these three, Andy and I did not initially share a lot about Colleen. We weren't being purposely evasive; we were simply at a life stage where Colleen seemed no longer the constant worry she had once been. Motherhood had brought out in her qualities we'd struggled fruitlessly for years to instil: concern for others (in particular her daughter), good manners (which she harped on constantly with Jaimie), a work ethic to which she at least paid lip service, and visible efforts to make the little person she'd created feel loved and cherished. Colleen read bedtime stories to Jaimie, enrolled Jaimie (with our help) in dance and skating lessons and heaped continual kisses and caresses upon her daughter. It was all good—wasn't it?

No. It was *not* all good. In 2001 when Lisa was sharing the Radcliff apartment with Colleen, she levelled with us about the situation there. Lisa's assessment, not one to inspire panic, *was* disturbing. While her sister unquestionably adored her niece, the living environment was far from ideal for raising a child. People came and went at odd hours and some were drinkers and drug users. All were smokers. Colleen too was smoking again quite heavily, despite that once-adamant vow that no second-hand smoke would ever enter Jaimie's lungs. To say the least, we were upset.

According to Lisa, Colleen also seemed inclined to grab at any excuse at all to keep Jaimie home with her. When the daycare centre Jaimie attended during Colleen's work and/or school hours had a head-lice outbreak, Colleen bought and used the proper shampoo, then dallied for weeks about returning her child—or herself—to the outside world. "These things happen. It's been dealt with. Get on with your life," Andy told her. "Not to *my* child," she insisted. "That'll never happen to *my* child again!"

"She's overly protective, yet neglectful," Lisa confirmed. "With all the smoking and noise going on, Jaimie gets sent to bed, but after that she's not really *supervised*. It's a bit scary."

What additionally scared Lisa was that her sister sometimes had episodes of acute paranoia that brought on a spate of recurring helter-skelter accusations against friends, acquaintances, everybody. Once, Lisa herself was accused of stealing cutlery from the drawers and another time of stealing some meat from the apartment freezer. Colleen yelled and cursed at her so vehemently that Lisa actually thought her sister might strike her.

What were the potential risks of this behaviour for Jaimie? Was there danger of physical harm being inflicted upon the child?

No! None of us was ready to believe that. If there was one little person Colleen would have done anything to *protect*, it was Jaimie. Besides, having Jaimie had wrought such miracles upon Colleen's character! We had all seen the evidence. *Jaimie* was the one who kept Colleen grounded, made her more responsible and gave her purpose…

But the child is a human being, not Colleen's psychiatric bandage. A voice within me (which would become more nagging and urgent in the future) said that distinctly the day Lisa recounted to us the cutlery and the meat stories. I shared Lisa's fears, even as I shared my elder daughter's opinion about her sister's genuine efforts to be a good mother: cooking nourishing meals, "kissing better" all Jaimie's normal childhood bumps and bruises and making sincere attempts to offer sound advice on Jaimie's various kiddy problems. When one of the two pet tomcats developed kidney disease, Colleen borrowed (and eventually paid back) money from Lisa to have it cared for by a vet. Unfortunately the cat died anyway—perhaps a mixed blessing, since it had started spraying furniture. But the other cat, a pitch-black Maine coon named Marley, was growing into a mellow gentle creature who loved being picked up and carried about: the perfect pet for a five-year-old.

All in all, the picture Lisa painted, plus the picture we ourselves saw when we visited the Radcliff place, produced unease at times but not dread. Neither legally nor morally was there justification for feeling our granddaughter belonged with anyone other than her beloved mom, particularly while her auntie was also around to watch over her welfare.

Her auntie's presence, however, would not last.

25. Colleen Will Not Spoil the Wedding

Lisa planned on getting out of the Radcliff place as quickly as possible. Living with Colleen was simply too stressful. As any teacher will agree, she needed all her faculties to cope daily with the challenges of the job; Colleen's wild lifestyle, along with those unpredictable moods, was turning her into a sleep-deprived wreck. "So what else is new?" she wearily kidded. "I've always been sleep-deprived because of Colleen."

We were fully aware it couldn't continue—despite the comfort it gave us that she was there. It wasn't her duty to supervise her sister. So we weren't surprised when she hooked up with the realtor aunt of her university friend Cat (the one who'd painted the flowers on Colleen's basement-apartment walls) and began looking into the ins and outs of assuming a mortgage. Once again to her credit, she went about this almost independently, only getting advice from her dad every now and then. Her research culminated in the purchase of a charming little townhouse in the Glamorgan area. Next thing we knew, dear Shawn reappeared on the scene!

After the breakup Lisa still saw Shawn occasionally but "only as a friend". Their social circles overlapped so they bumped into one another from time to time. Shawn had had some success at last in finding a job with a computer games company that agreeably tested his considerable skills as a graphic artist. I think he always loved Lisa but perhaps his sense of honour necessitated he feel secure about his future before he thought about making the bond between them more permanent. Neither do I discount the high probability that the prospect of having Colleen as a sister-in-law gave him the willies. Heaven knows it would have given *anyone* the willies! Shawn has since expressed to me his opinion of Colleen as "a toxic personality", one who always ruined family get-togethers with her temper, tears, or histrionic outbursts. He's right. And he seemed to relax much more with me, as a mother-in-law, when I acknowledged he was right.

But not to get ahead of myself, Shawn's reappearance on the scene when Lisa purchased the Glamorgan townhouse was initially as her tenant. He made her a deal to rent one of the bedrooms which would certainly defray some of her mortgage burden. Not unexpectedly, they didn't remain landlord and tenant for long. In Lisa's words, they soon "evolved into being a couple again". This time though, they decided to make it official. To our boundless elation, they announced their engagement.

They wanted a relatively small wedding: those invited included only us, Shawn's parents and siblings and assorted relatives, a few of their mutual close friends, and *our* close friends, the Dawson family. Lisa asked Grant if he'd consider being the one to perform the ceremony; after all, she'd known Grant and Dorothy and their two sons forever. And would he also consider performing it at Red Deer Lake United, rather than at Knox? Both Lisa and Shawn felt the little countryside chapel that was our church (prior to its ensuing expansion) would be perfect for accommodating their small guest list.

Grant replied he would be honoured to perform the ceremony. It was set for the seventeenth of August, 2002. Since our regular minister would be away on vacation at that time, even the matter of getting the incumbent's permission to use the church was no issue. All looked to be smooth sailing as the happy couple proceeded with their plans.

Mason and Kreger in their *Walking on Eggshells* book cite an account of the emotional dilemma undergone by a BPD sufferer's sibling. I include this account here in an attempt to exonerate Lisa, if she needs that, of any self-blame she may harbour regarding her reluctance to let Colleen participate in her wedding. In the account, the sibling confesses to experiencing difficulty loving her sister at all. Sometimes she's so angry at her sister's behaviour she almost wishes her sister dead, and then she feels guilty for wishing that. As she contemplates her upcoming wedding, part of her knows she should ask her sister to be a bridesmaid, and yet the thought terrifies her. What embarrassing socially-inappropriate act is her sister likely to commit at the ceremony? What is the miniscule chance her sister *won't* find a way to ruin her big day? Additionally she wonders: "Should *I* have children? What kind of aunt would she be? I couldn't trust her to babysit them. And—if this runs in families as some think it does—will my own children have this horrible disorder?"[10]

Lisa wanted, yet didn't want, Colleen in her wedding party. Shawn, I'm sure, would have been glad not to have her at the wedding at all,

10 Paul T. Mason and Randi Kreger, *Stop Walking on Eggshells: Taking your life back when someone you care about has borderline personality disorder* (Oakland, CA: New Harbinger Publications, 2010) 205, 206

but he was stuck with the reality of her being his bride's sister. In every way Andy and I shared their ambivalence. We realized how relieved we were about the small guest list—which meant we wouldn't have to worry about Colleen being a spectacle in front of *our* friends. Simultaneously, we disliked the part of ourselves that felt that way. It was already happening: Colleen was spoiling the wedding.

Our conscious decision as a family *not* to let it happen was a help. The Jack-and-Jill shower Andy and I held—which I videotaped—shows a bubbly six-year-old Jaimie excitedly handing presents to the bride-to-be and helping Auntie tear off wrapping paper while doting Mom looks on fondly. Some of the candid stills reveal Colleen's brittle smile and empty eyes but that expression is for the bride and groom, never for Jaimie. Colleen adored her daughter and was ecstatic the engaged couple wanted Jaimie to be their flower girl. Even her hatred of Shawn, who was stealing her sister, had modified to stiff politeness upon her realization that this marriage was happening with or without her approval. "It's about effing time," she even grinned at one point during the shower and all of us laughed and agreed.

As for Lisa asking Colleen to be a bridesmaid, she went through with it—having all the same reservations expressed by the sibling in Mason and Kreger's book. However, it was her close girlfriend Cat whom she chose as maid of honour and it was Cat—who *loves* organizing and preparing for such functions—who took charge of making sure everything went off like clockwork. "Lisa's the typical scatterbrained drama teacher," Cat giggled. "She needs *me*, the Wedding Nazi, to make sure she doesn't blow this!"

I had a lump in my throat the time I drove to meet Lisa and Cat at a bridal salon and watched while my eldest got fitted for her gown. Despite her independent streak, Lisa, bless her heart, made sure I knew she especially wanted me to be there. As well, she especially wanted both Andy and me to walk her down the aisle and give her away. In the beautiful young woman I beheld through tear-filled eyes at that gown fitting, I saw no vestige of the sulky teen who'd had to grow up in her sister's shadow. And I hoped with all my heart that her sister would not let her down when the big day arrived.

It was a perfect sunlit day. Jaimie was precious in her flower girl's dress, carrying her little petal basket and her favourite stuffed-toy bunny. Lisa, in lovely pearl-encrusted white, looked radiant. Shawn made as handsome a groom as any girl might dream of. And yes, Cat *and* Colleen, in their bridesmaid's outfits, were picture pretty. One thing only was wrong.

"I'm not feeling well," Colleen complained. "I think I might throw up as I'm going down the aisle."

"It's just nerves," I told her. "Don't think about it and you'll be fine."

"It's *not* nerves," she insisted. "It's stomach flu. I feel awful."

I didn't doubt she felt awful. I *did* doubt it was stomach flu.

As we were about to proceed into the sanctuary, she suddenly bolted for the nearby bathroom, causing a delay until she returned. Of course we were all concerned. Was she okay now? She wasn't sure. But down the aisle we marched as a wedding procession: Jaimie first, strewing petals, then Cat, then Colleen, then Lisa, with us on either side. Scott, the Dawsons' younger son, videotaped the whole thing. Thank goodness he did! When I watch that video, I can fully savour the once-in-a-lifetime thrill of watching my daughter and son-in-law take their marriage vows—a thrill I *couldn't* fully savour on the day itself.

With us flanking her, Lisa met Shawn, accompanied by his best man, at the altar. (To refresh my memory, I re-watched the video before writing this chapter and I cry anew at how lovely Colleen looked, yet how tragic was her expression going down the aisle.) "Do you, Lisa's parents, offer your promise of love and support to Lisa and Shawn as they enter married life?" Grant asked. "We do," both of us answered. Then we took our seats in the front pew. Colleen, instead of staying standing at the altar with Lisa and Cat, squeezed herself in beside us.

"I can't stand up," she whispered in my ear. "I think I might faint."

I nodded in reply and put an arm around her. It was fine if she sat there as long as she didn't cause a scene. As the most meaningful parts of the ceremony unfolded, she kept interrupting by whispering to me how horrible she felt. Her back hurt as well as her stomach. She had prescription pain medication but she'd left it at home. She wasn't going to be able to last through this without it. Was there some way we could take her back to her place right now so she could get it?

Right now? Colleen, are you nuts?

That she was ill and in pain—if that was true—made me upset but also made me angry. I was angry because I didn't really believe she was *that* ill and in pain. This had happened too many times before. I believed she mostly wanted to rip my attention focus away from Lisa and onto herself and her own troubles: par for the course. I also believed any illness and pain she actually *did* suffer was strictly of her own making.

At least she disrupted few others besides the two of us while in the church. At the reception it was a different story. Several times, after telling anyone who would listen how sick she felt, she made a big to-do of bolting for the bathroom. The first and second times I followed. She wasn't throwing up. But she *was* twitchy, restless and not pleased to see me.

Other guests at the wedding kept making solicitous enquiries about her health. She revelled in it. The frustrated bride was nothing but cynical. "She's just trying to grab the spotlight as usual. It's all an act. I was afraid of this."

Colleen had been scheduled to make a toast; someone else stepped in and took that over. Andy and I partook in several "bride-and-groom roast" speeches; then of course we had the pleasant duty of asking guests to join us in lifting their glasses to officially welcome Shawn into the family. "Now I have two beautiful daughters, Lisa and Colleen," Andy pointedly said, "*and* one quite nice-looking son-in-law, although he's not really my type." Right after the laughter, someone placed Jaimie on a tabletop so the audience could see her and handed her a mike, whereupon she delivered to the newly-married couple her own delightful little wedding gift, a piping rendition of this "counting-down" nursery school rhyme:

Farmer Brown had five green apples hanging on a tree,

Farmer Brown had five green apples hanging on a tree,

Then he plucked one apple and ate it hungrily,

And Farmer Brown had four green apples hanging on a tree....

On Jaimie sang, we listeners gleefully clapping rhythm, until the greedy Farmer Brown had consumed the last of his green apples. Applause was thunderous. Colleen (who had visibly grimaced at being called "beautiful" by her father because she never in her life saw herself that way) enthusiastically joined in the applause for Jaimie. It was the only time that whole evening I actually saw my younger daughter look dotingly and devotedly *happy*.

The happiness was short-lived. As soon as attention drifted from Jaimie's performance, Colleen began to whine again about needing her pain medication, feeling tired, wanting to go home *now* and take Jaimie with her. We called a taxi, paid the driver to return her to Radcliff and said we'd ferry Jaimie back once the festivities came to an end. No reason to penalize the poor child, who was really starting to get into the party spirit. Colleen's medication needs won out over her possessiveness of the little girl and she ceased arguing.

With Colleen's departure, the party livened up. It would be too unkind to attribute *all* the livening-up to Colleen's departure but some of it undeniably was, at least for Andy, Lisa, and me. Suddenly we could relax and allow ourselves to have fun. There was dancing, laughter, good food, and the cutting-up of a gorgeous wedding cake decorated with real flowers. All these, as well as many compliments about how lovely Jaimie *and* her mom both looked, our youngest missed out on because she couldn't bring herself to stay.

There's a stand-up comedian who jests about some individual being such a pill she could light up a room just by leaving. With aching heart I thought of this jest that night as I reflected on the mood transformation Colleen's departure had wrought in our family. We had said we weren't going to let her spoil the wedding. Our putting her in a taxi and sending her home had salvaged for us at least part of the evening's merrymaking.

Just before we left the reception hall, Andy and I gave huge hugs to Lisa and Shawn. We departed a bit earlier than many of the younger guests because our six-year-old charge was at last petering out. Shortly before midnight we drove across town to Radcliff and deposited our granddaughter back into her mom's care.

Colleen looked just fine when she opened the door. She said the stomach flu was gone and she felt a lot better.

No question she *did* feel a lot better. No question her miraculous recovery had nothing whatever to do with stomach flu.

26. Does She Take Us For Fools?

Having suspicions and being able to prove those suspicions are two very different things. There's also the reality of not *wanting* something to be true and finding ways to rationalize oneself out of believing it. In retrospect I did more of that than I should have. Colleen admitted to taking prescription Tylenol for chronic back pain, possibly caused by her refusal after puberty to wear a brace made for her weak left leg when she was very young, possibly an exaggeration or even a fabrication on her part. The pills, she said, were only for when her pain got really bad, the way it had been at the wedding. No way was she back into doing heavy drugs. But what about those other symptoms she'd displayed that day: the twitching and the nausea? Maybe she wasn't doing *street* drugs but any idiot could see she was over-medicating and—because she hadn't brought the stuff to the wedding with her—was starting to experience withdrawal.

In some ways I think I *was* a fool—on purpose. I desperately wanted the improvement in Colleen brought on by being Jaimie's mom to last. Lisa reported seeing her sister down far too much Tylenol at times; yet whenever I met with Colleen during that period she was clear-eyed and lucid. She was raising a secure and happy child. She was often strapped for funds but still gainfully employed as a server at Olive Garden and doing her best to support the two of them. Andy and I helped out, attempting to minimize her financial struggle without "enabling" (a fine line). When Colleen lost her job at Olive Garden (because, she said, the boss was unreasonable) we pitched in further to cover her while jobless. She wouldn't be jobless for long, she assured us. She was going to work for Telus, the phone company.

At Telus she lasted three months. When she started, the job was wonderful. Then the complaints began: her co-workers were boring and her boss was unhelpful. She quit—or more likely was let go. Following Telus, she went after a job with First Calgary Financial. Bright and articulate as always, she passed the interview with flying colours. Again the job was wonderful at first. Before the end of the three-month apprenticeship it had become terrible. The boss was incompetent; *she* was far better at the job than the boss was. (Did she tell the boss that? I wouldn't put it past her!) Once more she was soon unemployed.

"I'm moving to High River," she then asserted. ""Job opportunities are better in a smaller town. And the rent on this place is way too high. A friend of mine knows of a much cheaper place there. There's a good Catholic school close to it that I can get Jaimie into because Brad's family are Catholic. The Catholic system offers a more decent education than the public system." (This from the girl who'd barely attended the public system! But I kept my mouth shut.)

Colleen had lived for three years in the Radcliff place, longer than she'd ever lived elsewhere. To the best of our knowledge the move was *her* idea, not the landlord's. And it sounded as though she'd done some solid research. How could we not get behind the plan?

High River is a community about forty-five minutes south of Calgary. Originally a small farming town, it has burgeoned over the last fifteen or so years into a retirement haven and also one of Calgary's suburbs. Yet it still retains an air of country warmth and hospitality that makes it an appealing place to reside. The townhouse complex Colleen found there was a cooperative run by a board comprised of the tenants. Not only was rent substantially lower than what she paid at Radcliff, a certain percentage of its units were government subsidized and could be applied for by low-income renters. Colleen had already got her name on the waiting list.

Furthermore, these units were small but bright and modern, and the complex was only minutes away from a scenic man-made lake around which wound a pleasant trail complete with park benches. "We can walk this every day," Colleen enthused. "It'll keep us in shape. And Jaimie can easily walk to school from here. It's perfect."

Colleen moved to High River the summer of 2004, the year Andy retired. Pat and Sue, the same-sex couple who'd befriended her and already done so much to help her, were on hand to help her again. She professed not to need *our* help with anything physical—though she did need someone with a good credit rating to co-sign for a truck she planned on renting. We did this. The move took place without incident; the truck was returned on time; Jaimie was enrolled in Holy Spirit Academy; and Colleen was ready to embark on a new chapter of her life. We enthused right along with her.

Proud of the new abode, she invited us for coffee. We came with housewarming gifts and offered a few well-received suggestions for making the place homier. Andy repaired Jaimie's bed which we'd bought some time before and which had broken in the move. One of her new neighbours, a very sweet older lady, purchased material to sew her some floral curtains for the dinette nook windows, and then the dear soul made matching cushions for the dinette chairs.

Her first Christmas in High River is when Colleen decided she wanted to host the annual Christmas do which was normally either at our house or at the Dawsons'. She excitedly said she would buy the turkey and cook it, as long as I gave her instructions. We all thought this a fine idea, evidence she was getting it together and making a go of things. As I mentioned in a previous chapter (the one attesting to how harried we always felt on holidays by her astonishing mood swings) Dorothy and Grant brought a delicious pie, Lisa and Shawn brought a cheesy potato dish, and Andy and I brought a couple of vegetable casseroles. We ate a late-afternoon early dinner in the newly curtained dinette nook, sitting on the newly cushioned chairs. Marley cat had a grand time of his own, making repeated sneaky forays into areas of temporarily unsupervised food. Good cheer abounded, Colleen doing a bang-up job of being the gracious hostess. When the meal was over, we helped her tidy up and put away dishes, little Jaimie carrying plates and cutlery one-at-a-time from the table to the kitchen sink. The aura remained one of pleasant camaraderie right up until we hugged them both and said our final goodnights.

That's why I was so stunned by Colleen's words when I made a point of phoning right after we got home to thank her for the lovely time. It was too much trouble, she snapped, for us ever to expect her to do it again.

Used as I was to my daughter's mercurial nature—and desperate as I still was *not* to attribute such a marked mood swing to drug abuse—I was more stunned still when she added, "Christmas sucks. If it weren't for Jaimie I wouldn't even bother celebrating it."

27. The Diaries

Mum, my beloved best friend, passed away from pancreatic cancer in 2000. Dad lived on for another three years, his bad heart finally giving out shortly after New Year's Day 2004. I shall forever miss them both. They left me a huge legacy: numerous nostalgic memories of their love, warmth and caring. And Dad left a more tangible legacy: his daily journals in which he'd faithfully chronicled all significant events in his life right up to its end. His last entry was January tenth, hours before he suggested Brian call an ambulance. Two days later he was gone. On January twelfth, heavy hearted, I sat in what was now Brian's condo, opened up the barely-begun 2004 diary, and took up a pen. In Dad's memory, I that day became the new family journalist and I have been so ever since.

What I had no way of knowing then was how these diaries would assist me in the writing of this book. Not only do they help me recall the accurate sequence of various happenings, they provide an absolutely unvarnished portrait of how I wavered between sugar-coated naiveté and frustrated annoyance during the first two of Colleen's High River years. If I must be brutally honest—and I must—the diaries tell as much about *me* and the blinders I wore as they do about my daughter's gradual downward slide:

October 10, 2004: The kids came for Thanksgiving lunch. We drove Colleen and Jaimie back to High River. Jaimie showed me around her new place. It is very nice and bright. I do hope they'll both be happy there. A day to treasure!

December 25, 2004: We spent Christmas day at Colleen's with Lisa, Shawn, and the Dawsons. Lovely food! Colleen worked steadily getting things out on the table while Andy carved the bird. The meal was a great success. We stayed to help clean up and then left, just as the weather turned. But when I phoned to thank Colleen she said it was too much trouble; she'd never do it again. Also said, "Christmas sucks. I wouldn't celebrate it if it weren't for Jaimie." How could her mood change so fast? I wish she'd admit to her mental illness and get help.

February 24, 2005: Colleen phoned to say she's lost her job and the rent is due. So we'll have to help her out. Again! I can't help being resentful about giving her the retirement savings we worked so hard for, when we spent so much energy during her youth counselling her AGAINST ending up with a child and without a man to help with the support. I keep thinking: why should WE be penalized for her mistakes? It just doesn't seem fair.

March 30, 2005: Colleen had us over for Easter dinner. She had cooked a chicken with sausage stuffing and made cheesy potatoes. With my broccoli casserole and Lisa's pies we had plenty. Jaimie came back to Calgary with us because she was having a "sleepover" with Auntie Lisa. Great day!

April 17, 2005: Jaimie spent the night with us and we took her to church this morning. She enjoyed meeting our church friends. After church we took her back to her mom. Colleen had a neighbour visiting who was helping her clean up her messy place. They were both smoking like chimneys and the place stank. I hated to stay and breathe that stuff. Poor Jaimie!

April 20, 2005: Colleen called. She's had to quit her job because "the standing was making her hip too sore". Wow! She worked four whole days! I just don't know when—or IF—that poor girl will find her place in life.

May 28, 2005: Colleen phoned. Said she'd be sending her June budget. When will that girl become self-supporting??

June 19, 2005: Colleen had all of us over for Father's Day. She cooked a prime rib and made a lovely job of it. She also served baked potatoes and trifle for dessert. All delicious. Good on her! Maybe she'll be OK. I hope so...

September 1, 2005: We went to Colleen's. I think we got her out of bed! Her house was in a disgusting mess...

As the diaries reflect I, like Colleen herself, went through a whole lot of emotional vacillation in the course of those two years. But frankly they were years of transition, in a wider sense, for our whole family. In June of 2004, Shawn's company flew him to Montreal for a few weeks on a specific job; then in March of 2005 he was flown to *Germany* to do some troubleshooting and advising. By May of that same year he'd been offered employment in Edmonton, the company agreeing to pay costs for their move plus their first three months' rent until they were established. Lisa gave notice at her school and set about submitting resumes to education boards in the Edmonton area. Once more the couple so dear to us were deserting our vicinity to chase opportunities elsewhere. That's an inevitability dealt with by parents of grown children. Andy and I had done it ourselves. At least they were still fairly close. But I hated to see them go.

My two fondest recollections of 2005 were Mother's Day and Father's Day. Mother's Day marked one of our last visits to Lisa and Shawn's Glamorgan place. The kids, including Colleen and Jaimie, prepared me a fabulous brunch of eggs Benedict followed by a whipped-cream-topped fruit salad for dessert. Jaimie, a towel draped over her arm like a high-class waiter, escorted me to my seat, pulled out my chair for me, and dished up the food. Andy got the same treatment at Colleen's a month later in June when our youngest cooked up the delicious prime rib dinner described above. A few weeks after that dinner, Lisa and Shawn finalized their move, selling their townhouse and buying a starter home in Edmonton.

As for Andy and me, we'd purchased a winter residence in Casa Grande Arizona, halfway between Phoenix and Tucson. We liked the idea of escaping Calgary's November-through-March icebox, especially when that escape was to our own place in a small friendly community. My initial reservations about the monetary outlay dissolved in the face of Andy's logic: "The money isn't gone. It has just changed form. Let's try this. If we don't like it we can always sell."

Another factor swaying our decision was that Casa Grande was a mere three-day drive—and a mere three-*hour* flight—from Calgary. We could, and did, come back to spend important occasions like birthdays and Christmas with friends and family.

November 26, 2005 - Jaimie's Birthday Party: Just before 1:00 p.m. we set off for High River. A winter storm was predicted to begin dumping snow by late afternoon/early evening, but mostly to the north of us. By the time we arrived at Colleen's it looked pretty bleak and there was a raw wind. Right behind us, arriving about two minutes later, were Lisa and Shawn. Jaimie opened her presents at home; then off we went to meet eleven little girls in the McDonald's play area. (Bill footed by L & S. They are a most generous uncle and auntie!) We stayed till about 4:00, then left to drive back. L & S left also, to return to Edmonton. Great day!

When I wrote that I felt relieved that a major concern I had—Colleen feeling abandoned by us all—seemed unfounded. She looked reasonably well, as did Jaimie. Also, Jaimie was obviously settled in at school and was making friends there. Right after we acquired the Casa Grande home Andy had requested Colleen start submitting us a monthly budget of her expenses so *we* could budget for helping her. She'd been doing so regularly and her figures at that point, though sometimes higher than we liked, looked plausible enough. Maybe she was gradually getting better anyway, with or without professional help.

I had read enough about BPD by then to have come across several such statements as those made in one particular *American Journal of Psychiatry* article: that a diminution of symptoms occurs over time, particularly in the mid-forties, which—though continued therapy hastens improvement—happens *with or without* treatment.[11] I clung to that and I believe I *made* myself see improvements whether they were actually there or not. How eagerly in the passages quoted above have I grabbed onto Colleen's invitations and displays of culinary aptitude as evidence of both increased desire and *ability* to cope! How fraught with longing for positive change is all my selfish bellyaching about her failure to hold jobs and her persistent financial dependence!

Colleen communicated regularly by phone during our first Casa Grande winter. Jaimie's skating lessons were expensive; more money was needed to cover the cost of the required outfits. Yes, Jaimie seemed to like the idea of spending spring break with us in Arizona next February. More money would be needed for that, though, to buy Jaimie additional clothes and a bathing suit. Her application to receive funds from AISH (the provincially-administered Assured Income for the Severely Handicapped) had gone through, with her doctor attesting to her inability to work due to chronic pain caused by her weak leg and by back problems. Along with the federally-administered child tax credit she got for Jaimie, she was now in reasonable shape financially. However, she and Jaimie both needed new glasses right away so she'd be grateful for any extra help we could provide...

I had mixed feelings about Colleen becoming an AISH recipient. On the one hand, the guaranteed income would ease the drain on *our* pocketbooks; on the other, I wondered how "severely handicapped" she truly was and how much she was taking deliberate and unjustified advantage of the social welfare system. As well, the lack of necessity to expend job hunting efforts created much more time for her to brood upon and talk about her terribly disadvantaged life. Of course the captive audience for these reminiscences was Jaimie.

Several months before Jaimie's planned trip to visit us, Andy urged Colleen to get her daughter a passport without delay; otherwise Jaimie wouldn't be able to come. Colleen delayed. Then she told us the photographer who'd taken Jaimie's picture said Jaimie couldn't travel without a father's name listed on the passport. "That's nonsense and you know it,"

---

11 J. Christopher Perry, Elizabeth Banon and Floriana Ianni, "Effectiveness of Psychotherapy for Personality Disorders", *American Journal of Psychiatry 156 (1999)*: 1312 – 1321

Andy contradicted. "The photographer has no say at all about the issue." Only when Andy himself took Colleen and Jaimie to the passport office was the required procedure completed. Obviously Jaimie's enthusiasm for the upcoming visit was not shared by Colleen.

In February 2006 we welcomed our granddaughter to our Arizona home for the week of her school break. She was nine then, due to turn ten that November. From the moment we picked her up at Sky Harbor Airport in Phoenix we noticed a subtle difference in her. Always polite, she was now almost shy. Though she splashed happily with Grandpa in the community swimming pool and accompanied both of us on many a pleasant walk with our newly-adopted terrier Pepper, something in her manner bordered on wary. Colleen phoned each night from High River, talking at length to Jaimie. The calls, often wheedling and offering Jaimie various treats and bribes when she came home (a new hamster, for example) seemed to make the little girl uncomfortable.

February 18, 2006: Jaimie arrives. Picked her up at AP…She seems a bit reserved with us. Not sure what Colleen has been telling her…

February 19, 2006: Jaimie spends a long time in the bathroom and seems to have an obsession with washing her hands. Do I make too much of this…?

February 23, 2006: Colleen calls nightly. Her calls seem to upset Jaimie. Or am I imagining this??

February 24, 2006: We made a picnic lunch and took Jaimie to Old Tucson Studios. She loved the train ride, the old west show, the carriage drawn by a Belgian plow horse, and the staged bank robbery. She did NOT enjoy going down into the "mine", which was a bit of a "house of horrors" show. Seems she's still a bit young to handle that. There was a mechanical monster named "George" who especially frightened her. She had nightmares about him, poor thing! We let her sleep with her lamp on all night. She says she normally sleeps in her mom's bed back home. I don't like that…!

I began having difficulty sleeping myself, gnawing uneasiness about Jaimie being the cause. Yet juxtaposed with my worry was self-reprisal for making mountains out of molehills. When we returned to Calgary in the spring, I told Andy I'd enjoyed our first season away and the temporary oasis it provided from bad weather *and* from exposure to Colleen's ups and downs. But then I thought: what about Jaimie? She *had* no oasis. Her exposure to Colleen's ups and downs was constant and unrelenting.

Evidence it was causing damage—limited to the few small signs I'd noted in the diaries—was scant. Evidence of the tremendous *benefit* wrought upon Colleen by having Jaimie was abundant. Thus went my ride on the figurative seesaw of opposing feelings during those two years. Thus also hammered the increasingly persistent voice inside my head:

The child is a human being, not Colleen's psychiatric bandage.

28. Ovarian Cysts and Cancer

I have mentioned the brittle smile, the one that doesn't extend to the eyes. My years with Colleen have made me super-sensitive to what we all recognize: that if the eyes don't reinforce what the lips are doing, then the smile is vacuous and insincere. Tacitly the smiler is saying, "My soul isn't in this. I'm only going through the motions."

More and more frequently Colleen began to smile the brittle smile. To me it is the ultimate irony that, as a toddler, my youngest surprised and touched me with a remark she made while sitting in my mum's lap and closely examining Mum's face. Mum had some facial paralysis caused by surgery to remove a brain tumour so Mum was apologizing for not being able to smile. "It's okay, Gamma," piped precocious tot Colleen. "You're smiling with your *eyes*." Mum teared up at those words. How acutely sensitive they were! How sadly *unlike* the later Colleen!

Towards the end of 2006 Colleen told us she had ovarian cysts. She'd have to have surgery and spend a few days in hospital. We offered to look after Jaimie during her stay. For what date was the surgery booked? She gave us a date in mid-October and then phoned to say it had been delayed and then phoned again to say it had been *cancelled*. She was fine. We shouldn't put off our winter departure on her account.

Even for Colleen this was bizarre behaviour. Was she in need of hospitalization or wasn't she? Did she have cysts or didn't she? They weren't sure, she said; more tests were needed. She'd let us know. But by the time we flew back from Arizona for Christmas, her stories were just as vague. We asked if we could talk to her doctor and she crossly replied, "No way! That's privileged information!"

Christmas 2006 was strained. Lisa and Shawn arrived from Edmonton at ten a.m. The plan was for the whole family to enjoy Jaimie's excitement as she unwrapped her treasures. I already had the turkey in the oven and the accompanying casseroles prepared. We delayed the gift opening and awaited Colleen, who'd said a neighbour had agreed to drop off the two of them, also at ten. Eleven came and went; twelve noon ticked by with no sign of either one. It was nearly one before they appeared.

The neighbour—the same lady who had sewn Colleen's curtains and cushions—didn't hang around to speak to us. Jaimie, twirling an excited dance around the prolific present pile, was her happy-go-lucky self. Colleen smiled the brittle smile, grunted a greeting, and slunk out our back gate into the park for a smoke.

"Is your mom okay?" I asked Jaimie, guts clenched. Jaimie shrugged. More and more lately Jaimie shrugged when I enquired about her mom. We had recently requested Colleen's permission to treat Jaimie to another February holiday during school break, this time to Disneyland. Colleen had given it and had doted on Jaimie's wild elation when we'd sprung the news. But she'd turned dour since, which we'd attributed to anxiety about the medical tests she claimed she needed.

Because she wouldn't level with us we had no way of knowing the cause of her *real* anxiety or the extent of it. What I do know now is that she'd told the neighbour who gave her the ride that we were abusive people who were absolutely non-sympathetic about her *cancer*. She only wanted to spend a short time with us for Jaimie's sake because it sucked to be in our company too long.

When she'd finished her smoke and come back inside, we opened gifts. Jaimie, who loves playing piano, was thrilled with the new electronic keyboard from us and with various other cool toys and games from Auntie and Uncle. The Dawsons arrived soon afterwards. Once more Colleen smiled the brittle smile and deserted us all for the telephone, returning almost immediately to announce she'd been invited elsewhere; she and Jaimie had to go. "Dad, I'll need a ride back to High River," she added offhandedly.

It was the wedding all over again. My inner voice reiterated what it had said then: *Colleen, are you nuts?* Andy vocalized it. "No way am I abandoning my guests just because you feel there might be a better party elsewhere. Forget it." Colleen didn't forget it; she called up the neighbour who'd dropped her off and got that neighbour to return and pick her up. "Jaimie and I are going," was her curt announcement. What could we do? She was an adult of twenty-eight deemed legally capable of managing her own affairs—and of making decisions about Jaimie. As we helped them bundle up the gifts they'd both received, I choked down anger about Colleen's shameful conduct and about how my poor granddaughter must feel.

And again, as on the day of the wedding, something in the atmosphere lifted the moment Colleen left. Not that worry wasn't, as always, a lurking shadow but—as dear departed Dad once said—one can't live one's life on the edge of a cliff. Without the awkwardness Colleen created, the rest of us relaxed. The Dawsons, of course, were quite used to our troubled daughter's antics and, like us, had learned to weather them. Dorothy, as a nurse, had mentioned to her the treatability of ovarian cysts. Dorothy, in fact, made a point of mentioning it once again on New Year's Day when we reassembled for our customary dinner at their place.

That dinner was worse than Christmas day. Pat and Sue, the same-sex couple, dropped off Colleen and Jaimie, having agreed to pick them up right after the meal. Again we suspected (and have since had confirmation from these kind ladies) that Colleen was painting us as abusers whose company she tolerated only briefly for Jaimie's sake. At the table Colleen was dopey. Mom, Jaimie explained, had taken some pain pills; that's why she kept dozing off. She did stay awake long enough to partake generously of Dorothy's superb meal (and to hear Dorothy's repeated reassurances about the treatability of ovarian cysts) before the ladies returned to whisk her and our granddaughter away. However, as I've said, worry about ovarian cysts was not at all Colleen's problem.

What *was* the problem? I didn't understand it then the same way I do now. At the time I thought Colleen's preference for being an invalid plus her long-standing preoccupation with the dark and dire was causing her to dwell too deeply and morbidly on this "ovarian cysts" business. Unaware she'd already upgraded it to ovarian cancer for her High River neighbours, I actually did wonder—like Dorothy—if fear of possible cancer is what was preying upon her. But both Dorothy and I were thinking with the non-BPD mind.

The information I've since gleaned about BPD mothers from books that were not even published then leaves me no doubt about the real source of her worry.

29. Disneyland

That Colleen had found Disneyland too intense an experience as a child—and, as an adult, never really got over that propensity for over-reaction—made it seem improbable she'd want to accompany Jaimie on our February 2007 vacation. And indeed she *didn't* actually want to go. But the problem was this: she didn't want Jaimie to go either.

Her angst, which ultimately burst out of her in repeated phone calls to Lisa, was the same one that had caused her to hold up the issuing of Jaimie's passport the year previous. To her sister Colleen expressed it this way: "*I* should be the one to watch my daughter's wonder when she sees Disneyland!" Interspersed with that was her very real fear that someone in the dense crowds would try to snatch Jaimie away.

Lisa reported these conversations, concerned her sister's mental stability was deteriorating. Colleen's paranoid visions of would-be kidnappers lying in wait amongst the throng sounded overblown and histrionic as usual. I found myself reacting with impatience. Surely Colleen ought to be elated for her daughter, nurturing the sugarplum visions that dance in any child's head at the prospect of going to Disneyland—not filling that poor little head with "what ifs". And why had Colleen not been frank with *us* about what was bothering her?

Hindsight and the reading I have since done about BPD enables me to empathize more today with Colleen's feelings than I did then. I believe her lack of frankness stemmed from knowing rationally that she *should* be elated for her daughter—just as she knew she herself *should* have enjoyed Disneyland as a child. And more than that, her terror of abandonment, never far away, was closing in to engulf her. The little being she'd brought into the world and had fought to keep she saw as *hers*. Despite her words to us at her baby's birth, Jaimie was never supposed to leave her. Now, that was starting to happen. Jaimie was beginning to have experiences independent of Colleen, and Colleen couldn't deal with it. All her life she'd been rejected by others; now we were taking away—even if only briefly—the one person whose love and loyalty she'd been able to control. That was her reality.

Her disproportionate dread of kidnappers is further proof. Mason and Kreger cite the account of a BPD parent's adult child who says his mother viewed him as an extension of herself. All of his relationships were "about her" and she perceived all his friends and outside influences as a threat to *their* bond.[12] BPD parents, the authors state, are apt to feel threatened by a child's "normal" behaviour and these feelings increase in the BPD person as the child becomes more independent.[13]

A 2003 study published in the *British Journal of Psychiatry* looked at mother-infant relations when the mothers had BPD. Researchers watched BPD mothers interacting with their two-month-old infants. They found that the mothers with BPD were more intrusive with their children without being sensitive to their needs. The infants spent more time than babies of mothers without BPD looking away with dazed expressions. Even at this age, the babies were having trouble regulating their stress levels![14]

During that holiday, we saw mounting evidence of the stress levels Jaimie was enduring. Having met her plane at Palm Springs, we drove to our hotel, the Tropicana, right opposite Disneyland. We'd booked two rooms with a connecting door, so Jaimie had a separate room adjoining ours. She asked permission to leave the TV on all night to help her get to sleep. Since she normally slept in the same bed as her mom, she felt insecure about sleeping alone.

On her visit to us in Arizona the year before, I had mentioned to her that she was really too old to share her mom's bed but nothing had changed. Now I mentioned it again.

"You're ten, Jaimie, and you have your own bedroom at home. Don't you *ever* sleep in it?"

"It's too messy, Grandma. I can't even get to the bed. Mom likes me sleeping with her anyway." She scuffed her feet on the floor and seemed uneasy discussing this, either because she sensed this wasn't a normal practice or because the topic was one Colleen had specifically forbidden her to discuss, or both.

---

12 Paul T. Mason and Randi Kreger, *Stop Walking on Eggshells: Taking your life back when someone you care about has borderline personality disorder* (Oakland, CA: New Harbinger Publications, 2010) 42

13 Ibid, 180

14 Aguirre, Blaise A., M.D. 2007. *Borderline Personality Disorder in Adolescents: A Complete Guide to Understanding and Coping when Your Adolescent has BPD.* Beverly, Massachusetts: Fair Winds Press, 126

Her obsessive hand washing was worse as well. She spent longer than ever in the bathroom. Yes, she was approaching her teens and all teens take eons at their primping and preening. But this was more than that. Once, in a washroom on the Disneyland grounds, she raced out of a cubicle weeping hysterically. It turned out she had got a few drops of pee on her jeans. I helped her wash them off, telling her it was no big deal. The fact it *was* a big deal to her, I suspect, was a reaction to the disarray she dwelt in at home. Those limited environmental aspects she *could* control she wanted absolutely pristine.

Her mom had not supplied appropriate clothing, particularly footwear. Jaimie came with only one pair of shoes: stiff boots with a heel. She told us they didn't fit well and were uncomfortable so we bought her a pair of softer, more open shoes.

At Disneyland Grandpa took many photos of Jaimie in the company of several "princesses" whose autographs she was thrilled to get. He also captured Jaimie—and Grandma—on a multitude of rides. Jaimie's approach to rides was diametrically opposite to Colleen's: she would thoughtfully assess each ride in terms of scariness and babyishness. Then she'd make a decision. Once she'd decided, she had fun!

Of course many Disneyland rides are for all ages. Even the tamest ones were packed with children *and* their parents or grandparents. Jaimie loved them all, from *Dumbo* to *It's a Small World* to *Pirates of the Caribbean*. Her timidity—definitely greater than average—melted in the face of sustained wonder and delight. She kept saying things like, "Grandpa, get a photo of me and Grandma in front of Sleeping Beauty's Castle!" or "Grandma, take one of me and Grandpa on the paddle boats!" Several times my cheeks were wet with tears of gratitude. This was how it was supposed to have been with my own children. Better late than never.

I realized in the course of that trip that part of me nervously awaited a repeat of Colleen's Disneyland behaviour. Even as Jaimie seemed enraptured, I was braced for whining, complaining and public scenes. Would they start when she became tired of all the walking and waiting in lineups? Would she put up a fuss if we refused to buy her all the treats she wanted? What would she pick on to rant about? By the third day it dawned on me that, bless her heart, she wasn't going to rant about anything. On the contrary: she often said, "Thank you, Grandma and Grandpa. I'm having a great time!" My unfair pre-judgment of her was solely because she was Colleen's daughter.

We spent three days at Disneyland, one day at the equally captivating Universal Studios, and one day at the Crystal Cathedral. Since we were right next door to this stunning Reformed Church architectural landmark (seating over two thousand people and built by the congregation of Robert H. Schuller) we didn't want to miss seeing it. It has since filed for bankruptcy and been purchased by the Roman Catholic Diocese of Orange county, but back then there were guided tours of the campus as well as opportunities afterwards to visit a little gift shop.

On the Crystal Cathedral day we warned Jaimie, "This is something Grandma and Grandpa are interested in. You may be bored but we still expect you to be polite." Again, memories of Colleen's loudly-expressed contempt about the American Presidents pavilion at Disney World caused me to expect the worst. It didn't happen. Jaimie wasn't just polite; she asked questions of the tour guide and displayed recognition of religious stories portrayed in various paintings and sculptures. Of course religious instruction was part of the curriculum in the Catholic school she attended, but many kids receive religious instruction and don't take an interest. Based on her attitude and the questions she asked, we made a joyful discovery. Our granddaughter's good behaviour was more than just good behaviour. Jaimie had inherited her mom's articulateness and intelligence but had *not* inherited any of the mental roadblocks that held her mom back. Far from being bored at the Crystal Cathedral she was a sponge, eager to sop up every ounce of knowledge offered her.

And even more importantly, she was a sensitive caring person. On our way out, she asked if she could buy her mom something from the gift shop: a window-hanging inscribed with the words *I Love You.* "My mom would have liked to come," she told us. "She was disappointed she couldn't." Had Colleen said that? Was there reproach in Jaimie's tone?

We bought the window-hanging for her to give to her mom. We also explained that this was an expensive trip, one her mom had already taken as a child. "Now it's your turn," we added, wondering what else about us Colleen had said.

Soon enough I found out. That evening Andy ran into a convenience store to buy a newspaper while Jaimie and I waited in the car. Jaimie expressed a dim view of a passing mother who took a swat at her child's rear. "Maybe the kid was being sassy," I speculated. "That was just a harmless cuff." I even mentioned Dr. Benjamin Spock who had lived to regret his original unequivocal contention that children should never be spanked. Jaimie replied, "My mom says you should never hit a child."

"*Hitting* isn't the same as spanking," I countered. "Spanking might happen if a baby is reaching for a candle flame or a toddler is being openly rebellious. I once spanked your Auntie Lisa's diapered bottom in a TV store because I'd asked her not to touch the knobs on the display models and she deliberately did it again. The salesman thanked me. He said he wished more moms would discipline their kids." Her frown deepened so I added, "But parents have differing opinions about spanking and they're entitled to them."

Jaimie was suddenly tense. She said, "I'm not really supposed to talk about this." Then she shut up like a clam.

To what she *hadn't* said, I couldn't help responding. And I responded with the only thing that came to my mind. "Jaimie, if Grandpa and I were abusive people, you would have found that out for yourself by now. People can't hide what they are, especially when they spend long periods of time with each other."

My granddaughter made no reply. She'd decided the taboo subject was closed. I knew better than to pursue it. Later I said to Andy, "She wants to believe everything her mom tells her. What child doesn't? But she's getting old enough to see evidence to the contrary for herself. I'm so sad about how conflicted she must be!"

Andy shook his head. "Under the circumstances she's amazingly well-adjusted. I wonder what exactly the ugly tales are that Colleen has been telling her."

It was a long time later before Jaimie opened up to us enough to reveal those tales. And they were even uglier than either of us had imagined.

30. Wringing Our Hands

When the Disneyland vacation ended, we took Jaimie to Palm Springs and saw her onto her WestJet flight back to Calgary. She hugged and thanked us with tears in her eyes. How did the poor sweetheart feel about returning to life with Colleen?

"Their relationship may not be the healthiest," commented Andy on the drive back to our Arizona home. "But I doubt we could take Jaimie away even if we wanted to. She adores her mom. Colleen's efforts to turn her against us make me very angry but she's obviously beginning to understand—even if reluctantly—that her mom is misrepresenting us. The inconsistency of being told how abusive we are and then being left without hesitation in our care is starting to dawn on her. I think she's known it subconsciously ever since she was small."

I agreed—on both counts. Jaimie was conflicted. But Jaimie also felt a stubborn loyalty toward her beloved mom. Admitting even to herself that Colleen might be lying to her—about anything—constituted a sort of betrayal.

In matters of child custody, the law—as it should—heavily favours the parent. In the law's eyes and as far as we ourselves could judge, Jaimie was nourished, clothed, and sent to school. So her physical and educational needs were being met. As to her emotional needs, did her mom love her? Yes, obsessively! We knew we'd have no legal basis for contesting Colleen's right to Jaimie's guardianship even if we wanted to. And knowing what losing Jaimie would do to Colleen made us not want to. Colleen was still our daughter.

To this day I wonder if we looked the other way longer than we should have. Colleen called us right after she'd met Jaimie's plane (having pre-vailed upon someone to give her a lift to Calgary Airport) and launched into a tirade about what a terrible ordeal the airport experience had been. How dare WestJet let all the other passengers off first before dealing with unattended children on a flight! Didn't they realize what torture a waiting mother goes through? She was going to sue WestJet! Jaimie was never going to travel again!

WestJet has since made an executive decision to stop allowing unattended children on flights but that decision had nothing to do with Colleen, who never followed up on her threats. We, of course, saw through the complaints to the increasingly paranoid mind that had hatched them. Was her growing paranoia drug-induced psychosis in addition to mental illness?

Colleen's monthly budget submissions were sometimes higher than we liked but up to now had never been outlandish. AISH didn't cover anything but basics and Jaimie (said Colleen) wanted dance lessons, then skating lessons, then the required outfits for both, then an expensive doctor-recommended herbal remedy for an upset stomach condition. As long as Jaimie remained with her and remained subject to her influence, Colleen held a very effective blackmail card which she played at every opportunity.

The dance and skating lessons we'd handled in the logical way: by paying for them directly. And we ourselves had taken Jaimie shopping for the outfits. But certain requests like the stomach remedy, made by phone while we were in Arizona, we couldn't verify. We asked Colleen its name and the specific condition it treated. She flew into a rage, claiming we didn't trust her and couldn't care less about our granddaughter's health. What kind of people were we?

While the past legitimacy of Jaimie's lessons and outfits had been reassuring, the rage rang alarm bells. I said to Andy, "I don't buy this stomach medicine story. We've never seen evidence of stomach troubles in Jaimie." But Colleen continued to insist the symptoms had just developed and the doctor was sure this remedy would be beneficial. The same doctor was also recommending she, Colleen, take certain herbal products for her own general health. She would email us a list of all their names and their costs.

How do you argue with that? Well, you ask to speak directly to the doctor. After all, a list of herbal remedy names and prices one can get simply by walking into any health foods store. And if asking to speak to the doctor incites more rage, then the rat you've begun to smell positively reeks.

Yes, Colleen was furious. If that was how little faith we had in her, then she'd go elsewhere for help—to people who were compassionate rather than hard-hearted. She hated us. I'd never wanted her. I'd once said she should have been a boy, hadn't I? That was proof I'd never forgiven her for being a girl!

I was appalled. She'd taken a long-ago comment I know I should never have made and given it a whole different slant. This was a fried brain talking. "It's street drugs she's after; I'm sure of it," I said to Andy. My husband wasn't as sure. His trusting nature prefers to think the best of people. He found the decision not to send Colleen money even harder than I did but we made that decision together and stuck to it.

And now we needed to consider what to do about Jaimie. How deeply addicted *was* Colleen? Was she an unsafe parent? We had no proof of that. But when a child is involved, can you stand by and do nothing?

In the midst of all our verbal hand wringing, Colleen suddenly did an astonishing about-face. She called back to say she'd decided at last to seek counselling. We were thunderstruck. For nearly two hours she talked to me about how this was *it;* her life couldn't go on this way. She needed to learn some coping skills and she'd already been in touch with Mental Health. All her mood swings and emotional crises were very unfair to Jaimie. And I was right after all: maybe we *should* talk to her doctor.

I could hardly believe my ears. If true, this was a miracle. If a ruse to soften us up so we'd let down our guard (which of course I feared) it exceeded all her previous ploys. We didn't know what to think.

What I think today is that these periods of calm logic that we began to term Colleen's "reasonableness spells" were not a deliberate attempt to hoodwink us but an example of increased and unwitting drug use as *self-medication*. Dr. Robert Friedel, a distinguished clinical professor of psychology at Virginia Commonwealth University who serves on the Scientific Advisory Board of the National Education Alliance for Borderline Personality Disorder, points out that *dopamine*, one of the neurotransmitter chemicals affecting brain function, is under-produced by the BPD brain and that alcohol and many other addictive drugs have been shown to stimulate dopamine activity, alleviating depression and possibly *normalizing* the brain temporarily.[15] For me, reading this is huge. While I can't bring myself to say it *excuses* Colleen's persistent drug de-pendency, it at least *explains* it. I realize now that whenever Colleen told us her former non-productive life was over and then elaborated on all her grand schemes for the future, it was because she'd either taken a large dose of prescription medication or succeeded in coaxing a loan out of someone and had just given herself a substantial street-drug hit.

---

15 Friedel, Robert O., M.D., 2004. *Borderline Personality Disorder Demystified: The Essential Guide to Understanding and Living with BPD*. New York, NY: Marlowe & Company, Avalon Publishing Group Inc. 87, 88

Then, though, I was flummoxed. How could she be a screeching psycho one minute and the essence of calmness and common sense the next? *Had* she contacted Mental Health or was she lying? Did we dare hope she'd follow through on any of her promises?

A diary entry I made in mid-March of 2007 details my torment:

March 13, 2007: Up at 4:10 a.m. and off to work out on the machines here in Arizona. Couldn't sleep very well—too upset about poor Colleen. All her life she has internalized and dwelled on the negative and let it get her down. She's still weeping over my once telling her she'd be less trouble if she'd been a boy—something I NEVER should have said even if angry—but the "why" of her inability to get over things and move on is something I'll never understand and am helpless to change. Her telling me she hated me and wished I'd die so Dad could marry someone else I doubt she even remembers. (Or, if she does, I doubt she thinks it has had much effect on me.) And when I reminded her that I'd frequently had talks with her about how much I loved her and I'd also frequently tried to help her get over her heartache over the teasing at school, etc., she DID remember that. I only wish she could train herself to focus on the positive and not be defeated by the negative. It is the one thing I've wished for her all my life!! And I am powerless to make it happen.

We took advantage of a "reasonableness spell" to get Colleen to reveal the name of her doctor. With her consent I called his office and made us an appointment. It would not be until April. Meanwhile, she would *not* consent to my having a conversation with him on the phone. Upon our arrival back in Calgary and the approach of the appointment date, Colleen twice cancelled. First she claimed she had the 'flu and then she claimed Jaimie had it. Not until May, when we refused to be put off again, did it finally take place.

Pulling up at her townhouse we were surprised to see Jaimie—at home on a weekday—clamber onto the back seat ahead of Colleen. "She's got a bit of a bug," Colleen grumped. "Let's go." Jaimie looked perfectly okay to me but one issue at a time.

While we sat in the doctor's waiting area our daughter deliberately turned her back on us, gossiping with the receptionist who lived in the same townhouse complex. Today I'd say she was battling enormous angst; then I took it personally and felt snubbed. Eventually the three of us were ushered into a consulting room while Jaimie stayed where she was, happily reading.

It was a grim session. The physician, whom I'll call Dr. Jones, looked chronically ill himself and the most generous light in which I can paint him is to say he probably empathized with patients who told him they were in constant pain. Jones admitted to prescribing for Colleen large doses of OxyContin, a trade name for the opium-based drug oxycodone hydrochloride. He also admitted to having taken at face value her statements that she had a weak leg and bad back that hurt her constantly. He was aware of no previous medical history on her; otherwise he'd have known better. I had words with this doctor, told him he shouldn't be practicing medicine. He said he soon wouldn't be and I realized the man was telling us he was dying.

From this sad excuse for a doctor, Andy and I managed to gain the information that Colleen had never had ovarian cysts, had never been booked for a hospital procedure, had never been told she might have cancer, and had never had any herbal remedies recommended by him, either for herself or for Jaimie. Throughout the exchange Colleen made frantic attempts to divert the conversation. No wonder she'd been so desperate to cancel!

Okay, she was sorry she'd deceived us. But the pain in her weak leg *and* her back, she maintained, was often unbearable. She regretted not having worn the leg brace prescribed for her as a child. She would work with Dr. Jones to try and lower the doses of OxyContin she was taking and replace it with something less addictive. Jones promised to support these efforts.

As to street drugs, she denied ever buying them, with the exception of once trying a hit of crack cocaine that didn't agree with her. Vehemently she also denied lying about the herbal remedies she'd often had to borrow money to buy. When she'd hit up people she knew for loans to purchase these (which she now said had been recommended by a friend in the health food business, not the doctor) she'd thought prospective lenders would be more likely to contribute if the remedies were represented as doctor endorsed. I didn't believe her. But again, there was no way to disprove anything she said.

"The doctor will help me step down my pills, Mom," she vowed. "Now I have to get Jaimie home so she'll get over her bug and back to school as soon as possible." Spoken like the paragon of good intentions and conscientious parenthood!

The "reasonableness spells" increased in frequency after that. Lisa had a teaching colleague who'd started a monthly youth magazine; he was going to pay Colleen to write articles for it from her home computer. She said she was putting together a properly formatted resume (I helped her with this) so she could apply for a position at the local library. She had several other job leads as well. She was going to become a self-supporting contributing citizen for Jaimie's sake.

In June of 2007 our son-in-law was offered a job in Vancouver working on the graphics for *Santa Buddies*, a Disney direct-to-video movie series aimed at young children and featuring talking puppies. A prequel and several sequels were planned, promising him sustained and lucrative employment. The opportunity excited him as did the fact he'd be able to live in Surrey close to Terry and Jen: his dad and his dad's second wife. It would be a chance to re-establish that relationship as well as branch out into a new application of his expertise. Lured by the prospect of a stimulating life and career change out west, Lisa shared his excitement. Colleen felt her sister was deserting her.

"I may move there too," she told me. "I never get together with you and Dad anyhow, so I have no one." She said it as though *we* were the ones repelling *her*, rather than the other way around. Even had I known then what I know today about the typical "I hate you; don't leave me" BPD behaviour, I think I would have found it hard not to be annoyed.

Shawn had to leave his wife temporarily behind in Edmonton so she could complete her teaching year. Meanwhile he drove to Surrey and roomed for a few weeks with Terry and Jen who helped him find an ideal house for sale right in the same neighbourhood where *they* lived. Lisa viewed the photos Shawn sent and gave her blessing. She began the process of packing up their stuff and putting their Edmonton house on the market.

Lisa invited Jaimie to spend the final week of July in Edmonton—a last chance for aunt and niece to share some time before Lisa moved further away. Colleen was lukewarm, but with Jaimie out of school for the summer, could find no excuse not to agree. Lisa drove down to High River to pick Jaimie up.

"I hardly ever get invited past the front door of that townhouse," our elder daughter reported on the following Saturday when, after their week together, she and Jaimie stopped at our place for lunch and a movie before

Lisa headed back to Edmonton. "And Colleen lives in stygian gloom in there with all the blinds drawn to shut out the sunlight. I got a grand lecture on how careful I have to be that kidnappers don't try to snatch Jaimie if I take her out anywhere. And every night I got calls. I had to put Jaimie on the phone to say good-night and they'd have long conversations that often seemed to be about the *real* fun they'd have together after Jaimie came home. I think Colleen's paranoia is getting worse. I have to admit I'm getting to hate taking Jaimie back there."

We could not agree more. Hand wringing, it seemed, was not confined just to Andy and me. At that moment I got a brief flashback of a much younger Lisa's stricken little face and her pleading query when her sister misbehaved: *Why don't you do something?* But now she knew as well as we that, without proof and without Colleen's cooperation, we were powerless to do anything.

Earlier in the day we had offered to fetch Colleen and have her join us for lunch; she'd declined, as was often the case, saying she wasn't feeling well. So Andy and I drove in our car to see Disney's newly-released animated picture *Ratatouille,* while Lisa and Jaimie went in Lisa's car and met us at the movie theatre. After the movie, Jaimie transferred to our vehicle for the journey back to High River so that Lisa could make an earlier start on the return trip to Edmonton. Our elder daughter parted from us with a hug, the worry we three shared hanging over our embrace like a cloud.

We drove to Colleen's townhouse. Andy rang the bell several times. We then tried knocking. Neither produced results. Andy sighed, taking from his pocket the spare key he'd insisted Colleen give us since Radcliff days. Drugged or not, Colleen had always been a heavy sleeper; it was her way of escaping the world. Her tendency not to wake up in time for prearranged appointments or invitations had caused Andy so much irritation—and worry—in the past that he'd set ground rules. One (preceding any real concern we had about drug use) was that any time we were supposed to meet her somewhere we would simply leave after twenty minutes if she hadn't shown up. Another was that if we came to her place and couldn't rouse her we had the right to walk in and wake her ourselves.

We unlocked the unit, entered and called up the staircase leading from the front hall to the second floor. No answer. The place smelled stale and was alarmingly messy. Marley cat picked his way through piles of tattered clothing to greet us. As I was about to ascend to the master bedroom Colleen appeared at the landing.

She looked terrible. Her matted hair had obviously not seen a comb in several days and her skin, peppered with red blotches, had a prison-like pallor, as though it had never been exposed to sun or fresh air. Her weight was ballooning to obesity and she was dressed in rags: a stained low-cut top she half fell out of and a pair of stretched-tight sweat pants full of holes. My heart lurched.

"It's okay. I'm up!" She gave one of her forced laughs and limped her way downstairs. "I had to take some painkillers for my leg and back. They've been giving me real trouble." She pulled her daughter into her arms. "Hi, angel, I missed you. Did you have a good time with your auntie? Let's hear about the movie you saw."

The little girl hugged her back and obliged as Colleen listened dotingly; then Jaimie went over and stood by the stairs stroking the cat while Andy and I cleared a space on the living-room couch and sat down to talk with our daughter. Now fully awake, Colleen displayed her usual oratory skill and spun a tale rife with pathos: she'd been buying herbal remedies for the pain, which left her with money enough only for food; she couldn't afford clothes as well. I felt the pressure of tears behind my eyes.

This was a person whose sole motivation for maintaining a hold on life was centred in her precious daughter. It was too great a burden to ask the poor child to bear.

"Colleen," I whispered, "you need intensive help. Jaimie could come and stay with us while you get it."

My daughter stiffened defensively. "I'm already getting help, Mom. I've started to see an addictions counsellor about my dependence on the pills and Dr. Jones is gradually stepping me down. Besides, I couldn't stand being away from my baby for any length of time. We're fine."

Loud choking sobs suddenly convulsed Jaimie. She hadn't been close enough to hear our murmured conversation so those sobs were startling. Lowering herself to the bottom step of the staircase, she clasped her knees to her chin and cried as though the world were about to end. With a quickness her mom couldn't manage, I leaped up and went over to her, putting an arm about her shaking shoulders. "What is it, sweetheart? What's wrong? Tell Grandma."

For several moments she continued to sob before she could answer. When she did at last, it was with these eight heart-rending words:

"I want to go back to Auntie Lisa."

31. The Phone Message

Colleen began to cry for her baby and I began to cry for *my* baby. In a rush of empathy I was transported back to my own painful days of rejection by my own children. "Lisa and you guys can show Jaimie a good time," Colleen sniffled. "You have the money and the mobility to take her places and do things with her. I don't have either. No wonder she doesn't want to come back here. But I'm a good mother and she knows how much I love her! And besides, she's all I've got."

The words had their effect. I told my granddaughter quietly, "It's always a bit sad to come back to ordinary life after a nice holiday. But we all have to do it, sweetheart. There'll be other nice holidays." The poor darling nodded and stopped her crying. Colleen hugged me saying, "Thanks, Mom." I felt utterly torn.

I went shopping and bought Colleen several new tops and new pairs of pants: an attempt—Band-Aid though it might be—to give her self-esteem a boost. She again thanked me, said she loved them, and wore one set in August 2007 when we picked her and Jaimie up to go and meet Lisa at a mid-point between Calgary and Edmonton: *Smitty's* in Gasoline Alley, Red Deer. Andy and I treated our elder daughter, along with Colleen and Jaimie, to a farewell lunch there before Lisa moved to B.C. (Shawn, already living in the Surrey house they'd bought, flew back shortly thereafter to help pack up the last of their belongings so the two of them could make the return trip together in Lisa's car.) Colleen seemed better at that lunch. She'd combed her hair and applied makeup, and her manner was fairly cheerful. Squeezing her sister's shoulder with a grin she said, "We can still talk on the phone. It won't make any difference that you're changing provinces."

Today I'd say her nonchalance was almost certainly an act, a cover-up for those engulfing feelings of abandonment. But she pulled off the act very well. When Jaimie clung crying to Auntie, she stroked her daughter's hair and soothed, "It's okay, angel. We'll do something fun together, you and I." Jaimie swallowed and accepted the inevitability of Lisa living further away.

The little girl had already learned by then that Mom's follow-through on promises was poor to non-existent. She looked glum throughout our ride back to High River. Colleen tried to jolly her into a good mood by teasing, prodding and tickling: something that had worked fine when Jaimie was younger. It wasn't so effective any more. I remember thinking that Jaimie's emotional maturity level seemed to be approaching Colleen's. Maybe it had already surpassed it.

Like a light bulb that burns brightest on the brink of failing, Colleen had some of her best "reasonableness spells" during the next several months. Just before we left for Arizona in September she actually invited me for lunch right after my sixtieth birthday, which she apologized for forgetting. It was great, she bubbled, that Lisa had succeeded in getting a one-year-contract job (hopefully to become permanent if all went well) at Fleetwood Park Secondary, a Surrey high school within walking distance of their residence. The townhouse living-room and kitchen looked worlds cleaner and tidier. Jaimie seemed happy-go-lucky and told me school was going well. What a relief! Maybe Colleen really *was* cutting down on the pain pills as she'd vowed to do. Amazingly, phone conversations between us went from rare to moderately frequent and were full of the success she was having. As a mother who desperately wanted her daughter to get better, I was easy prey to self-persuasion.

When we returned from Arizona for the Christmas holidays (which Lisa flew back to spend with us, Shawn being unable to get sufficient time off), I still saw in our youngest a much more "together" young woman, inclined as always to oversleep but presenting as having a handle on herself and her life. She would have completely fooled outsiders—and often did. At Grant and Dorothy's annual Christmas dinner, she went on at length about her self-improvement plans for 2008, including getting to bed much earlier so she wasn't tired all the time. Shortly after that speech she dropped off, still sitting up in a chair, and spilled coffee all over Dorothy's rug. We all helped mop up, amid our daughter's profuse apologies. "It's okay," assured Dorothy. "It could happen to anybody."

But it happened again to Colleen the very next day. She and Jaimie had spent the night with us after our evening at the Dawsons'. She slept in while the rest of us—Lisa, Jaimie, Andy and I—took our little dog Pepper for his morning walk. When she limped into the kitchen just before noon and poured herself a coffee, she promptly spilled it all over the floor. Again she apologized, blaming it on pain in her back and leg that had forced her to take painkillers. In my diary entry for that day I describe her as looking like "an empty shell of a person, doped to the gills". I say it's a heartbreaker about which I can do nothing. And yet she swore things would be better in 2008. She and her doctor were going to address the physical causes of the pain as a further measure to reducing her pill dependence. I believe she was trying to convince herself as much as me.

"When you get back from Arizona in three months," she declared, "things will be totally different. You'll see."

It was hard to leave again for Arizona. In the chapel service we attended there we regularly requested prayers for Colleen, frustrated at not having more tangible avenues for helping. She continued to phone often, saying she was really working on her "issues" but was finding the herbal substitutes for OxyContin prohibitively expensive. Usually these phone conversations included requests for money—not only for the herbal remedies but for taxi fares to and from Foothills Hospital in Calgary. (Jones, she said, preferred Foothills to the High River Hospital.) X-rays and various other tests, she claimed, were being done on her leg and back.

In February, sounding perfectly lucid, she told us her account was overdrawn and she needed grocery money. She'd had to use taxis a lot lately for regular appointments with a psychiatrist she was seeing who said she suffered dissociative episodes as well as multiple personality disorder. This psychiatrist wanted to talk to us about Colleen's childhood when we returned, and Colleen said she'd agreed to it. We were all scheduled to meet with him in April.

Mainly because of Jaimie, Andy arranged with the Bank of Montreal in High River for BMO overdraft protection for Colleen—a line of credit in the event of emergencies. I'd be lying if I said we did this in good faith; of course we didn't. But for the next two months until we returned home, it ensured Colleen remained solvent. What it might really be doing, I conceded to Andy, was insuring her ability to buy street drugs.

"Well," he replied, "let's see how she handles this line-of-credit situation. She has sworn she won't use it unless some big unanticipated expenses come up, and time will tell if she remains true to her word."

She used it up in both February and March.

Her story in March was that she'd had two episodes of vomiting blood and finding blood in her stool. Suspecting side effects from some of the anti-inflammatories Jones had her taking, the doctor had again sent her to Foothills Hospital to be checked out. Twice she'd had to use taxis to get there and back: a good 64 km, or 40 miles altogether. They'd released her right away after each examination and her doctor had now taken her off all medication that might be causing the problem. She was feeling much better.

Jaimie confirmed her mom had been ill and had had to take taxis into Calgary but was now okay. They didn't have much in the fridge though because Mom had used up all her money on hospital trips.

"Let's sell this place," I said after that conversation. My husband concurred. Our hoped-for escape from the torment of being Colleen's parents simply wasn't happening any more and our concerns for Jaimie's welfare were building. We needed to be closer at hand all year round in the event something happened that demanded our intervention.

Phone calls from Lisa in Surrey magnified our worries. Did we know Colleen's townhouse complex had issued her with an eviction notice? (We didn't, and when we questioned Colleen about it she said it wasn't a big deal: some failure to meet a safety code that she had attended to.) Did we know Colleen had asked Lisa and Shawn to finance a move to B.C. and that Lisa was considering doing so for Jaimie's sake? Would *we* be open to helping out with such a move?

It was overwhelming. We'd always known Colleen kept things from us but this was her greatest deceit so far. We closed up our Arizona place and headed immediately back to our home in Calgary. There we found a phone message left only hours before—a message from Jaimie's school Principal that revealed greater deceit yet. Since December our granddaughter's school attendance had all but ceased. The truancy board had been notified but Colleen wouldn't meet with them, wouldn't even answer their calls. The Principal had our number in Jaimie's file as the emergency contact and had therefore decided to turn to us.

I felt blood draining from my face as I listened. My eyes met Andy's and he looked equally pale. And I remember a moaning utterance coming out of my throat to which he only nodded in reply.

"We have to get that child out of there."

32. Ultimatum

It's one thing to decide you have to act. It's quite another to just go ahead and carry out what you've decided to do. When it involves a doting BPD mother who is a superb actress and a child who loves that mother very much, nothing is so simple.

We tried Colleen's phone and couldn't get an answer. We couldn't even leave a message because her machine was full. Should we rush right over and pound on her door, using our key to open it if there was no answer?

No, we shouldn't. Colleen had a habit of not answering her phone and of making it impossible to leave a message when there was something she was hiding from. We already knew what she was hiding from.

As to returning the Principal's call, it was now after school hours. We'd have to wait until the next day. Both of us spent a fitful night and I made the call the moment I could the following morning. Jaimie's Principal, a gentle-sounding lady named Dorothy White, wanted to meet with us right away. We could hardly get there fast enough.

In Dorothy White's office we learned that Jaimie's teachers thought of her as a lovely girl with great potential to do well at school, but—when she showed up at all—it was without clean clothes and without a lunch. Some kids laughed behind their hands at the way she dressed, which Jaimie was certainly smart enough to realize. Ms. White speculated that Jaimie had probably reported these negative incidents to her mom and Colleen—who'd had mainly negative experiences herself at school—had responded by opting to keep Jaimie home.

On the few rare occasions they'd managed to contact Colleen, our daughter claimed Jaimie was too sick to come to school. They had sent her a package of home-schooling materials which they doubted had ever been opened, since no completed assignments had been returned for marking. Several truancy hearings had been arranged which Colleen didn't attend. We were a last resort.

There may be those who wonder why the school didn't get in touch with us much sooner, well before things had reached this point. Me, I applaud the efforts they *did* make and I shall forever be grateful to Ms. White. Nowadays the laws are very strict regarding protection of privacy; they were strict enough while I was still teaching. Intervention on a student's behalf in cases of perceived neglect or abuse can sometimes be turned back against the teacher by enraged parents who threaten to sue or to have that teacher de-licensed. (Indeed, Colleen *did* threaten to sue when she found out, though—as with the WestJet situation—it was all bluff and bluster and she never acted upon it.)

Ms. White said the school psychologist had been trying to talk to Colleen but had so far not managed to contact her. Perhaps it would be good if we could sit in on that meeting as well, if and when it took place. It was obvious Ms. White would have approved of our trying to take Jaimie out of the poor child's present living conditions, but she also mentioned the efforts Colleen ought to be making to improve things and how the law favours parents except in circumstances of "clear and present danger" to children. It was an ambiguous picture that left us to arrive at our own decisions about a course of action.

From Jaimie's school we made our way straight to Colleen's townhouse and did what we'd considered doing the night before: banged on the door, with the spare key at the ready. Our daughter answered, once again in tattered clothing, hair uncombed and those red lesions all over what we could see of her skin. She admitted to not answering her phone, saying she'd been receiving "harassment" from those who ran the complex. Despite her efforts to fix things up, a few mean people still wanted to evict her and had circulated a nasty letter about her. They had no right to be so mean in view of how hard she was trying to improve herself and to kick her drug dependency. In fact she wanted us to accompany her to the AADAC lady she'd been seeing.

From what we were able to observe of her unit's condition—which was not much because she'd gone back to not admitting us past the threshold—desire on the part of some to evict her was understandable. It was in a disgusting mess: clothes, shoes, and various odds-and-ends strewn all over, the sound of a faulty kitchen tap running constantly (which she said the plumber "refused to repair") and, confirming Dorothy White's suspicions, Jaimie's home-schooling materials in a box at the foot of the stairs, still in their plastic wrappings. The air smelled stale and the blinds were once more closed, shutting out the world.

"Let's go," she said, thwarting any discussion. "I'm supposed to meet the AADAC lady in fifteen minutes. Come on, Jaimie."

Jaimie said she'd been too sick to go to school for a while: the story her mom must have coached her to give out. We drove Colleen to her appointment and went in with her to see the counsellor, a lady about our age who listened while Colleen, amazingly, said all the right things: her self-image was in the toilet; she was regularly seeing a psychiatrist to address some issues; no, she wasn't on street drugs but her family doctor was helping her conquer her dependency on prescription pain medication. Par for the course, she came across as articulate, mentally competent, and in the process of working on improvement. "I feel like I just want to go home. I've hit rock bottom now and know I could lose my daughter if I don't turn my life around." The gravity in her voice as she said those words would have convinced anyone.

By "going home" did she mean coming back to live with us? The counsellor didn't think that was such a good idea at her age and we certainly agreed! Could we survive further intrusion into our lives by Colleen other than what already existed? I doubted it. Aloud I made a remark I later felt was unnecessary and unbecoming a supposedly supportive mother. I said, "If we were to go back to fighting over who was in charge at home, I think I might have to kill myself." In my diary I write, *Why did I say that? Poor girl! She doesn't need anyone making her feel any worse than she does.* But Colleen merely nodded and then took a different tack, stressing how she knew she had to make it on her own. The counsellor applauded her entire speech, seeming to take her at face value, as had Dr. Jones.

"I feel privileged to have been part of this conversation," the well-meaning lady said. "You have a wonderful attitude and I'm sure you're a great mom to your daughter." How do you enlighten people who have never experienced living with a BPD sufferer, people who swallow whole the sufferer's Academy Award-deserving performance?

As for the psychiatrist Colleen professed to be seeing and the appointment she professed to have made for us all, it turned out to be pure invention. The man had moved offices, she now said, taking all his patient files with him. She didn't know where he'd moved, didn't even know his last name, since they'd always interacted on a first-name basis. Yeah, right!

Sounding like a broken record I said it anyway. "Colleen, how can you expect others to help you when you continue to tell stories and lead people down the garden path? Stop lying to everyone, including yourself, or you *will* lose Jaimie! When she was born you said you were going to take the best care of her and you asked us to take her away if you ever failed to do that. Well now you're failing to do that! If you don't show us

177

and the truancy board that you're through playing games, we're going to have to do what you asked us to do!"

It was a threat I wasn't sure we could legally carry out but I made it anyway. The daughter she doted on was the only accessible avenue by which Colleen could any longer be reached. In a rage and declaring she'd sue the school for interfering with her parental rights, she accompanied us back to Holy Spirit Academy. Jaimie sat and waited in the secretarial area while we again saw Ms. White. Sulkily Colleen listened as the Principal stressed the importance of Jaimie not missing any more school days between that time and the end of June unless Colleen wanted her daughter to fail the grade-six year. Colleen acknowledged that passing was important and swore she'd make sure Jaimie attended every day from then on. We all discussed such things as the necessity of clean clothes and a wholesome lunch. Andy and I made a commitment to tutor our granddaughter on weekends so she could catch up with material she'd missed—I in Social Studies and Language Arts, Andy in Maths and Sciences. Ms. White had Jaimie's teachers prepare for us a package containing the necessary materials.

We also discussed what would happen if Colleen should fail to live up to her end of the bargain. We gave her no wiggle room. It was abuse, we said, to make a child live in a dingy and disorderly environment with a parent hooked on medication, prescription or not. She must clean up both the place and herself without delay. It was further abuse to deprive a child of an education, particularly a bright child like Jaimie. We'd be watching carefully, as would the truancy board. If there wasn't an immediate reform, removal of Jaimie would be our only option.

"*Should* we have agreed to let Colleen come back to live with us?" I asked Andy after that weighty exchange. "I know the AADAC counsellor didn't think so but I'll never stop feeling like the worst mother in the world…!"

"You know how Colleen loves us to feel like bad parents," Andy replied. "No, I agree with the counsellor. She's thirty years old. If she doesn't start solving her own problems she's doomed." The poor man looked haggard. "I'm not sure she isn't doomed anyway. *Jaimie* is the one we have to concentrate on saving now."

Though feeling drained dry, I remember once more weeping torrents when he said that. I wept for the suffering I saw in my husband's face, for the plight of our cherished granddaughter, and for a daughter who, I strongly suspected, was already beyond rescue.

33. More Summit Meetings

The ultimatum day at Jaimie's school should have made Colleen contrite and willing to cooperate. It didn't. The crystal clarity of my hindsight sees that BPD combined with drug-induced psychosis ruled now. She sought ways to appear an object of pity against whom everyone was ganging up. Right after the school meeting someone purporting to be Mark Donnelly, Colleen's AISH worker, phoned me. Colleen was short funds, he stated, because of several taxi rides she'd had to take to Foothills Hospital to be treated for stomach ulcers. He was calling to tell me he had the taxi receipts right there in his office so I need not hesitate to reimburse her since he could verify the truth of her story. I thanked him, phoned the AISH offices, and spoke to the *real* Mark Donnelly—who had no idea what I was talking about.

Did being caught in a lie induce shame in Colleen? No. She brazened it out, insisting she'd had to get a friend to impersonate Mark Donnelly because she was desperate. The costs of food and of trying to get the unit back into shape were just too much for her. There was a lot she couldn't do for herself because she was handicapped: something we and her equally hard-hearted neighbours refused to understand. Some of them had even circulated a petition demanding her immediate eviction. Next week there was to be a hearing of her case by the tenants' co-op board and all the tenants would get to vote on whether she should be thrown out. If the vote went against her, then Jaimie wouldn't be able to finish the school year and it would be all *their* fault, not hers.

That she had finally shared this much information meant things were closing in on her. So long had she kept hidden from everyone the true extent of her downhill slide that all the deceptions, built upon other deceptions, were cascading her false front into collapse. We attended the tenants' co-op board hearing on an evening in early May and physically dragged a reluctant Colleen there. "It's going to be a lynch mob," she glared. "Why should I go and listen to their insults? They all hate me! And *I* hate all of them!"

"Enough with not facing up to things," Andy insisted. "You're coming!" The meeting room was almost next door to Colleen's unit so we were able to leave Jaimie home watching TV. Throughout the very civilized proceedings Colleen sat stone still, eyes downcast. Photos of her unit, both inside and out, were on display and the difficulty of gaining access to her unit due to her hostility was discussed. Concern for Jaimie was also mentioned, one neighbour shouting out, "I see Colleen's parents are here. Where have they been and why don't *they* do something?" That neighbour was almost immediately shushed by others. We didn't attempt a response, our purpose there being not to justify ourselves but to buy Jaimie enough time as a High River resident to allow her to complete her school year. Besides, as I've said before, how do you attempt to explain any of it to someone who hasn't walked in your shoes and couldn't begin to understand?

One of us only was granted audience at the hearing so Andy spoke. The content of his speech was brief: we were not contesting the eviction but were simply requesting a grace period that would allow our granddaughter to finish her school year. In return for this consideration we were prepared to help Colleen clean up the unit.

"There's no point," one of the other neighbours said. "We've all helped Colleen at one time or another and our efforts never pay off. She just lets things go right back to the same sloppy state. We were sorry for her because she told us she had cerebral palsy, then ovarian cysts, then ovarian cancer, then MS. She often uses a cane and says how hard she finds it to walk—but I've sometimes seen her walking just fine! We don't believe her stories any more. They were just ways to get our sympathy."

"They were also ways to avoid paying rent," someone else contributed. "She's always behind in her rent." That was news to us.

These neighbours were forthright enough with their opinions at the public hearing but were very wary of us one-on-one. As we later learned, Colleen had told them what one individual termed "unthinkable things" about the abuse to which we had subjected her as a child. No doubt they didn't know what to think or believe any more. Even if Andy and I *seemed* normal enough, how could we have produced such a screwed-up person as Colleen unless we were screwed-up ourselves?

We could understand how they felt—both in their attitude toward us and in their advocacy for the removal of an undesirable tenant. Two or three spoke in favour of letting us have a go at cleaning up the unit and of at least allowing Jaimie to complete her school year. After all, these people said, Colleen had started out being such a nice person when she moved in. She'd even expressed interest in serving on the tenants' co-op board herself. They just couldn't figure out what had happened.

A secret-ballot vote was taken amongst assembled members of the cooperative. We were told Colleen would know the results as soon as possible. Our daughter was asked if she had anything at all to contribute before the meeting ended. Hollow-eyed and emotionless she replied, "None of this is my parents' fault." The pronouncement shocked me and I almost choked on the lump in my throat. It was as if an alien presence in control of her mind had momentarily released its hold—"momentarily" being the operative word.

The instant we left the meeting room she reverted to hostility, railing against all who'd spoken in favour of evicting her. She hated these people, hated this place, *wanted* to move out. Let *them* clean up the unit! Jaimie's schooling or well-being, we noticed, didn't figure at all in the content of her rantings. Yes, Jaimie had been going to school every day—with a lunch—since our meeting with Dorothy White (and we knew that because we'd asked Ms. White to call us in the event Colleen didn't live up to the agreement) but Colleen evidently held no real belief in the value of schooling. She was merely going through the motions because her back was to the wall.

The vote went against her. She had sixty days in which to vacate. When she showed us the letter, she smirked and re-echoed the words of her childhood the day she'd been "sentenced" to community service. "They'll never see me broken. That's plenty of time for Jaimie to finish the school year and for me to move somewhere better than this dump!"

If it weren't so sad it would have been funny. Isn't that what black humour is? Her accommodation had been lovely before Colleen herself had turned it into a dump.

Regardless of the vote's outcome, we told Colleen we were going to help her make the place more liveable for the next sixty days. Strongly suggesting something to our daughter normally guaranteed resistance to the idea—which, since the day she'd gained adult status, had always meant our hands were tied. Now, however, she was in a corner. Without us she had no one. And what we were suggesting was both to her benefit and to Jaimie's. Resentful though she was ("Let *them* clean up the unit!"), she capitulated.

Andy and I brought cleaning supplies from home and, over the next several days, worked on the downstairs: the living-room area, the dining nook, the kitchen and the bathroom. It wasn't just sloppy; it was filthy. Dirty dishes were piled high in the kitchen sink as well as in the dishwasher. Mold was growing over unemptied grounds in the coffee machine's filter. A thick layer of dust blanketed everything. Under the living-room furniture were desiccated food scraps that had obviously been there for weeks, if not months. The bathroom toilet was disgusting. And there were clothes strewn everywhere, clothes that had once been clean and crisp but were now bedraggled, having not seen a hanger in ages.

Declining to hear any excuses about being handicapped, we insisted Colleen do her share. Shamed into it she proved capable, as we knew she was. Gradually, a phoenix of respectable-looking rooms began to emerge from the ashes of slovenliness and grime.

One of these cleaning days was a Saturday so Jaimie was at home. We never interfered when Colleen disciplined Jaimie but we often noted the inconsistency of her disciplining: too picky and harsh one minute, cloyingly apologetic the next. That Saturday was one of those days. Colleen seemed to find fault with everything Jaimie did. Finally the little girl flounced away to pout in the kitchen and I followed.

"Your mom is having some problems right now," I told my granddaughter, wishing I didn't always have to make excuses for Colleen. Brow furrowed with anger, Jaimie took my hand and led me over to a white board that hung on the wall between the kitchen and the foyer, a board Colleen had entitled, "House Rules". That board stipulated several behaviours Jaimie was expected to live by such as "No lying" and "Clean up every mess you make". Andy and I had certainly chuckled ruefully at the irony. That day Jaimie's words made me certain big trouble was on the horizon in this mother-daughter relationship.

"See that?" Jaimie pointed to the board. "*She* doesn't follow a single one of those rules!" I had no choice but to hold out comforting arms, mumbling something about hoping Colleen would get help very soon. Jaimie was not rebellious by nature or inclined to stay angry for long but the teen years *were* approaching. And teen years or not, no child with any brains could have failed to be incensed at the double standard. "That's not fair" is a favourite teen line anyway. In Jaimie's world the feeling was totally justified.

Right after that weekend the school psychiatrist contacted Colleen and arranged to meet with her. She consented to our sitting in on the meeting. But as we were about to set out for it on the Monday morning, Dorothy White phoned. Colleen had kept Jaimie home again, claiming the child was sick with 'flu. "There's a lot of 'flu about," Ms. White reported. "It could be true. But I wanted to notify you."

Thanking her we went to Colleen's, still on our cleaning mission and now on a truancy investigation. As it turned out, Jaimie really *was* sick: listless, red-eyed and mildly feverish. We abandoned mops and pails in favour of giving Colleen and her daughter a ride to Dr. Jones's office.

Jones would not see Jaimie. Due to a compromised immune system he was seeing only patients without contagious conditions. He recommended Colleen take the child to the town hospital's walk-in clinic. Because Jaimie told us she didn't feel too bad, we first kept our appointment with the school psychologist. One of the secretaries offered to sit with Jaimie while the rest of us talked.

Jaimie had low self-esteem, the psychologist said, and exhibited signs of depression, anxiety, and feeling trapped in a bad situation from which she couldn't escape. She evidently loved her mom very much but he had concerns about the nature of their bond. Jaimie had mentioned sleeping in her mom's bed which he felt was not a healthy practice for a child of nearly twelve. Colleen became defensive, having heard this from us numerous times.

"She gets scared at night," our daughter sulked. "She needs comforting. There are lots of cultures where it's just fine for children to sleep with their parents."

"Not ours," the psychologist said. "Jaimie has reached an age where she deserves some independence and privacy: a room to herself and a chance to confront whatever night fears she may have." What I'm sure he suspected but didn't say was that the practice probably served the needs of Jaimie's mom, not the other way around. And my present knowledge of BPD tells me there'd be no better solution for allaying a sufferer's chronic feelings of emptiness than having a warm little body pressed up against that sufferer's own. If I'd known then as much as I know now, I'd have been certain Colleen intended to continue the practice forever, despite her concession on that occasion that it should end.

As things were, Andy and I couldn't help suspecting Colleen's avowal to the psychologist that Jaimie's welfare came first was once more an act of going through the motions because her back was to the wall. We never doubted Colleen's adoration for Jaimie. But we *had* begun to doubt that Jaimie's welfare truly *did* come first with Colleen any more.

Was this the time, then, to make our move and take Jaimie away? Such an upheaval in the little girl's life would be enormously upsetting, even in view of her minor rebellions and her questionable environment. Other than her brief stays with us and with Lisa, that environment was all she knew. Mom as the doting number-one figure in her life was all she knew. She loved us. But we did not delude ourselves that taking her away would be an enormous struggle—in the physical sense. We were by no means certain she would come with us willingly.

After we left the psychologist we went to the walk-in clinic. Jaimie's fever had increased and the poor child had the shivers. "Look how busy it is!" Colleen said disgustedly. "We'll be waiting forever!"

"Well you better take a number then," advised Andy. Colleen ignored him, grabbed her daughter by the hand and left. She wasn't willing to sit around in a chair for hours, she declared, and Jaimie would be better off home in bed. They'd come back tomorrow.

"When you and Lisa were children and became sick," Andy argued, "we sat around for as many hours as it took to get you seen by a doctor and put on whatever medication you needed! That's what parenthood is about."

"She's not that bad," Colleen insisted. "Are you, darlin'?" Jaimie gave a bare shake of the head. "Let's go."

Our objections were useless; Colleen would not be swayed. She seemed very fidgety, and both of us suspected the *real* reason she was so adamant had to do with needing a fix. We could have dug in our heels and refused to provide a ride home but that would have resulted in a huge scene—the last thing our poor sick granddaughter needed. So against our better judgment, we complied. Jaimie *did* go straight to bed and Colleen reiterated that she'd take her daughter back to the clinic first thing in the morning. She knew someone she could count on to give them transportation.

"We're coming tomorrow anyway," we pointed out, "to continue with the cleaning."

"That's fine," she said. "You can let yourselves in with your key and carry on working downstairs. Jaimie and I will be back right after we've seen the doctor."

And that was the way things were left on the evening of Monday May fifth, 2008. Andy and I drove back to Calgary, took Pepper for a long walk, and discussed for the trillionth time our worries about Jaimie and our dilemma about what we should do.

Tuesday May sixth is a day I shall never forget. It was so horrible its details are etched forever in my memory.

34. The Worst Day of My Life

W riting about this day forces me to re-live it. Where is the good in that? How can it possibly benefit anyone, least of all me?

To be honest, I considered abandoning the whole project rather than re-living this day. Then I decided that would be cowardice after I've come this far. As to where the good is, it lies in the lesson to be learned from letting BPD rule unchecked, from turning the other cheek for too long to an illness in need of treatment. Since denying the problem is part of the illness, it takes a special fortitude on the part of the sufferer to access the rational part of himself that tells him he must seek help. And it takes a special fortitude on the part of those close to a BPD sufferer to keep pushing him to seek help before it is too late.

My friend Kathy from church has had that fortitude. She has learned to ignore the part of her mind that tells her everything is everyone else's fault. With therapy and the right medication—two things Colleen always refused—she is managing her illness. She describes it as a one-day-at-a-time battle, like that of a recovering alcoholic. Hard as we pushed Colleen to seek help in the early years, we could probably have done much more for her today. There is greater optimism amongst mental-health professionals that BPD sufferers *can* be helped. But as with all serious diseases, if one doesn't engage in the battle the disease wins.

On Tuesday May sixth 2008 I rose at 4:30 a.m. after almost no sleep. I took Pepper for a walk; then I burned nine-hundred calories on my elliptical machine, followed by a session of lifting weights. It had become a pattern with me: the more worried and helpless I felt, the harder I exercised. Three hours later I called Colleen and let the phone ring until her dopey voice answered. *(How can you sleep when your child is sick?)* Yes, she told me, a person she knew would give her and Jaimie—who still had a fever—a ride to the clinic right away. As discussed yesterday, Andy and I could come over to the townhouse, use our key to enter, and continue cleaning downstairs.

My husband hadn't slept well either. When he got up the two of us packed more cleaning supplies into the car, drove to High River and let ourselves into the empty unit. Despite our ministrations to this point, the ubiquitous stale smell prevailed. We threw open windows to air out the place. The downstairs now looked miles better, though the kitchen, foyer and bathroom floors still needed damp mopping. "I'll go and take a quick look around upstairs while you're doing that," Andy said, "and see what sort of shape it's in."

Had Colleen been home I'm sure she would have stopped him. She had specified we remain *downstairs*, and I myself had assumed most of the mess would be on the lower floor which was the larger area and the area where food was eaten. I mean, besides strewn-about bedding, another layer of dust, and probably another toilet desperate for a scouring brush, what was likely to demand our attention up there? Andy ascended the stairs to get a head start as I continued mopping.

Not more than two minutes later he reappeared at my side. One look at his anguished face told me something was terribly wrong. "Come upstairs with me," he choked. "This is beyond belief."

Heart hammering, I followed him. With every step I climbed the miasma of staleness increased. By the time I'd reached the top it had turned putrid. Clothes were piled up everywhere and through the piles lay a narrow pathway leading to the master bedroom. No such pathway led to the adjacent room that was supposed to be Jaimie's; it obviously hadn't been entered in ages.

The clothes mounds and Jaimie's unused room were not what got my attention. The nauseating stench emanating from behind the half-closed master-bedroom door was. Andy pushed it fully open so that I could see inside. I would never wish to behold such a sight again as long as I live.

Months' worth of discarded fast-food boxes, most containing un-consumed and mold-ridden leftovers, littered the floor, the window sill, the computer desk and the unmade bed. Dirty plates, their contents hardened to cement, occupied whatever space was not taken up by the boxes and were interspersed with cartons of curdled and fetid milk. Marley cat played our escort, treading delicately through half-chewed pizza crusts and chicken bones to an area beside his sodden, brimming litter-box—an area which I realized he was now using as his bathroom, having no other choice. The clothes mounds in that area were wet with cat urine and covered in cat feces. I literally gagged.

"That isn't all," my husband grimaced. "Look at the *dunes* of cigarette butts and ashes. Look at the number of burns on the carpet and the bedclothes. Look at the *melted* computer keyboard! She's not just living in filth; she's passing out with lit cigarettes between her fingers. It's lucky this place hasn't already gone up in flames!"

I swallowed. "We can't let Jaimie stay here a moment longer, can we?"

"No, we can't. Luckily, I've got the camera outside in the car. I'll start taking pictures of this *clear and present danger*. We'll need evidence because we know Colleen will fight us tooth and nail."

"I'll call Social Services," I said. "I'll explain what we're doing and why." I was actually shaking, and my teeth were chattering. I was probably in a mild state of shock.

No one was available to speak to me at Social Services so I left a message with my name and phone number. Just before he began taking photographs Andy found a piece of paper amongst the rubble and, using the pen he always kept in his pocket, composed a note authorizing us to have temporary guardianship of Jaimie and giving us permission to okay any further medical treatments she might need. He left a line at the bottom for Colleen's signature. Minutes after he was done with the photos, we heard the front-door latch click and Colleen came in, leading a tired and ill-looking Jaimie by one hand and clutching a pharmacy bag in the other.

"The doctor says it's probably bacterial," Colleen said. "This should take care of it." We wasted no time getting a spoonful of the liquid antibiotic down the poor sweetheart's sore throat. But when Colleen then told Jaimie to go upstairs to bed we intervened. Asking the little girl to lie down on the living-room couch where she instantly began to doze off, we took our daughter aside and talked to her in the foyer. We'd seen the horrific state of the upstairs, Andy informed her. If she as an adult wanted to live like that we could do nothing to prevent it. But we *could* remove our granddaughter from such unsanitary and dangerous conditions and we intended to—immediately. Jaimie was coming with us.

As we'd dreaded, an ugly scene ensued. Colleen's mental illness had progressed beyond her having the decency not to involve the child in the scene; her own needs superseded all other considerations. Her shouting awoke the dear little girl who of course wanted to know what was going on. To our devastation Colleen answered, "They're kidnapping you! I knew this would happen someday!"

Jaimie began to scream in terror. Getting up from the couch, our granddaughter ran to her mom and flung herself into Colleen's arms, hanging on tightly and sobbing. "You see?" Colleen glared triumphantly.

"She loves *me*! You're *not* taking her away! I'm calling Social Services!"

"I've already done that," I said, keeping my voice as calm as I could. "There was nobody there but I left a message to explain. Remember how you asked us to remove Jaimie if we ever decided it was necessary…?"

"I hate you both!" Colleen screeched. "You're the meanest and most terrible people on earth!" Her rage started Jaimie screaming again. Colleen directed her next words to her daughter. "If they've called Social Services, they intend to turn you over to them and you'll spend the rest of your life being raised by strangers!"

"No! No! No!" the terrified Jaimie wailed, clinging harder than ever. Mental illness or not, I found it difficult to forgive Colleen putting her beloved child through that rather than allaying the little girl's fears as a mother alone has the power to do and reassuring Jaimie that things would be all right. I found it even harder to forgive Colleen's refusal to turn over to us Jaimie's medicine and her wrathful remark: "I'm not *helping* you do this!" I responded that depriving a sick child of medicine was not the way to prove she deserved Jaimie back and then I simply took the medicine. When the dispute threatened to turn physical, Andy held Colleen at bay while I also gathered up some of Jaimie's cleaner-looking clothes.

Getting Colleen to sign my husband's hand-written note was another challenge. "Whether or not you sign it won't change what we feel we have to do," Andy told her. "Agreeing to sign it doesn't mean you *lose*. It just means that if Jaimie has to have medical treatment we'll have the authority to make sure she gets it." Ultimately his calm persistence (and, I believe, Colleen's growing need for a fix) held sway. Teeth gritted in fury, she signed.

Detaching Jaimie's iron grip on her mother was our next obstacle. Colleen made things worse by shrieking profanities while clasping the child against her chest. "I'll call the police!" she spat. "I'll press charges! I'll sue you! You won't get away with this!" That renewed Jaimie's crying. Andy had no choice but to detach the little girl's grip himself, pick her up in his arms, and carry her struggling and screaming to the car.

I can only imagine what that was like for the poor sweetheart. Her mother, the primary figure in her life, had told her awful things about us and our abusiveness—and now, in her helpless sick state, those reputedly abusive people had forcibly seized her. How Andy managed to get the seat belt around her thrashing body I shall never know, but he achieved it. I sat in the back seat with her and talked to her—again as calmly and softly as I could—with the tears streaming down my cheeks while my husband drove us back to Calgary.

"We're your family, Jaimie," I remember saying. "We love you very much and we would *never* give you away to strangers. I hope you believe me because I wouldn't lie to you." To that I got no reply, hardly to my surprise. Jaimie was used to being lied to. Like Colleen's neighbours, she no longer knew what to believe and what not to believe.

"Your mom is ill," I reiterated. "She's not managing her life at all capably right now. She's not taking care of herself or you."

"She's handicapped!" Jaimie protested. "She needs *me* to help her! It's *my* fault about the mess…!"

"No, sweetheart, none of this is your fault. It's been going on since before you were born. Your mom has to get professional help." I felt sobs grip me and had to force myself to continue. "Jaimie, I've said I wouldn't lie to you. You're old enough to understand this. If your mom doesn't decide to go for the help she needs right away, she's going to die."

Voicing it brought its reality crashing down on *me* as well. Sobs escaped my throat as Jaimie began a fresh bout of weeping. In my mind for the ten millionth time, I pleaded with God to stop putting our family through this torture. What had we done to deserve it all? Would it never end?

Eventually pure exhaustion overcame our granddaughter and she slept. As we approached town she woke up enough to ask if she could have tortellini for supper. That request released the dam on my sobs. As before at the hospital, it was as though God had nudged me. Tortellini was one of Jaimie's favourite meals; she'd frequently asked for it during her brief stays with us. That request I saw as a sign that, despite everything, she *did* trust us. We stopped off in the pasta section of the Co-op grocery store and picked up a package, along with a four-cheese sauce of her choosing. The moment we arrived home Andy cooked it up while I gave her a second dose of her medicine.

However, she was unable to eat. Overcome by fatigue, she sat at the table in the kitchen nook nodding off and several times narrowly missing doing a face plant into the plate. We abandoned the effort, took her to the spare bedroom where she was used to sleeping and made up the pull-out couch there. She does not remember our putting her to bed; she was unconscious before she hit the pillow. Andy gave Pepper a brief walk while I stayed with her. When they returned, Pepper went immediately to her bedroom and jumped up onto the bed beside her. Himself an SPCA rescue from a life of horrific neglect, our little cream-coloured mixed-breed terrier somehow seemed to know she needed him.

He stayed there at his post all that night and did not desert it for the entire time Jaimie was in our care.

35. "I'm Happy"

Once we ourselves had retired to bed, exhaustion claimed us as quickly as it had Jaimie. So did more bouts of weeping. I found myself very moved by Pepper's insistence on staying with our granddaughter. Having his warm little body pressed up against hers was bound to be comforting if she woke in the night.

She didn't. In fact, she didn't stir until nearly noon of the following day. Five hours earlier I sneaked into her room, put on Pepper's leash, and coaxed him in a whisper to come with me for a walk. He obliged with reluctance and then returned eagerly to Jaimie's side as soon as he'd done his business. How adorable!

Three hours before Jaimie woke Colleen phoned, her voice icy. "I've called the police. You have until tomorrow morning to bring Jaimie back or else." Wiping my eyes and pushing down the sadness I replied, "Colleen, if you're to save your own life you belong in rehab. You can deny it till the cows come home but Dad and I know you're a hard-core addict. If we'd properly seen the state of deterioration in your place before yesterday, we would have taken Jaimie sooner. Renfrew is where you should be calling—and *now*. We're going to look after Jaimie for as long as it takes until you get clean." And I hung up.

How much reality was behind Colleen's "or else"? *Had* she called the police? We didn't doubt she had. Andy spent the morning on the phone talking to various law offices and being passed along the line from one person to another. It was a frustrating business. Ultimately he was advised to go downtown to the courthouse and fill out a form requesting an ex parte (without the contesting party present) court order for Jaimie's removal, which a judge would sign if presented with convincing evidence that the removal was necessary. Taking with him the photos of Colleen's premises, he departed without delay. Maddeningly, so much time elapsed wading through all the folderol of finding out where to get the form and how to fill it out that the courthouse was closed for the day and no judge was available when it was finally done. He was instructed to return as soon as the courthouse re-opened the next morning. A judge would see him then.

Of course I stayed behind with Jaimie, checking on her occasionally but letting her sleep until she woke of her own accord. When I heard the toilet flush I went downstairs and found her sitting on the family-room couch hugging Pepper. I remember saying, "How are you doing, sweetheart?" to which she replied, "Not good." But she referred to her emotional state. Physically she looked much better and when I felt her forehead she had no fever. I brought down her medicine and gave her another dose; then I suggested she might feel better if she put on clean clothes. She still wore what she'd had on the previous day. Under the circumstances we'd decided sleep was more important than getting her to change into pyjamas. She said she was okay dressed as she was so I didn't pursue it. Instead I made my voice as matter-of-fact as I could. "Let's go upstairs then and get some breakfast."

She was hungry: a very good sign. I sat with her while she ate a bowl of cereal and told her how much I hoped her mom would see the urgency of getting help: "I'm not going to tiptoe around this, Jaimie. Your mom is addicted to drugs. She needs to go into a rehab program. Grandpa and I suspect it may take her a while to get clean."

Jaimie shrugged. "It's just pills the doctor gave her. She takes those for pain."

"No, sweetheart. She abuses those pills and takes far too many. And she also buys and uses street drugs."

Jaimie's mouth fell open. For several moments she just gaped at me. And I suddenly realized the reason for her astonishment. (She has since confirmed it.) Jaimie *knew* her mom was using and had been enlisted by Colleen to keep the fact hidden from us. She'd repeatedly received dire warnings never to mention it or she'd be in big trouble. That morning as she sat at our kitchen table she was thinking, *"They know anyway! So why have we been lying and covering it up all this time?"*

After breakfast she looked tired again and asked if she could go back downstairs and watch TV. All that day she alternately watched and dozed, Pepper on the couch beside her. From the upstairs phone I informed Dorothy White what had happened, saying we'd bring Jaimie back to school as soon as she was properly over her bug. I also spent time explaining the situation to a paralegal and confirming we were taking the correct measures to ensure we weren't arrested for kidnapping. Jaimie was oblivious to all of this, as I wanted her to be.

Later on Colleen phoned. "I want to speak to my daughter," she rapped out. Jaimie had just finished eating the tortellini she hadn't been able to eat the day before and was looking brighter than she had all day. Sleep had done her worlds of good. Even her emotional state was improving.

Yes, she nodded; she would like to talk to her mom. Colleen made her go to a different room out of our hearing. When she returned to the kitchen, her mood had suffered a relapse.

We didn't ask what Colleen had said to her. We didn't have to. The poor child had obviously been guilted into wanting to go back to her mom and yet somehow realized she was far better off where she was. My helpless anger at Colleen seethed. How unfair to torment the little girl that way! But would it not be more unfair still if we denied Jaimie the chance to talk to her mother? As usual, Colleen had us all over an emotional barrel.

That night Andy and I both chatted with Jaimie for quite a while before giving her her medicine and tucking her into bed. We steered clear of heavy topics, limiting the exchange to things that interested her. At one point she said, "You can get yourself out of a lot of bad situations if you're a good liar." That one disturbed us and we refuted it right away. No, Andy told her, lies will always catch up with you sooner or later. Then you're in worse trouble than ever. Neither of us mentioned her mom as the example.

She told us of the friendships she'd formed at school, admitting some of the boys teased her but saying she hung out with several nice girls. They would all talk and laugh about how dumb and immature the boys were. She told a few funny stories about the boys' antics and remarks the girls had made—and for the first time since we'd had her with us we began to see a re-emergence of the smiling upbeat little person who'd had such fun at Disneyland. At one point the three of us actually burst into laughter in unison.

Though she was willing to brush her teeth and wash her face, she still would not change out of the clothes she was wearing. "These are the clothes my mom put me in," she explained. We understood. Those clothes were the only link she still had to her mom and she was afraid to break it. I said, "Okay, sweetheart, I won't push. But clothes get smelly and dirty if one wears them for too long. You'll need to change them eventually. *You* can decide when."

Andy took Pepper for his final walk while I sat at Jaimie's bedside and gabbed. Hilary Duff was her favourite singer back then and she also enjoyed painting: a hobby I myself had recently taken up. Once we left the subject of her mom she brightened again. Pepper resumed his post on her bed as soon as Andy brought him back. She hugged him very lovingly and gave *us* a hug each as well. After we'd said our good-

195

nights to her and gone upstairs, Andy and I agreed she was recovering emotionally as well as physically.

"It won't last if she goes back to Colleen," Andy lamented. "As I've said before, no matter how this plays out we've got to be able to look in the mirror and say to ourselves that we did all we could. So it's back downtown to the courthouse for me tomorrow morning."

At nine o'clock the following day, he spoke to a Family Counsellor and then sat in a room and patiently waited his turn to be called before a judge. A number of cases were on the docket ahead of ours so that didn't happen until nearly noon. The judge asked if the child's removal had been reported to Social Services and was assured it had. However, Social Services had such a backlog of data to input into their system there was as yet no computer record of the report. It took some time to clear that up. The judge then looked at Andy's photos of Colleen's place and also at a copy of Jaimie's school attendance record we'd obtained from Dorothy White. He signed an ex parte court order for a period of one week. At the end of that week Colleen was to appear before him and would have the chance to make a case for getting her daughter back.

We'd been told the law weighs heavily in favour of the parent and we found out the truth of that statement. Colleen herself spoke to Social Services—telling them heaven-knows-what about us—and latched onto a sympathetic young case worker willing to state that Colleen was a loving mother with a physical handicap who would receive government assistance in getting the place cleaned up and fit for a child to live in. My guess is that Colleen was stoned when she spoke to the case worker, probably triggering that dopamine release in the brain that temporarily "normalized" her behaviour. I'm sure she came across as capable, clear-headed, and doing the best she could to overcome a terrible childhood. Who *wouldn't* be moved to help her in such circumstances?

Meanwhile, Jaimie and I spent a pleasant day together. We had break-fast, made a cake, and then got out my watercolour palette and did some painting. Jaimie has natural artistic talent and was soon caught up in her picture. She wanted to paint a sunrise over the ocean and listened carefully to my suggestions, though she had her own mind about the choice and blending of colours and came up with an effective combination. In the afternoon, her Auntie Lisa (who knew what we'd done and applauded it) phoned and reassured her for a long time, telling her we were all go-ing to try to make sure things turned out all right. What a lovely older daughter we have! In late afternoon, Jaimie and I took Pepper for a Fish

Creek Park walk. By the time we returned Andy was home with his ex parte order.

That night when Colleen called demanding to speak to Jaimie, we told her about the order—and the opportunity she would have in a week's time to plead her own case. She went ballistic, screaming *she* would get a court order declaring us dangerous people not fit to have Jaimie. Furthermore, if we didn't give Jaimie back immediately she would make public all the awful things we had done to her. Par for the course now when she ranted into our ears over the phone, we hung up. Lisa reported later that she then called her sister, who only repeated exactly what we had said. Unaware of all this (thank heaven), Jaimie played piano downstairs, Pepper on the mat at her feet.

I speculate Colleen had a hit of something after speaking to Lisa because she called us back in a while sounding perfectly calm and reasonable. Could she please say good-night to her daughter? Yes, Jaimie wanted to talk to Mom when asked. Our granddaughter took the call downstairs and spoke in low tones, the words inaudible. As before, the conversation adversely affected the dear little girl's mood.

Trying to buck up her spirits I again sat on the bed with her (and Pepper) after doling out bedtime medicine and tucking her in. "Let's have a *Grandma chat!*" I said as brightly as I could. She still had not changed out of her clothes but of her own accord she *had* brushed her teeth, washed her face, and combed her hair. It was a start. That "Grandma chat" marked the beginning of what became a nightly ritual for the rest of her stay with us. She loved the Grandma chats and would pointedly request them. Unwritten ground rules were that the chats remained as positive as possible—though, as they continued, the sweetheart began to open up to me more and more about her fears for her own future.

On the occasion of that first chat though, I found it difficult to hold myself together when, as we said final good-nights, she sat up in bed, put her arms around my neck and murmured, "Grandma—I'm happy." Choked, I hugged her back, declared it was lights-out time, patted Pepper, and made a brisk departure.

Then I went upstairs to our own bedroom and, in Andy's arms, sobbed myself to sleep.

36. Jamie's Panic and Colleen's Terror

Andy went to High River on the morning of Friday May ninth to deliver one copy of the court order to Colleen and one copy to Jaimie's school. He informed the school that Jaimie was over her 'flu and would be returning to classes the following Monday. Me, I stayed home with Jaimie—who had finally changed her clothes—to give her breakfast and to tell her it was time to go back to Holy Spirit after the weekend. Using the materials Dorothy White had provided, her grandpa and I had started conducting daily school sessions at home as soon as she was well enough to commence them. She'd made good strides towards catching up on what she'd missed and she'd proved to be an apt pupil. As we'd realized when we took her to the Crystal Cathedral, Jaimie was a naturally bright individual and was *very* thirsty for knowledge about her world.

To be fair to Colleen whose doting parental love had resulted in the young child's receiving much exposure to books, Jaimie had a good grounding in basic reading skills which flourished in the presence of her natural aptness. Schoolwork came easily to her. However, I still had qualms about telling her it was time to resume formal instruction. My lifelong unsuccessful battles with Colleen about regular school attendance braced me for an argument or even a tantrum.

So with great firmness I made my case to Jaimie that morning. She was legally required to be in school, I said. Passing her grade-six year was at stake and the matter was not up for debate. She shrugged, took a bite of her toast and replied, "Okay." I nearly fell off my chair!

That Sunday was Mother's Day. How sad! Andy offered to pick up Colleen and bring her to church which would afford an opportunity for the two to visit and for Jaimie to give Mom a card and a little present. (Jaimie and I went separately in my car because I had early choir practice.) Colleen agreed to come but behaved like a restless kid throughout the service, prodding her daughter and continually whispering into the child's ear. Again it occurred to me that Jaimie was now the more mature of the two. A retired psychologist colleague—and our own Lisa who has earned her Master's degree in psychology since beginning her teaching career—confirm that drug addiction stalls brain development and a hard-core teenage addict may become forever "stuck" in the teenage groove.

We had thought church to be a safe venue for avoidance of unpleasant scenes. We were mistaken. In the parking lot afterwards as we were parting company—Jaimie coming home with me and Andy driving Colleen back to High River—our daughter clasped *her* daughter and burst into loud wails. "I know you're heartbroken about being away from me," Colleen wept. "But I'll get you back. You'll see!" The words and the tears started Jaimie sobbing as well, clinging hard to Colleen in a repetition of that terrible day we'd had to take her away. It seemed forever before we talked them apart and, though Jaimie's mood while I drove her home recovered faster this time, mine didn't. Trying anew to comfort my granddaughter, I was swept with such pity for both of them it was difficult to keep from breaking into fresh sobs myself.

"*I* pity Colleen as well but it makes me so angry the way she manipulates that child and tells her how she *should* feel," Andy quite correctly stated later that day. By then Jaimie was busy playing a game on the computer, having successfully re-escaped into her own world. (She has since told me how she learned to do that from a very young age—and also how she learned to "lay low" whenever Mom was "in one of those moods". The survival skills of even very small children are amazing.)

We drove Jaimie to High River the next day and dropped her off at school. She wore clean clothes of her own choosing and had brushed her hair until it shone. With enthusiasm she was welcomed back. Giving us each a hug, she went off to classes. We prayed nothing would interfere with that regimen between now and the end of June; heaven knows the dear little girl needed to be able to count on some stability. But still to come was the judge's hearing of Colleen's case. And still to come was the day of Colleen's eviction.

Colleen had been given until June fifth to move out. Flouting authority as always, she sneered that they couldn't *make* her leave until several weeks after that. Besides—since we wouldn't let her come and live with *us*—she had nowhere to go, right? Yes she did, we insisted. *Rehab* was the place to go and she had better get busy making those arrangements because the alternative was a women's shelter. We would come over with groceries if we had to but we were *not* supplying her with any more money.

Doubtless she bemoaned our hard-heartedness to her sympathetic social worker, who testified in court a few days later that Colleen's place was now clean enough, not for a baby but for an older child. Talk about supreme irony: Andy gave our daughter a ride to the courthouse so she could stand before a judge and accuse her father of kidnapping! (Proof of the extremity of her mental illness, she also made the ludicrous claim that the judge was bound to find in her favour because he was a friend of hers! She backed off that when Andy pointed out that a judge couldn't hear a case involving a friend and would have to recuse himself.)

And how did the judge decide? It went as we'd told Jaimie it would probably go: our granddaughter was allowed to return to her mom at least for the time being, on the proviso that Social Services regularly monitored the place to ensure it met minimum cleanliness standards. Caught up in her victory, Colleen hardly seemed to hear the judge's additional comment that we had been quite correct to remove the child from the original disgusting environment.

My diary records my frustration about the decision and yet my surrender to its inevitability. If Colleen had presented as an incompetent spaced-out addict, no judge would have allowed the child to go back. Here again is an example of supreme irony: I'm sure our daughter was coked to the gills that day and was therefore rational, remorseful about the mess and sincere about trying hard to get help and learn to make it on her own despite her handicap. Her convincing demeanour did the trick. We were ordered to return Jaimie right away.

Two weeks later in the middle of the day, our granddaughter made a long-distance phone call to her aunt in Surrey. The little girl was beside herself, sobbing hysterically. It was a school day but by great good luck Lisa was at home ill and picked up. Our elder daughter's first dreadful thought was exactly what mine would have been: Jaimie had found her mom dead. But no, that wasn't what terrified the poor sweetheart. It was that her mom had gone out hours and hours ago, promising to return very shortly, and was still not back.

Lisa stayed on the line with Jaimie until Colleen came in. The question of what her niece was doing home from school *this* time was inconsequential in the face of the other question. Where had Colleen been and why had her sister abandoned the child for so long? Colleen said Jaimie exaggerated and all was okay now. Lisa hung up and telephoned us.

I was upset that Jaimie had chosen to call her aunt instead of us when *we* were the ones close enough at hand to rush over there and help. (Jaimie has since said she didn't call because her mom always forbade it and would have been very angry to walk in and find her in an unsupervised conversation with us. Again, how sad!) We thanked Lisa for letting us know, asked after her mild bug which was getting better, and decided we'd lean more heavily on Colleen about entering detox once and for all.

And it was our leaning on Colleen (kicked off by Jaimie's panic at being left alone) that caused the terror torturing our child to show its unmasked face at last. "Renfrew is an awful place!" she screeched. "They cut you off cold-turkey, throw you into a room by yourself and laugh while you suffer!" Even *she* must have realized how outlandish those remarks sounded. "Besides, they said it's going to be hell and with my level of addiction they can't guarantee I'll come out of it alive."

Had they told her that? It's possible. Whether they had or not, the first time my poor baby ever confessed to having a "level of addiction" she was half convinced it was already be too late to save herself.

I kept emotion out of my tone. I simply said, "Colleen, you're admitting how bad your drug dependency is. That's the first step. They've got good medical supervision at Renfrew. There are ways to lessen the withdrawal symptoms. You have to go there—because if you carry on as you're doing, you *won't* come out of it alive. You won't be around to see your daughter grow up."

Before that conversation terminated Colleen actually *agreed*—not to go to Renfrew but to look into rehab centres in general without resentment and with a view to accepting their help. That was significant.

I can't claim optimism. But at least it was her first *good* decision in a while. We could only pray she would follow it through.

37. The Rehab Ruse

Our prayers soon proved futile. Empathetic to Colleen's very real terror of rehab, I still can't gloss over how she planned from the outset to use rehab centres to her own advantage—not for their intended purpose of getting and keeping her clean but as avenues for obtaining free room-and-board, making contact with individuals just like her, and yes, *dealing* drugs to those vulnerable people in order to finance her own habit. Did she purposely set out to do those things when she decided to seek rehabilitation? That I don't know. But what I now *do* know about BPD leads me to speculate that, even if part of her wanted help, Colleen in her heart of hearts didn't consider herself worthy of rehabilitation.

Her rejection of Renfrew remained firm but now became based on its Alberta location. As her eviction date approached, she voiced what she'd already discussed with Lisa: that she wished to leave the province and go to live in B.C. near her sister, who could care for Jaimie until she was clean. Dear Lisa, who adores Jaimie, was fine with this idea even though she and Shawn had their own worries at the time. Shawn had been laid off work (the computer graphics industry being just as volatile and economy-driven as the oil industry) and Lisa's teaching job was still in its probationary period. It was a repeat of the financial-stress-on-top-of-Colleen-stress that *we* had endured in Colleen's childhood; yet our lovely elder daughter didn't flinch at agreeing to look after her niece.

"I'm Jaimie's godmother," Lisa stated. "Somehow I've always known it would come to this." And Shawn supported his wife's position. What an outstanding couple!

Still, they had no idea what they were in for. Knowing her sister was mentally ill as opposed to dealing daily with that mental illness not as a sibling but as an overseer were two very different things for tender-hearted Lisa. She envisioned regularly pitching in to help her sister—once Colleen was drug-free, on proper medication for her BPD, and established in an apartment—with such chores as housework and grocery shopping. She envisioned the two becoming closer friends and forming a mutually beneficial bond strengthened by their common love for Jaimie. Those were wonderful visions and bless her for having them! But we warned about the disruption to her life that Colleen's proximity would be bound to create.

It took very little time before she and Shawn realized how grossly they had underestimated the extent of both the mental illness and the disruption. When Andy and I visited them in Surrey the next month, Shawn put it this way: "We have a whole new respect for what you've been going through all these years." I shall always regret that they had to go through it themselves but they wouldn't have had it any other way. The family Lisa had held in such contempt as a teenager she now stood by without hesitation.

Colleen got in touch with several B.C. rehab centres and was probably extremely eloquent about wanting to be near her daughter's caregiver and wanting to turn over a new leaf. A place called Glory House in Port Coquitlam said they had an opening and were willing to admit her right away. This was encouraging, besides providing the perfect solution to her upcoming need of a roof over her head.

Like the Alberta facilities we'd dragged Colleen to as a youngster, Glory House has as its mission to "rebuild lives, restore families and improve communities" by working with the addict in an intensive twelve-month residential program setting. There is ongoing support available for an additional ten months or "as long as it takes" after the patient has "graduated" the program. Assistance with re-establishment in the outside world is provided, such as finding the newly-rehabilitated person a place to live, a job, and a different social circle outside the drug culture. But there's the standard caveat: all this takes patience, persistence and commitment. No "quick and dirty" method exists for breaking a long-standing dependency. Colleen was looking at being in treatment—and having her daughter under her sister's guardianship—for at least a year. This doesn't sit well with the instant-gratification proclivity typical of BPD.

Nevertheless, Colleen arranged with a counsellor to pick her up in Port Coquitlam on June fifteenth, ten days past her official eviction deadline. And here is yet another supreme irony: the same person who had gone to court to accuse us of kidnapping now asked if *we* could take Jaimie again until the end of the school year and then fly her to Lisa in B.C.! Careful to get written permission with every "i" dotted and "t" crossed, we agreed. We also agreed to pay the transportation costs to Port Coquitlam—but by *bus*, not plane. (Colleen had the nerve to complain about that!) It was part of our needing to feel we were doing everything we could no matter what the outcome.

So on June fifteenth—Father's Day—we drove to High River to load up the van with her belongings, including Marley cat and a hamster named Bear-Bear which we'd said we'd keep until we ourselves motored to B.C. in the summer to visit Lisa and Shawn. Her furniture she was leaving behind; the co-op board planned on selling it to offset some of the considerable cost of cleaning up and fixing damage to the unit. She'd told us a neighbour had offered to help her pack but we arrived to find much of the packing still not done and Colleen sitting in her living-room watching the DVD *Sweeney Todd*, starring Johnny Depp. "Mom's been watching this over and over," Jaimie informed us. "She says Johnny Depp is a friend of hers and she's going to make sure I get to meet him." The neighbour looked distraught.

We had only a couple of hours before the bus was due to leave and Andy and I put our backs into finishing the job. The neighbour, a pleasant older lady, thanked Colleen for "the gifts". (Colleen revealed during the trip to the bus station that those gifts were strictly to spite the co-op board for evicting her, leaving them with less to sell. And the neighbour later telephoned us saying she herself was on the board and hadn't realized accepting the gifts was a conflict of interest. The board was threatening to sue and the hapless neighbour wished she'd never heard of Colleen. We recommended the lady simply relinquish the gifts to the board to save herself further stress.)

All the way downtown, Colleen grumbled. First she'd forgotten her lip gloss. (Jaimie hastily supplied her some to avert a tantrum.) Second she was hungry. (We'd advised her to make sandwiches for the bus but she hadn't. I bought her a sandwich-and-fruit combo at the bus station.) Third she re-hashed our stinginess in not supplying a plane ticket. Finally, just before boarding the bus, she made her customary public scene: clinging to Jaimie and loudly bemoaning their separation. We disengaged them, hugged Colleen and exhorted her to get herself better.

"Here." She handed me a paperback she'd had in her pocket. "I think you should read this, Mom. I really think you should."

"Sure. Okay." In the emotion of the moment I nodded and shoved the book into my own pocket without even glancing at it. Some things could wait till later.

Jaimie, upset but not traumatized, accompanied us back to the van, installing herself in the rear seat amid Colleen's belongings, the caged hamster and the crated Marley cat. En route to our home she asked, "Grandpa, how come I had to leave *all* my stuffed toys behind?" When Andy reacted with bewilderment she disclosed that her mom had said Grandpa wouldn't allow her any stuffed toys because space was too limited. So Jaimie had had to sacrifice every one of her precious stuffed friends and had been told it was her grandfather's doing! That was the last straw. Mental illness or no mental illness, I felt my daughter had become an unethical spiteful person, without gratitude for help received and totally heedless of anyone else's feelings other than her own. In my diary I write: *I am physically sick about the amoral and spineless human being I've brought into this world.* Thank goodness I had the diary as a venting tool because I would have found it unthinkable to say such a thing either to Jaimie or to Colleen.

Naturally we corrected Jaimie's misapprehension. I lent her a stuffed moose (a Christmas gift from one of my French classes) to tuck into bed with her at night. I also *gave* her—with Andy's permission—a little stuffed bear carrying its own stuffed toy that my husband had brought me in hospital when I'd had my hip replaced in 2001. That bear was to alleviate the poor child's distress at suddenly remembering a now-abandoned bear Great-Grandpa had given her on his last visit to us: the only tangible token she'd had left of my dad. Many other items the little girl had treasured—including a photo album we'd prepared for her as a memento right after her Disneyland trip with us—were lost due to Colleen's carelessness or malice or both.

But Jaimie was no more inclined than we to nurse grudges or stew in useless resentments. She loved her mom and now accepted our statement that Colleen was ill. We praised her attitude, and Andy (who still had the digital Disneyland photos saved in the computer) made her a substitute album—which today resides with Lisa and Shawn because, wonder of wonders, a kind member of the co-op board found and rescued the original before cleaning crews went in with gas masks to strip and fumigate the unit.

During her remaining time spent in our care before we transferred that care to Lisa in early July, Jaimie returned to school and with our assistance as tutors *did* pass her grade-six year. She agreed to let us find an interim home for Marley cat—who was having issues with Pepper—just for a few weeks until she went to live with her auntie. We asked at church and had no less than *six* offers from the good-hearted people there. Dear Sharon Mansfield, daughter of Elaine and Tom Mansfield, one of our lovely congregant couples, lived closest to us and was happy to let Jaimie come and visit Marley whenever she wanted. (Sharon, too, struggles with moderately severe mental health issues, and Sharon's compassion for Jaimie's situation was truly heart-warming.)

On weekends Jaimie helped me prepare meals. She especially loved a salad I call "mango-tango" made with avocadoes, cheese, lettuce, shredded carrots, and various nuts (besides the mangoes). Since it's healthy fare I readily complied when she requested it. (She still requests it when she visits!) To our delight her naturally happy disposition reappeared and her appetite skyrocketed. Malnourishment, we'd suspected, had started to happen while she lived with Colleen and this was substantiated by her telling us Coke and potato chips was all there'd been to eat lately in the townhouse. Within a half year of her living with Lisa and Shawn, our granddaughter's percentile readings on the medical growth charts catapulted from fiftieth to sixty-fifth.

That isn't to say we were out of the woods with Jaimie. It *is* to say we had rescued her in time. Physically she bounced back quickly; psychologically there was work yet to be done. She had an almost pathological fear of being left alone, which is why if Andy wasn't home she would accompany me wherever I went. Once while we were walking Pepper she wanted to stop at a playground and go on the swings. I told her I'd continue with the dog to the end of the green space (five minutes) and then turn around and come back for her. She agreed but panicked the moment I was out of sight, enlisting the aid of a nearby parent to go with her and find me. Filled with a distrust of the world instilled by her mom, she saw dangers lurking everywhere.

And she still spent far too long in the bathroom washing and re-washing her hands until they were raw: an obsessive-compulsive habit doubtless a reaction to the filth and chaos she'd endured for so long. Her mindset in that regard was as it had been at Disneyland the day she'd treated a few drops of pee on her jeans like a crisis. Yet the school psychologist, who met with us again, remarked on the *amazing* difference he and her teachers already saw in her. On the last day of classes when the town fire department showed up in a truck to spray the kids with their hoses (cool—in both senses of the word!) she was as excited a participant as any, sporting the new bathing suit we'd bought her for the occasion. Yes, Jaimie had been saved in time.

Colleen on the other hand, despite claims of wanting rehab, resisted being saved from the outset. Upon arrival at Glory House she phoned the same neighbour we'd advised to relinquish the gifts and told that neighbour she planned on using the place as shelter only as long as it took for her to talk Lisa into letting her come and live in Surrey: two weeks at the most. Then she'd have free shelter *plus* her daughter back. The neighbour phoned us to let us in on the plan. We phoned and warned Lisa.

Inured as we all thought we were by now, this latest breach of good faith and ethics brought a crushing disappointment.

38. I didn't Hug Her

WestJet no longer permits children to fly unaccompanied, so in early July Jaimie and I—and Marley cat in his crate at our feet—made the trip to Vancouver together. Lisa and Shawn met us at the airport where I bought coffees all round (juice for Jaimie) while Shawn piled Jaimie's suitcases and the cat crate onto a trolley. Briefly we discussed Colleen, not wanting to get too intense in front of the little girl. Lisa said she'd made clear to her sister that living with her and Shawn in Surrey was not an option. Colleen had been furious but that was too bad: Colleen was stuck with staying in rehab, the best possible place. I hugged them both and gave a huge parting hug to Jaimie. WestJet lets adult chaperons fly at half price but—fair enough—only if they agree to turn around immediately and go back to their point of origin. My return flight was leaving right away.

Teary, my granddaughter clung to me hard. I assured her we'd continue the Grandma chats by email and we'd see her in a couple of weeks when Grandpa and I came by car to visit, bringing Bear-Bear hamster with us. Then I went briskly through the departure gate, reversing my gaze only once to wave at the three of them. Jaimie was hugging Lisa by then. Momentarily I flashed back to *our* airport-parting experiences with the child Colleen. Was Jaimie about to subject her new guardians to a gut-wrenching don't-leave-me episode? No. Of course she wasn't! Jaimie might have a few psychological hang-ups but she most assuredly was *not* Colleen.

In the intervening period between my farewell wave at Vancouver airport and our reunion of the whole family two weeks later at Lisa and Shawn's Surrey home, Colleen caused big trouble at Glory House. She pestered her sister and brother-in-law to provide her money to buy OxyContin, claiming the doctors there thought it best to wean her off it gradually. Met with blanket refusal, she then had a Glory House counsellor call *us* asking if we were willing to provide Colleen cigarette money (because giving up her chain-smoking habit at the same time was too stressful) as well as finance the medically-supervised OxyContin step-down process. The B.C. government's health-care system does *not* pay for OxyContin, period.

Having verified by calling back that we were indeed talking to a Glory House counsellor and not some impersonator, we agreed. But the arrangement lasted only briefly. Glory House telephoned again shortly thereafter to say they didn't think Colleen had any real desire to step down her drug intake. Anyhow, Colleen was the only patient there argumentative enough to have talked one of the doctors into allowing her the drug itself and the only patient there to resist being given methadone instead (an alternative synthetic opioid used to help decrease withdrawal symptoms when stepping down from dependence on other opioid drugs such as heroin, codeine and morphine). She was a bad example to others, not to mention a source of temptation. We stopped the drug payments.

Simultaneously, Lisa and Shawn, through email and telephone communication, relayed that Colleen was badgering them with constant demands to see Jaimie and declarations about leaving Glory House and coming to take her daughter away to where none of us would ever see either of them again. Her accusations against her sister and brother-in-law for stealing both her daughter *and* her cat were a source of upset to us all.

Next came threats of legal action. Lisa and Shawn were brainwashing her daughter, said Colleen, poisoning the child's mind against her. Visits by Lisa to Port Coquitlam proved an ordeal fraught with wild accusations and public scenes. Colleen would sue! They would pay for what they were doing!

Of course Colleen's drug-addled BPD brain wasn't functioning normally but still, one had to pay attention to these threats. At our expense, Lisa found and retained a lawyer. Lisa and Shawn were already doing enough; financially they weren't in a position to pay the legal fees a custody battle involved. Conversely, Colleen had free access to legal aid whenever she requested it because she was an indigent. In my diary I write: *Where is the justice? For this we put in blood, sweat and tears building up a decent retirement fund. I am devastated.* But we had no choice. We could foresee Colleen wouldn't last at Glory House and we knew she might be silver-tongued enough to convince someone to help her "rescue" her daughter. We couldn't let that happen.

The lawyer advised Lisa and Shawn to open a file on Jaimie with the B.C. Child Protective Services and start recording any "behavioural aberrations" in Colleen deemed undesirable and/or dangerous to the child. We, at the same time, were instructed to prepare a history documenting the many problems Colleen had had since childhood and specifying any diagnosed mental or psychological instabilities. Much as part of us felt like traitors to our own flesh-and-blood for doing this, we did it. The battle lines had been drawn. Again, we had no choice.

As Jaimie adjusted to life with her aunt and uncle, her growing attachment to them as guardians became evident. Her responses to my Grandma-chat emails were full of the antics of their four Italian greyhounds, how Marley cat was gradually getting used to the dogs, and how Uncle Shawn had enrolled her in swim classes at the YMCA. (Jaimie and I still email one another sometimes and banter back and forth on Facebook, but those regular reassuring Grandma-chat missives, I rejoice to say, are no longer necessary.) Shawn's dad Terry, and the dad's wife Jen, lived only five minutes away and their twin daughters Megan and Nicole were close by as well. All readily befriended Jaimie and became her extended family. Andy and I, who had met them at Lisa and Shawn's wedding, were delighted to renew that friendship when we visited in late July.

By then Colleen had transferred out of Glory House into "Stepping Stones", a women's residential rehabilitation facility located in Abbotsford. The rules at Glory House were totally unreasonable, she informed her sister (with whom she still maintained some contact since Lisa had her child) and at this place she could start over. Andy and I wondered if we ought to drop in and visit her there while we were in the area. It's about a forty minute drive from Surrey to Abbotsford and it couldn't hurt to show her we were still rooting for her despite everything. We called first and were allowed to speak to her. Yes, she would see us. We set up a day and time. I wasn't anticipating a warm welcome but her agreement to see us at least meant family still counted for *something* in her eyes.

On the morning of July twenty-seventh 2008, Colleen called Lisa's place to say she'd changed her mind; she was too sick to see us after all. In fact she was on her way to the hospital. Maybe we could do it another time; she had to go now. End of conversation. Left hanging in that anxious state, we decided we'd drive to Stepping Stones regardless. Maybe we could get some answers out of someone in charge there.

Like every other facility Colleen has been in, Stepping Stones is not a prison. A house supervisor named Aisha ushered us into a sitting room and spoke with us pleasantly but frankly. Yes, Colleen had talked someone into giving her a ride to the hospital, claiming to be in extreme pain from a fictitious tumour on her spine and needing some medicinal relief. Aisha made clear to us that Colleen was on borrowed time at Stepping Stones for a number of reasons. The other residents found her pugnacious and difficult to get along with. She refused to follow rules about sharing chores. She balked at entering the detox program and showed not the slightest serious desire to end her addiction. She was up to stunts like this hospital trip all the time and had been caught "double doctoring" (seeing two physicians and obtaining from each an identical pain-medication prescription) as well as *dealing* within the facility itself. I had thought that in today's computer age double doctoring would no longer be possible but apparently not all pharmacies are electronically linked—or weren't at that time. I had also thought that *dealing* within a centre for recovering addicts was too reprehensible an act for a daughter of mine to stoop to, and it saddened me immensely that I was wrong.

While we were still talking to Aisha, Colleen arrived back from her hospital outing. Her weight had ballooned further and her skin, covered with the red lesions, had a more ashen pallor than ever. Stunned—and certainly *not* pleased—to see us, she turned belligerent when Aisha, before going off into another room to let us have a private family visit, conveyed the gist of what we'd been discussing. "I hate Aisha!" she screamed. "She tells lies and she gets her kicks watching people suffer!"

Andy ignored the slur. "Colleen, you have to stop resisting detox. Scary as it is, you know it's the only way to save your own life. You have to bite the bullet once and for all and just *go*."

She shook her head. "I can't right now. The detox centre is full. I'm on a waiting list to get in." Could there be any truth to that? Certainly the term "waiting list" is one applied to all aspects of health care these days. But no, as Andy had pointed out, Aisha had just said Colleen was *resisting* detox. The two accounts didn't jibe and I didn't doubt which one was accurate. Neither did my husband.

"How long is the wait likely to be?" he pursued. "Would Aisha have any idea? Shall we ask her?"

I didn't hang around to hear Colleen's response; I was already on my way to knock on the door of the room into which I'd seen Aisha disappear. When the house supervisor opened up and came into the hall, I asked her myself. She eyed Colleen narrowly and replied, "I can make a phone call *now* and have her in by tomorrow morning. It's up to her."

"Way to go Mom," sneered Colleen. "It's sure nice to know you have such faith in your daughter's word that you need to check everything I say with someone else! That gives me real confidence in your support!" The ridiculousness of that remark in light of having just been proved a liar seemed to elude her entirely. Familiar frustration tightened my jaw.

"Colleen, you're an addict and right now I *don't* believe a word you say," I concurred. "Maybe someday…"

"I'm through talking! Get out!" She unleashed a stream of profanities relating to what both of us could do to ourselves and flounced away into an adjoining kitchen area. It was indeed time to go.

Andy followed her into the kitchen to give her a hug. "Colleen, you're still our daughter and we still love you," he said sadly. Cursing afresh she pulled roughly away from his embrace.

"Well you have a very funny way of showing it. Get out, both of you!"

"Come on love," I urged him. "It's no use. Let's go." I admired his gesture and his words but I could not follow suit with the hug. Considering all I'd tried to do for her all her life, why subject myself to that kind of ingratitude and rejection? What was the point?

Aisha saw us to the door and stepped outside with us for a moment. "I feel for you," she said. "It's very tragic. But I'm sure you've heard this before: you can't save her if she won't save herself." We nodded, thanked the house supervisor and drove back to Surrey.

Many times since I have thought about the hug I chose *not* to give Colleen that day. I know now that I would have given it to her in spite of everything had I realized that that was the last time I'd see her alive.

39. "And I don't Want to Live This Life"

Children of BPD mothers, like Jaimie, feel understandably torn. While loving and wanting to please their moms, they simultaneously recognize that by a certain age it is natural for them to seek their own independence. If they pull away they cause their moms anguish; if they *don't* pull away they cause themselves anguish. It is truly a Catch 22. Colleen dealt with it by not dealing with it. Jaimie, at twelve, started to face it *and* to accept help. Lisa took her to a counsellor, whom she began to see regularly.

In late August, Shawn made a road trip to Alberta for a short visit with his mother who lived near Edmonton. He brought our granddaughter along and dropped her off in Calgary on his way, picking her up a week later on his way back. This time Jaimie actively *enjoyed* being with us and was much more open about her conflicted feelings. We validated those feelings, emphasizing as before that she wasn't wrong to love her mom but that she was *right* to want a life of her own. We saw a different girl emerging, one whose poise had begun to blossom. She talked patiently and calmly to Colleen (who phoned every day but only to speak to her, never to us) and pointedly stayed in the same room with us so as not to make the conversations secretive. She told us Lisa had been taking her for counselling and it was helping. And she shared with us the story of the crack pipe.

"One time Lisa and Shawn had a tire-pressure gauge on the dashboard of their car," she related. "I saw it there and I started to cry. It looked like a crack pipe to me. All I could think was: *Oh no! Not again!* It was such a relief when they told me what it really was and showed me how it worked." Andy and I were enormously impressed both by this forthright revelation and by the new self-assurance in her behaviour. These were miraculous milestones to have attained in such a short time.

Shawn had a good talk with us as well, just before he and our granddaughter departed for Surrey. He said a new job was on the horizon for him in the coming month and Lisa's teaching contract at Fleetwood Park Secondary School had been renewed for the upcoming year. He said he too had been uprooted from his home as a child due to family problems, and he had shared with Jaimie his anger about it. They had formed a bond. This was all wonderful news. On the not-so-wonderful front, he told us Colleen continued to say she was going to abduct her child for whom she was still the legal guardian. Apologizing about the expense, Shawn felt the time had come to put to further use the lawyer they had retained.

Andy turned over to him, for the lawyer, our prepared document detailing Colleen's troubled history, her mental health problems and our reasons for removing the child from the home and taking out an ex parte order against Colleen. If the lawyer asked for anything else, Shawn and Lisa would let us know.

September brought more mixed news. Enrolled now at Fleetwood Elementary School—the grades one-to-seven feeder school for Fleetwood Park Secondary and almost next door to it—Jaimie soon made friends there and began to excel academically. She had expressed concerns to us about how the amount of school she'd missed in grade six might hold her back in grade seven; her concerns proved groundless. It chokes me up to write it: this was final proof that we had, indeed, saved our granddaughter.

But as we feared, the more happiness and success Jaimie started to acquire in her own right, the more enraged and off-the-wall Colleen became. Thrown out of Stepping Stones, she had to spend one night at the Salvation Army before transferring into "Step By Step Recovery House", another residential rehab program based in Surrey. Being in the same town as Lisa and Shawn she was now in a better position than ever to harass them and she did so unceasingly. She renewed her demands to have Marley cat back (despite being unable to keep him at the residence). She told Lisa she'd spoken to her same-sex couple friends who had agreed to let her return to Alberta to live with them and bring Jaimie with her. (Later, these kind ladies affirmed she *had* spoken to them and they hadn't known what to believe or what to do—though they phoned Lisa for an update and decided Colleen was best off in rehab and they shouldn't interfere.) She left an "anonymous tip" with Social Services that Shawn smoked marijuana and was therefore an unfit guardian. She somehow connected again with the same fellow she'd persuaded to impersonate Mark Donnelly and she said she and he would soon be grabbing Jaimie away by force.

Through all this Lisa and Shawn had to hold down their respective jobs as well as provide a steadying influence for Jaimie whenever the poor girl became frightened. They too became frightened by the stepped-up threat bombardment, as did we. Immediate action was called for. Andy forwarded by Fed Ex, at the lawyer's request, a certified copy of the closed ex parte order from June, along with another copy (notarized, this time) of Colleen's troubled history and the BPD diagnosis. The lawyer also requested, and received, a copy of Jaimie's assessment from the psychologist at Holy Spirit Academy in High River.

At a hearing held on the last Friday of September 2008, Lisa and Shawn were granted temporary legal guardianship of Jaimie until October thirtieth, on which date a case for custody would be heard. Their next task was to go to the Step By Step Recovery House and to serve Colleen with the legal papers requiring her court appearance at the custody case. Of course Colleen created a monstrous scene and Lisa and Shawn were treated very coldly by the female director there. When one is a recovering addict, the director reproved, losing custody of one's child is hardly an incentive to get clean.

After Lisa related to me how she'd been reproached, I diarized my anger thus: *Poor Lisa! With all she's doing, to have people who know* diddly-squat *about the situation passing judgment on her…! Never mind. I know both Lisa and Shawn have the strength of character to handle this.* And so they did. Andy and I talked to them on the phone that night until well past midnight—long after dear Jaimie had been tucked safely into bed.

So it was that step one of obtaining Jaimie's emancipation had been initiated—at great expense, both emotionally and financially. We still had a long way to go. In our own situation, none of us adults felt any less torn up than did Jaimie in hers. Lisa sobbed, "How could my own *sister* do this to me?" and we all shed tears of empathy. But we cried just as hard with sorrow at Colleen's mental and physical deterioration, so destructive as to force the rest of her family into the role of antagonists.

Was the director right? By trying to stop Jaimie's destruction were we hastening Colleen's?

It was during this angst-ridden time that I remembered the paperback my younger daughter had thrust at me just before boarding her bus for Port Coquitlam. Then, I had put the book into my jacket pocket from which I'd later transferred it to a shelf in our study. Colleen had occasionally recommended to me in the past various examples of her standard reading fare: dark or grisly tales that were not to my literary taste. Without even glancing at it I'd assumed this paperback to be one of those and I'd consigned it to the proverbial back burner while Andy and I dealt with more pressing issues. Now, in my conflict-wracked state, I took it up from its shelf and for the first time examined it thoroughly.

Deborah Spungen, mother of Nancy Spungen, was its author. Its title, one I believe Colleen had come to feel applied to her, was *And I Don't Want To Live This Life*. Its subject matter was the true story of Deborah's mentally-ill daughter who, in the late nineteen seventies, was stabbed to death in a New York hotel room by her famous mentally-disturbed punk rocker boyfriend Sid Vicious. Vicious, charged with Nancy's murder, himself died of a heroin overdose before the case went to trial. Much speculation attended their deaths. Did they both agree to put one another out of their mutual misery? Was there a suicide pact which Vicious had reneged on but later fulfilled? In her book Deborah refers to the pair as "two lost souls who had found each other" and adds that their relationship "came out of their inability to find what they wanted in the outside world."[16] The book's title derives from words in a poem Vicious wrote about Nancy after her death and just before his: *And I don't want to live this life/ If I can't live for you.* [17]

I recalled Colleen's urging as she'd placed the book into my hand. *"I think you should read this, Mom. I really think you should."* She'd felt strongly, more strongly than about other books she'd previously promoted. And as I began reading, I discovered why. The margins of some printed pages were covered with copious scribbling in my daughter's handwriting.

Deborah Spungen's account of Nancy's childhood history is hauntingly familiar. She describes Nancy's defiance of all authority, Nancy's outbursts of declared hatred followed by almost frantic and cloying declarations of love, and Nancy's persistent problems at school. She describes repeated parental efforts to get Nancy help and the reluctance of mental health professionals to "label" a child by diagnosing a mental illness. She mentions various facilities where Nancy briefly stayed before running away. She documents her growing concern about the "bad boys" to which her daughter was attracted and her increasing feelings of alienation toward her daughter, as well as her need to distance herself and find retreat in other activities. It was like reading a carbon copy of my own maternal experiences.

---

16 Spungen, Deborah. 1983. *And I Don't Want To Live This Life*. Toronto, Canada: Ballantine Books, 323

17 Ibid, 391

At each point in the story where parent-child conflict occurs, Colleen has made a derisive note about how awful this mother is, how Deborah "deserves a mother-of-the-year award" for ignoring her own child's misery and for withdrawing both emotionally and financially from her daughter. *I* am that awful mother, I guess. But a large part of me believes Colleen's eagerness to have me read this book was based on something other than a desire to berate my parenting skills. In fact most of me believes that, in her heart of hearts, my baby loved me very much and was crying out to be understood. She wanted me to know that *she* was Nancy. Like Nancy, her brain didn't manufacture the "happiness" chemicals. Like Nancy, she was the product of a time when hesitation by professionals to attach stigmatizing labels had kept her from being helped early enough or aggressively enough.

And like Sid Vicious, if the one individual she felt most attached to in this world was going to be taken from her, then she wanted to die.

217

40. The New Boyfriend

Colleen didn't last at Step By Step any longer than she had at the other centres. By October she was somewhere else but not sharing her whereabouts with either us or Lisa and Shawn. All we could gather from tidbits she imparted to Lisa whenever she demanded a visit with Jaimie was that the place was co-ed. People struggling with addiction are cautioned *not* to form bonds with other addicts; ergo Colleen, ever defiant, formed one almost upon being admitted.

I'll call the new boyfriend Joe. Andy has spoken to him once on the phone but we have never met him. From what Jaimie has said he was a sad sack who grew up in an unstable home, had several failed relationships and ended up returning to that home to live with his ailing mother. He was nearly forty, ten years older than Colleen. And he was totally taken in by our daughter's tragic tale of her entire family's evil plot to steal away her child.

Considering how Lisa was being maligned, I would hardly have blamed our eldest for not lifting a finger to bring about further visits between Colleen and Jaimie. But that is not dear Lisa's nature. For Jaimie's sake, Lisa drove to this rehab, located in a neighbouring community, and—having established it was overseen by qualified persons and its professed 'child sleepover' policy was actually the truth—dropped off her niece to spend a night there.

Jaimie felt duty-bound to accept her mom's invitation of an overnighter but both the place *and* the boyfriend "creeped her out", as she reported to Lisa. Almost at once Colleen spirited her off to the bathroom, closed the door behind them and showed Jaimie the court documents Lisa and Shawn had served. "Look how they're lying about me!" her mom ranted. "*They* are the crazy ones!" Much as we'd all been trying to keep Jaimie as uninvolved and unburdened as possible, again it was Colleen who resorted to preying upon the poor child's divided loyalties, begging Jaimie to keep telling everyone how much she wanted to go back to her mom. Unmindful of collateral damage, our youngest sank herself by the very act of choosing that way to try and further her cause.

The bathroom episode troubled Jaimie greatly—but not as much as Colleen's revelation that she and Joe were going to get married, move into their own place and then bring Jaimie to live with them. "Do *I* get a vote in this?" Jaimie asked. "Well no, you're my child," was Colleen's reply. "Of course you'll want to come and live with us. We'll get a big dog! You'll like that, right? Joe and I are going to court to fight everything they're trying to do to keep you and me apart!"

That visit brought back all the little girl's anxieties. And sure enough, Colleen and her new ally accessed legal aid and had a statement prepared containing some horrendous allegations. Andy and I had always been cruel parents who beat and abused her. We had roughly and savagely snatched her child away even though the child hated and feared us, and had then brainwashed our captive with lies in order to turn the child against her. Lisa and Shawn were a similarly cruel sister and brother-in-law, in league with us. *They* now had the child and were abetting the brainwashing despite the fact that she, Colleen, was drug-free and well able to provide Jaimie a secure home.

Wow! When Lisa and Shawn were served this statement in mid-October, their lawyer had them write a rebuttal and also asked for a rebuttal from us (signed in the presence of a notary public) which we immediately provided. We offered to fly out and attend the October thirtieth hearing if necessary but were assured our sworn affidavits would be sufficient. Colleen and Joe showed up together at that hearing where Colleen staged a magnificent portrayal of a long-suffering, hard-done-by victim. Although the male judge did rule in Lisa and Shawn's favour, he was obviously moved to some sympathy for Colleen's supposed predicament because he placed stipulations on his ruling. Lisa and Shawn could not take Jaimie out of the province or country without Colleen's written consent. Good only until mid-December when it would be reviewed, the judgment dictated *twelve hours per week* of visitation time between Colleen and Jaimie in the presence of a court-appointed supervisor—costs of said supervision time (nearly $2,000 per month) to be borne by Lisa and Shawn!

It was enough to make anybody gulp. Our elder daughter and son-in-law had already lost a day's pay each by taking personal leave to attend the hearing; now they were faced with expenses that had the potential to bankrupt them, or us, or both. What if the mid-December review had the same result? How long could our collective bank accounts hold out?

Lisa and Shawn assumed most of the supervision fees while we continued to pay the hefty legal fees. Lisa went to see the manager of the company that arranged the supervision to fill out all the paperwork. He spoke to Colleen as well about the procedure. "Your sister doesn't seem too bright," he later remarked to Lisa, who repeated the remark to us with shock. If there was one quality Colleen had always possessed it was mental acuity. But her drug habit had obviously reached a level where even that part of her brain was in trouble.

An eight-hour supervised-visit day held in neutral territory such as a shopping mall (to which Lisa had to drive Jaimie) took place each Saturday, and a four-hour supervised-visit evening, under identical circumstances, took place each Tuesday. Costly and inconvenient as these visits were, they *did* have a positive side: an objective observer was present to witness any inappropriate behaviour on Colleen's part and to record how faithfully—or not—she kept the appointments with her daughter. The supervisor's log book was soon full of incidents where Colleen used foul language, threw tantrums about how restrictive the conditions were, or simply failed to show.

During one such visit, the supervisor was actually forced to intervene and steer discussion in another direction. "The day you start to use drugs—and you will—make sure you tell me about it," Colleen advised Jaimie, "so we can share the experience together." The supervisor put the kibosh on further utterances of that sort and committed the occurrence to print.

Jaimie grew to hate the visits and yet they had their positive outcome for *her* as well: she was forming a more realistic picture of the extent of her mom's illness. "Joe is ugly and he smells," Colleen told her. "But he's the best I can do." (That's so sad!) About Colleen's failures to show up for visits Jaimie observed, "Mom says I'm the most important thing in her whole world. But this proves I'm not. Drugs are." Painful as it was for her eyes to be opened, her words proved she was old enough and mature enough to *have* them opened.

One night Colleen phoned Lisa and Shawn's, screaming imprecations and demanding to speak to Jaimie. Tense, Jaimie took the call. Colleen told her they (Colleen and Joe) had both left rehab and were living with Joe's mom, and they were on their way *right now* with the police to pick up the little girl and "take her home". Jaimie's tension became terror. She was afraid she might throw up. Aunt and niece stood together over the toilet bowl while Lisa soothingly explained that the police would not interfere in any matter that was being contested before the courts and this was all a bluff. Sure enough, neither Colleen and Joe nor the police ever materialized.

Regularly during this period I had my "Grandma chats" with Jaimie as well as "Mum chats" with Lisa. We made up for a lot of lost time, Lisa and I, talking meaningfully as we couldn't while Lisa was resenting growing up in her sister's shadow. We cried together. Ever supportive, Andy and Shawn contributed to the chats. Many a young husband in Shawn's shoes would have bailed, but not Shawn. What a dear man he has turned out to be, a man as strong and noble-natured as his father-in-law. He hadn't realized he was signing on for this when he married his high-school sweetheart, but bless him, he hung in there!

As for Colleen, she overdosed twice in the month of November and ended up in hospital. Joe called to inform Lisa. Anxious and upset, Jaimie carried on with her counselling sessions—and Lisa entered counselling with her. More and more, Jaimie levelled about how bad things had been in High River. "There were people coming and going in the house all night long and we were living in *squalor*," she told the psychologist. (At risk of putting comic relief where it doesn't belong, that's a beautiful descriptive noun for a twelve-year-old to know!) "Once, I got out of bed to go pee and found a strange man in the shower. It was very scary." My knees turned to water thinking about that strange man in the shower and what might have happened to my granddaughter.

And as with the supervised visits, their counselling sessions had a positive outcome, not just for Lisa and Jaimie who bonded even more closely, but for us as well. "Get out the Kleenex, Mum," Lisa warned one night. "I wish you'd been there today. Jaimie had a bout of tears. She said she'd spent years believing the horrible things Colleen claimed you and Dad had done and holding herself back from becoming too attached to you. Now she knows that you're wonderful people and she's *so* sorry for ever thinking those things about you." Yes, that warranted wads of Kleenex all right.

We discussed inviting both Jaimie and Lisa for a visit to Arizona next March during their school break just before we listed our unit there for sale. Shawn, who couldn't get enough time off work, encouraged the women in his life to take advantage of this opportunity, saying he'd be with us in spirit. Colleen used the legal club she held to threaten withholding from Jaimie permission to make the trip. And Lisa's lawyer took note of this detail for the upcoming review hearing.

The hearing, held on December seventeenth 2008, revisited the matter of Jaimie's guardianship and was conducted this time by a female judge.

Having gone over the material presented by Lisa and Shawn's lawyer, this judge then asked why Jaimie's mother was not present in the court. No one knew. Colleen had been apprised of the hearing's date and time but hadn't appeared. Not to be deterred, the judge contacted Colleen's most recent place of residence and engaged in a teleconference then and there! Colleen made excuses, slurred her words and sounded stoned. The judge asked if Colleen could think of a single reason to deny Jaimie a nice holiday with the family down south next spring. Cornered, Colleen admitted there *was* no good reason.

"Right, so you'll be giving these folks a written note to that effect and signing it," the judge ordered. She also lifted the visitation restrictions and granted Lisa and Shawn guardianship of Jaimie *indefinitely* until medical tests showed Colleen drug-free. The onus was now on *Colleen* to demonstrate worthiness of being a dependable guardian, not the other way around. What a relief! What a well-deserved reprieve for darling Jaimie—whose first Fleetwood Elementary report card, despite everything, was nearly all 'A's.

I could almost have been happy were it not for my ever-present heartache about my youngest. Colleen had hoped to use Joe as proof she was getting on her feet and working towards being able to provide for her child. Alas, she had instead proved just the opposite: her downslide had gained momentum since her association with Joe. If anything—much as I shied away from the comparison—the new boyfriend was shaping up to be Sid Vicious to her Nancy Spungen.

41. Alee of the Storms

I think it would be fair to say that the greater the turbulence looming on our horizon, the more we practiced employing those internal stabilizers Colleen had been born without. The act of divorcing oneself emotionally, like any other skill, keeps improving the longer you do it.

Colleen obeyed the judge's dictate and gave Lisa signed permission for her daughter to make the Arizona trip in March 2009 but then said she was going to rescind permission because, with the lifted visitation restrictions, Jaimie didn't want to see her as often and now insisted on having a supervisor (usually Lisa) present.

"Blackmail won't change my mind," Jaimie declared. "After all the lies I've been told I don't want to see Mom *or* the troll (her name for Joe) without a supervisor. If they *ever* try to make me go and live with them and say I don't get a vote, I'll just vote with my feet. I'll run away." Her resentment was natural and bound to come out but we urged her not to get too angry. March was three months away. Situations and attitudes can change within three months.

One situation that did change is that Andy's Crohn's disease doctor found a lump in Andy's bowel requiring further investigation, so our winter migration got put on hold anyway. Lisa, Shawn and Jaimie faithfully called to ask for updates. Thank goodness the lump turned out to be a fatty deposit and Andy was given the doctor's blessing to travel. Possible cancellation of *Jaimie's* blessing to travel remained a potential impediment.

We began to see evidence that Colleen's mood swings were getting wilder and more out of control. She went to watch Jaimie in a stage production of *Thoroughly Modern Millie* and was all beaming maternal pride; then she was back in hospital, presumably from an overdose. Upon being released, she got kicked out of Joe's place and re-entered rehab for a four-week residential evaluation period at the Crossroads Treatment Centre in Kelowna.

Crossroads Treatment Centre has since had to close its doors due to lack of funding. At the time, it offered the four-week program to assess the client's level of addiction as well as accompanying mental health problems; then recommendations were made as to how to best treat these problems. Colleen's first stay there came to an untimely end when she persuaded Joe to let her move back in with him.

Andy and I sent her Christmas gifts that December, as we had sent gifts for her birthday. Jaimie and Lisa made sure the gifts were delivered but she never acknowledged them.

My diary entry for the end of 2008 reads: *The year has been eventful: a terrible downslide for Colleen but a wonderful gain of confidence and self-esteem for Jaimie. We must focus on that and just keep hoping that someday Colleen will see the light.* When I made that entry, I know I had very little real hope remaining for our youngest.

In January 2009, Andy took a chance and booked Lisa and Jaimie a flight to Arizona. (We covered the cost of Lisa's ticket as well as Jaimie's: her birthday present. She certainly deserved a vacation!) Joe had again thrown Colleen out by then and she was back at Crossroads—though only briefly. She was apparently informed she had to leave due to discovery of a contraband substance in her possession. "Whatever," I told Lisa over the phone. "We say exactly the same thing here," Lisa agreed.

The waves of Colleen's storms got larger and our adeptness grew at staying alee. As our Parent Support Group had taught us, this was survival. Paralysis would not do, so we went on with our lives. Lisa and Jaimie *did* come to Arizona in March and we had a great time taking them to places such as Tombstone, the Desert Museum in Tucson and the Hale Theatre in Gilbert where *The King and I* was playing. Lisa had brought along Colleen's signed note allowing the trip and Colleen never followed through on rescinding it. I think the maelstrom of her own life took up all her attention.

In April, Andy and I revised our wills. (Colleen never learned of this revision.) Our originals had left most of our estate to our children on a fifty-fifty basis. Now we put Colleen's money in a trust fund to be doled out to her only as needed at the trustee's discretion, and we composed and signed a letter explaining why. Originally Lisa was to get my diamond engagement ring and Colleen the eternity ring Andy gave me for our twentieth anniversary; now I left the eternity ring to Jaimie. Colleen, I knew, would have pawned or sold it to buy drugs.

Given yet another chance in the four-week residential evaluation program at Crossroads, our youngest begged for, and was granted, a fifth week. At the end of that, she was told she couldn't simply use the facilities as a rent-free place to stay; she had to make a decision to address her mental health issues and to get clean. If she made that decision, they would place her in a one-year supervised program where she would receive intensive help. And if she completed the one-year program successfully, she'd then be able to look at getting her daughter back.

Colleen outright refused. She wanted her daughter back *now*, and she didn't need the intensive help. She claimed she'd never used drugs in the first place and had only taken advantage of the centre as a living accommodation, whereupon she was, of course, asked to leave. She also claimed she'd be contesting Lisa and Shawn in court once more and going for sole guardianship of Jaimie. "Whatever," Lisa said grimly.

Andy and I made a present of singing lessons to Jaimie, which she enjoyed. She passed grade seven with honours that June—a "graduation", because in B.C. grade eight marks the beginning of high school. She was asked to perform a valedictory solo before her entire graduation class and their parents. Our faces were wet as we watched the DVD and marvelled that this poised young woman in the chic dress and the fashionable hairstyle was what the timid traumatized little girl we'd rescued had become.

In July, Lisa came to Calgary to take some qualifying courses for her psychology degree at U. of C. and stayed at our place for three weeks. Jaimie came along and spent the days with us while Lisa attended classes. She contacted Pat and Sue, the same-sex couple who'd known her since babyhood and they invited us all over for coffee. Jaimie wanted these kind ladies to realize that when as a child she'd told them how bad things were at home and then took it all back and said she'd lied, she had in fact told the truth in the first place. Her mom had forced her to take it back and say she was lying. Pat and Sue were touched that Jaimie so valued their opinion of her as to want to set the record straight. Andy and I found the whole experience very moving.

Granddaughter and grandparents prepared meals, enjoyed miniature golf and midway rides at Calloway Park, and (Lisa included) took in *Man of La Mancha* at Rosebud Theatre. There, Jaimie and Lisa together bought for me (as a surprise) a beautiful Egyptian pendant I admired in one of the gift shops. "I used some of the allowance I get from Uncle Shawn and Auntie Lisa for doing chores," Jaimie told me. "Lisa and I *wanted* you to have it, Grandma." That pendant I treasure as much as I do the stuffed monkey Colleen gave me so long ago.

On the same day at Rosebud, Jaimie also bought a metal treble clef to hang on her bedroom wall. "Auntie Lisa and Uncle Shawn say I can decorate the room the way I want," she revealed. "They're even letting me choose some new furniture!" Lisa told us later that Jaimie had burst into tears one night and asked them if there'd be enough space for *her* if they ever decided to have children of their own. They'd told her the room was hers as long as she wanted to stay there and they decided between themselves to quell her insecurities by letting her decorate it to her taste. Every day I am thankful anew that such lovely people are my daughter and son-in-law.

As to whether they plan on having children of their own, it's none of my business but I have my doubts. If there's the slightest chance of their having a child with BPD as severe as Colleen's, I can understand them avoiding pregnancy like the plague.

"Mom has sworn she's changed her mind and is going back to Crossroads to complete a twenty-eight-day detox program and then the follow-up year-long life skills program," Jaimie told us during that same visit. "I don't have any faith it will happen." I'm afraid we had no faith either.

Colleen telephoned Jaimie a few times while she was with us. Not only did our granddaughter stay in the same room, she vocally expressed her displeasure at her mom's request that she take the phone to a more private location. "No, I won't," she said. "There's nothing I can't say to you right here in front of family." We didn't purposely eavesdrop but obviously Jaimie didn't mind being overheard. At one point she talked of being insulted that her mom would think her susceptible to brainwashing. Proud of my granddaughter's assertion of independence, I still pitied my younger daughter's flailing and futile efforts to turn back the clock and regain the naive and totally controllable little being Jaimie used to be. That little being was gone forever.

Before starting high school in September, Jaimie attended a horse-riding camp—again, a present from us. Right away she became passionate about riding, saying she favoured it to singing lessons. The camp ended with a show to which parents were invited. Jaimie told her mom about the show but asked Colleen *not* to bring the boyfriend—a request guaranteed to incite Colleen's perversity. Sure enough the two appeared at the show, where a furious Jaimie informed her mom she didn't want to live with them *ever* and would never change her mind.

"I've written up a record of the event and filed it with the lawyer," Lisa told us. She sounded very down. "When I'm not worried about how this will end, I'm worried about all the expenses—to us as well as to you." Andy and I sat down and talked after that conversation. We decided, in addition to paying the legal fees, to make a monthly contribution to Lisa and Shawn's bank account from then on to help them out with those expenses. Colleen had always been a drain on our funds; it was time to start putting money towards a cause that (sad as it was to say) promised a brighter future.

The same academic success she'd displayed in grade seven soon attended Jaimie's efforts as a Fleetwood Park Secondary School student. Colleen continued to agitate for a return to court, causing Lisa and Shawn's lawyer to recommend they go for sole custody. That was where things stood when Andy attended the United Church Men's conference in Banff and spoke with Dr. Densmore about how recent brain-imaging techniques have shown clearly the defective neural pathways in impaired brains. Andy's telling me of that conversation caused a figurative deadening to the neural pathways of *my* brain—those connecting emotional heartache with rational certainty that my baby was headed down the road to death.

Yet emotion can only be kept at bay for so long. I remember having several meltdowns during 2009, totally out-of-proportion to the actual cause. Once while trying to do a watercolour representation of a waterfall, I was suddenly choking and my hands were shaking. *I can't get this right! I'll never get this right!* I inwardly mourned. Another time, I had a disagreement with the church choir director who wanted me to sing a part too low for my voice. *I can't sing this! I sound like a frog!* I protested to myself while my eyes filled with tears. A third time, I sat with Andy, Lisa and Jaimie at church in mid-July and we listened while Wendy Johnson, a beautiful gentle lady in the congregation, read a children's story aloud. "God doesn't make mistakes," Wendy read and then she herself, moved by the tale, started to cry. Jaimie, Lisa and I joined her. We were all thinking of Colleen.

And of course there was Mother's Day that year which featured special music sung by a group of young mothers. *In my daughter's eyes I am a hero,* was a line from that song. I lost it, as did another lady in the audience. We ended up sobbing in one another's arms and asking the heavens what on earth we had done to deserve daughters who not only didn't esteem us but hated our guts.

In November 2009, Andy and I got an offer on our Arizona place that we couldn't refuse and we sold it. We would miss the warmth and the friends we'd made there but mostly we were relieved. Now we could direct all our energies where they belonged. Again we sent a Christmas package to Colleen and again we received no acknowledgment. Lisa heard her sister had been in hospital recently but was now out. Twice in December, our eldest took our granddaughter to pre-arranged meetings with her mom, and twice Colleen didn't show. Poor Jaimie!

But we were all very thankful—despite how excruciatingly sad it was—that Jaimie too was definitely becoming as good at shrugging and saying "whatever" as the rest of us were.

42. Heartbreakers

And now we face 2010. What lies ahead? Those are the first words I diarize for that year. We had our usual New Year's Day dinner with the Dawsons and I shared with them my apprehension that worse was to come than we had already endured. Still, what happened one night in early February blew me away.

Andy and I were spending a quiet evening watching TV when the phone rang. I picked up, not thinking anything. The receiver in that room showed no call display. "Hello," I muttered, half expecting some telemarketer. The next moment I was clutching the arm of the sofa convulsively. The voice at the other end was Colleen's.

She had not spoken to us in a year-and-a-half. Now, as though she'd never borne us the slightest ill will, her opening enquiries were pleasant and solicitous. How had we been? What was new? Was Dad's sore ear better? (It was *my* sore ear she was thinking of, and it was nothing serious.) She hoped we were keeping well. It was good to talk to us. Et cetera. You would have thought we were on the best of terms and she was phoning just to chat!

Completely bewildered, I waited. What was she after? What kind of trouble was she in? At the best of times Colleen's phone calls had usually had an ulterior motive. Her feigned concern about our welfare was a buttering-up technique she'd used before when she wanted something of us—usually money. I was braced for it the whole time—whatever "it" was.

And then it started to unfold: an ocean of self-pity. She was losing "little one" because of Lisa and Shawn's traitorous conduct. "Little one" was her whole world. No one understood that, not even the boyfriend. Her "baby" used to love her so much and now that love was being destroyed. Colleen's voice rose to hysteria. "Mom, do you have any *idea* what it feels like for a mother to lose her child, to feel that her child has turned against her and is gone from her forever?"

I didn't know whether to laugh or cry.

Collecting myself, I said, "Colleen, the devil of it is…"

I got no further. "I'm not a devil, Mom!" she screeched. Stunned, I took a deep breath. I was dealing with raging paranoia and a mind that no longer listened properly. Misinterpretation happened before a sentence was even out of the speaker's mouth. I doubted she could ever be dis-

229

suaded from thinking I'd called her a devil, any more than she could be from thinking I'd told her she should have been born a boy. Then she said something that stunned me even more. "I guess that's why you told Lisa you wish I would die."

Shock made me dizzy and my hands were sweating on the receiver. "Colleen, I've never in my life said such a thing! And I didn't call you a devil just now. It's just an expression! I was going to say: 'the devil of it is that no mother can build her whole world on her little one because children grow up'. And there's no traitorous conduct going on. Jaimie has a good head on her shoulders and she's starting to think for herself. That's a *good* sign. It's part of becoming an adult." My next-door neighbour and dear friend was dying of cancer and my heart was heavy anyway. To my own ears my voice sounded exhausted. I'd had a bellyful of Colleen's self-centredness and her preference for delusion over reality. "There are people in this world who have problems they can't control and don't deserve. *You* are causing all your own problems."

She wasn't receptive to that argument. I didn't expect her to be. Lisa and Shawn were the real villains, she said. She'd thought they'd help her once she got to B.C. and instead they'd turned on her and stolen her child. That she herself had placed her child in their care seemed to have completely gone out of her mind.

I told her this discussion was pointless. Andy talked to her for a while with no better results. Actually she had never been an addict, she insisted. And she and Joe were now well able to provide for Jaimie's needs—maybe with a little help from us.

There. *That* was what I'd known was coming.

"We're not helping you get Jaimie back when we believe Jaimie is better off where she is." Andy's voice was as weary as mine. It was like talking to a brick wall. "But we love you and we're still hoping you'll persist with rehab and get better. We'd have to be sure you're completely better before we'd support Jaimie going back to you. Jaimie is old enough now, though, to be making her own choice about such matters." That was another reality Colleen simply could not grasp. She didn't agree, she said, but she'd keep in touch. I think she was convinced we'd cave if she kept working on us.

Two weeks later, my neighbour died. The day after the funeral, Colleen called again. It was past midnight. She said if we didn't give her money she'd soon be on the streets. Her relationship with Joe was falling apart.

They fought all the time and he was doing horrible things to her. He had stabbed her in the arm with a knife and she'd had to call the police and be escorted to a women's shelter. "I have no way to get money," she wept. "I used to get a child government allowance for my baby and now that Lisa has stolen my baby I don't even get that anymore! Lisa doesn't get it either because she and Shawn earn too much to qualify. What a waste…!" Then her voice turned cold and the naked amoral sociopath emerged, raising the hairs on the back of my neck as though I were in the presence of a malignant alien. "They won't beat me. I'll beat *them*. I can get pregnant again and have another baby; then they'll *have* to give me money. They'll *never* see me broken!"

It was a terrifying announcement. Anger suffused me. To the malignant alien I said, "Don't consider it. If you get pregnant again, that child will be taken away just as Jaimie has been. And that child will grow up, just as Jaimie has done. But I doubt you can get pregnant anyway. You've abused your body far too much."

Andy took the receiver and said, "We're tired, Colleen. You woke us up. Don't phone at such ridiculous hours with the same old whining. Good night." And he hung up.

Colleen then phoned to whine to the traitor Lisa, but her story was different from the one she'd told us. There was no mention of the police or the boyfriend attacking her with a knife. Lisa was sure that was all fabrication, the usual attempt to up the ante when she didn't get what she wanted.

I don't know if we treated that phone call the right way—or the letter that followed it. I shall never know. Were we too curt? Were we too dismissive? At the Banff Men's Conference, Dr. Densmore advised Andy of the importance, always, of making someone like Colleen feel she was still loved and valued even if unacceptable to the family in her present state. We should keep encouraging her to get professional help with both her mental illness and her addiction, but we should never give her the idea that we washed our hands of her entirely. If people like Colleen read that kind of message, he warned, there is a high danger they will "successfully suicide".

Walking that fine line is harrowing. There is risk of sending the wrong message without meaning to. But Dr. Densmore equally emphasized to my husband that parents have to make clear to an adult child such as Colleen that they have their own lives and—unlike poor Bertha in the

Parent Support Group—will not put up with being lied to, manipulated or held perpetual hostage. How can one be sure that a firm yet loving stand is being conveyed and that correct interpretation will be put on that stand by the severely-afflicted BPD mind? The answer is that one can't. One can only do one's best.

The letter arrived by email on April sixth, addressed to me only, and came from Crossroads. So she'd split with the boyfriend—or he'd thrown her out again—and she was back in rehab. It began "Hi, Mum"—spelled with a "u", the way "goody two-shoes" spells it! It talked of being "emotionally broken" rather than defiant, as she'd been on the phone. And, like her telephone calls, it was a litany of lies or self-delusion mingled with self-pity—truly a heartbreaker:

Hi Mum:

I am currently at Crossroads using one of the computers at the library. These past two and a half years have been the toughest of my life, and they seem to only become worse and worse. I have been calling little one nightly, and though she was receptive to my calls and wanted to talk to me at your place, now things have once again changed. Yesterday, she told me not to call her anymore, that I would only fail again once I left, and thus, she didn't want to get her hopes up. Here's the great part: I could send her, you, Lisa, Dad, drug tests that defy this ill-fated rumor of constant relapse, but have doubt what sort of use the truth actually has these days. I told the truth about needing help 8 months after using for the 1st time, it won me my baby taken, no home, and very little to hope for.

I see women all the time, been on crack or heroin for 20 plus years, and they clean up with their families behind them, their children not told half the fairy tales Jaimie's been subjected to, and they want them to have a good life and be good parents. I can't help but ask myself why it is I am so horrible my family believes it better that my Jaimie believe lies, and that they themselves loathe me so much they don't want any part of my sobriety.

I know I haven't done an eighth of what these women have done to their families. I know, or at least used to believe that I'm not a terrible person. So please, Ma, tell me what it is that makes me useless sober??? What is it that refuses me the right to my little girl despite being clean and staying that way for over two years??? Do you want the drug tests? Or does the truth of the situation matter so little they would fail to change anything anyways???

You know we do goals in recovery, and back when I still believed in justice, I had them. I'll get a job, and I'll do whatever it takes…I know clean and sober my family *will support me. Now that the reality is $600/month, cut to $230 once it goes through that I've left him, no money to get a place, disabilities preventing me from full time work, emotionally so broken I can't even begin to imagine working as hard as I can to come home to a bachelor suite with no Jaimie's voice, no sweet little one who makes each day worth it…it all seems impossibly painful, and so undoable.*

I never dreamed this is what my admitting to having a problem, wanting to make Jaimie's life better by getting and staying clean would look like. This is a nightmare I cannot awaken from. I don't understand, because the truth…well, the truth should make you guys proud and happy, not telling me you'll do anything to keep my daughter away from me. What did I do so wrong in wanting to, and succeeding in long-term sobriety to earn your hatred? To earn Jaimie's??? Please, Mum, just tell me, and if you want, I'll stop talking to you too…but I just need to know. I need to understand why…because I still love Jaimie so, so much, and I still love you both…and I honestly believed you'd be proud of me for my sobriety, for leaving him…not wanting to punish me for it again and again and again.

Please, just tell me why??

I love you,

Colleen

The response, written by both of us after much tearful soul-searching, much temptation to yield to the pity she wanted, and great care taken in the wording, is a point-by-point rebuttal of the arguments the letter presents. Is it too hard-hearted and emotionless? I admit we were inured enough by then that it may read that way. Does it harp too much on Colleen's past wrongs? Do we come off sounding as though we bear grudges that we can't get past?

I'll never be able to get inside Colleen's head to know the answers for sure. All I *do* know for sure is that we fired off a copy to Lisa for her feedback before we sent it to Colleen. While not an objective party, Lisa was now a qualified psychologist who knew her sister inside out. We took stock in her opinion. Lisa felt the letter's tone was down-to-earth and forceful, listing the behaviours that had alienated her from us and others and must change, yet not disowning her but saying we still loved her. Ambivalent all the same and torn up inside with torment at my baby's pain, I sent it:

Hi Colleen:

We received your plaintive letter and we decided to answer it carefully and frankly. That your situation is truly sad is undeniable, but the reason it is sad is not that we haven't supported you. Neither is it that you don't, at this time, have Jaimie with you. It is that you are refusing, as always, to admit the truth to yourself and move on.

The truth, to be brutally honest, is that you have never in your life faced up to reality. And reality, as you will remember, is that over the years we have spent vast amounts of both time and money in trying to help you. We were willing to spend more on intensive psychotherapy, but you didn't want any part of that. We poured thousands and thousands of dollars into rent money for a nice apartment in High River so you could make a happy home there for Jaimie. You poisoned your relationship with the people there with your many lies to them about having cancer and MS, presumably to gain sympathy. You trashed the apartment and spent our rent money on drugs, even getting your friend to defraud us out of more money by posing on the phone as your AISH worker. (That's a criminal offense, for which we decided NOT to press charges because you're our daughter.)

And Jaimie has told us that she felt neither safe nor happy at your apartment in High River. Allowing Jaimie to miss over half of her school year in grade 6 and totally ignoring your responsibilities for her home schooling was an abrogation of your duties as a mother. You nearly stole Jaimie's future by these selfish actions. She lost both education and the chance for school friendships. As you know the school psychologist diagnosed Jaimie with depression, a low self-image and a feeling of helplessness. We are so grateful for Dorothy White's efforts to help Jaimie by contacting us about these issues. Since you really do love Jaimie, you should be so too. With all of Lisa's and Shawn's efforts this has now been reversed and Jaimie is a well-adjusted, confident, and happy person.

It is you, not Jaimie, who is living in the fairy-tale world. Jaimie has a practical and pragmatic nature. Counselling has helped her to think for herself and make her own judgments about things, but we have no doubt she would eventually have done that anyway. She is highly intelligent and not subject to "brainwashing". She loves you and is sorry for you, but she has repeatedly expressed to us that she doesn't hold much hope for your recovery because you refuse to get proper help and are always looking for shortcuts. She has also expressed to us that she would not live with you as you are now. We agree with her.

In your letter you refer to Jaimie as "little one" and "my baby". She is neither of those things anymore; she is a teenager, well on her way to becoming a young adult. She gets straight 'A's at school, has lots of friends, and—again, through counselling—has learned not to yield to the guilt trip you've always put her on and to re-claim the life she's entitled to. Do you remember Jaimie herself recently expressing to you on the phone that she considers your thinking she can be brainwashed insulting? We do. We remember her saying it to you while she was here with us.

As for the "support" you think we still owe you, we presume you mean money. Your pattern has always been not to speak to us unless you want money. Even when you were regularly getting money from us while living in High River, you were saying awful things about us to your neighbours there. You also said awful things about us to your friends Pat and Sue. Again, you're living in a fairy tale if you think these facts don't eventually come to light. Furthermore, as we keep telling you, we are now retired and on a fixed income. We have worked hard all our lives to ensure that we'd be okay in our old age. You are an adult of 32. We don't owe you putting ourselves in the poorhouse. We have already given you far, far more than what we owe you—to no avail—and that well is dry.

Our advice to you is to see what you can do about arranging to live in a place with a couple of roommates so you can all put your government incomes towards rent and expenses. This is not a "punishment" but a down-to-earth suggestion based on your present situation. We aren't into "punishing" you—we are just concerned with our own survival and getting on with our own lives. Jaimie's concerns are the same. You should be very proud of her AND grateful to your sister, not nursing grudges over non-existent wrongdoing on her part. True love for a child is selfless, not selfish and possessive. Jaimie's present happiness and success should be cause for your rejoicing in her behalf, not wanting to pull her back into a life where she was depressed, insecure, and guilt-ridden.

We trust this leaves you no ambiguity as to our feelings on the matter. You are still our daughter and yes, we are heartsick over the bad decisions you have made. We haven't given up hoping and praying that you will start making some better decisions, and soon. One of those should be facing the fact that you'll NEVER get back the innocent trusting baby you used to have. That is called LIFE. All mothers lose their babies eventually, because babies become adults.

Move on and begin to establish a life for YOURSELF. Happiness cannot centre on being with just one person, and particularly not your child. Learn to think in terms of developing a good relationship with your young adult daughter. That is reality, and nothing you want or feel you need is going to change it. No doubt your psychologist at Crossroads (whom we would be glad to speak to, should he wish help with background and past history) would tell you this as well, were he aware of these facts.

WE are not punishing you, Colleen; you are punishing yourself. Stop doing that and start trying to build some self-esteem. We know it will involve long-term effort on your part. There is no "quick fix" for a long string of bad decisions, but you'll never fix it at all unless you decide to try.

We fervently and sincerely hope you'll begin to do that.

Love,   Mum and Dad

Colleen's reaction to the letter was probably to leave Crossroads (if that is indeed where she was), find a drug dealer and get stoned. I surmise this because her next call was another "reasonableness spell". She didn't agree with everything our letter said but yes, we were right: she should seek help. Joe held that opinion also. (So she was back with him.) Her counsellor would be glad to meet and talk with us. He would be in touch soon. We didn't hold our breath. And it never happened.

On May ninth, Mother's Day, one of my neighbours left a beautiful card in our mailbox. Another gave me a fervent hug. I shall always be so grateful for the kindness and caring of our neighbours here in Evergreen. Lisa, Jaimie, and Shawn called and sent an exquisite bouquet of flowers. My darling husband gave me chocolates. From Colleen no one heard anything. *About* Colleen, Lisa said she thought her sister was trying to engage yet another lawyer to force the courts to give Jaimie back. The latest "reasonableness spell" had gone the way of its predecessors.

Sunday June thirteenth dawned an ideal day. I rose early and went for a long endorphin-producing bike ride. Weather was perfect for the scheduled church picnic: table-and-chair groupings were set up outdoors; the standard hamburgers and hot dogs were cooked barbecue style; there was an ice-cream stand, balloons, face painting and various races for the kids; and the adults got to visit over pie and squares. It was a day of laughter and high spirits. Only once did I succumb to a wave of sadness when Elaine Mansfield—the mother of Sharon, who had so generously looked after Marley cat for us—put consoling arms around me and whispered in a breaking voice, "I'm one who knows exactly how you feel. My heart bleeds for both our daughters."

I wasn't aware of it yet, but as the two of us held onto and comforted one another on that beautiful picnic day, my baby was already dead.

43. Full Circle and Beyond

And so I end where I began. It is a painful place to be but in truth less painful than all the years I spent agonizing after I'd found out my baby was mentally ill. Her thoughts couldn't torture her any more. Unable to be happy in life, she was at last at peace in death.

When we returned home from the church picnic to Lisa's phone call, I was at first numb. It took me a while to cry and I didn't cry for long. What I *did* do, after only two days, was write the introduction to this book. But then I couldn't carry on writing. The ache was too throbbing, the wound too fresh. I felt the day might arrive when I would be able to write the rest, so I went into "wait and see" mode about the whole project.

Lisa got the call with the news from Joe. He had returned home after a jaunt to buy beer and cigarettes to find Colleen lying unresponsive on the bedroom floor. Colleen had called his cell while he was out and had asked him to come quickly; she needed him. He'd said he'd be there soon and had ended the communication. Sick of Colleen's complaining and constant emergencies, he took his time about going back—something that was plaguing him with remorse.

Joe told the EMT team he was her fiancé, so he was the one to accompany Colleen on the ambulance ride to Royal Columbian Hospital in New Westminster. Attempts to re-start her heart failed and she was declared dead-on-arrival there shortly after one o'clock a.m. Joe agreed to cremation of the remains at government expense because both of them were living on welfare.

Numerous words of consolation were exchanged amongst our family members. Jaimie told me between sobs how she'd been expecting this and just wished she'd had more time to say good-bye to her mom. We got Joe's phone number from Lisa and said we'd call them back later—after all of us had had time to process the shock. We phoned my brother Brian and Andy's brother Steve; both were grief-stricken but semi-prepared, like Jaimie. Steve made a graphically memorable comparison. He said, "It has been like watching a freight train without brakes plunging down a steep hill. You know what's going to happen when it reaches the bottom but you're absolutely powerless to do anything to prevent it." How tragically true!

Finally, we phoned Joe. Andy alone spoke to him, saying we shared his loss and grief. Joe's voice cracked as he admitted he and his fiancée had

had many arguments, always about her heavy drug use. She'd brought drugs into his home, sabotaging his own efforts to free himself of the habit, and she had overdosed several times, causing him to have to drive her to the hospital. He loved her and, like Steve and all of us, had dreaded more and more lately that this was how it would end. And yes, he was consumed with self-blame. Welcome to the club!

I could overhear enough of his voice on the phone to get an impression. He probably has his own mental health issues, which is why he and Colleen were soul mates. But Sid Vicious he isn't. There can be no certainty of course, but I don't believe he ever attacked Colleen with a knife or did "horrible things" to her, any more than we did. I *do* believe what he said about the cause of their fights being Colleen's heavy drug use.

Joe thanked us for getting in touch and said he could not afford the cost of a funeral. If we were going to retrieve the ashes and hold a service ourselves, could he have half the ashes to remember his fiancée by? Of course he could.

When we again spoke to Lisa and Shawn later that day I told Jaimie, "If I were in your shoes, sweetheart, what I'd be feeling right now would be a mixture of guilt and relief. I'd be so sorry to have lost my mom and not to have had a chance to tell her I loved her, but I'd also be relieved to have all the conflict over with and my future settled once and for all. Don't feel guilty about feeling that way, sweetheart. It's a normal and understandable way to feel." I think I was trying to comfort myself as much as my granddaughter. But I came to be glad I'd uttered those words. A couple of weeks afterwards Lisa said to me, "Mum, thank you so much for validating Jaimie's feelings. During one of our walks she told me that you knew *exactly* how she felt. And she realizes none of the blame for this rests on her, which is very liberating for both of us. We're going to continue going to counselling together."

The memorial service was held in August rather than right away. That gave us two months to plan, as a family, what we wanted to do. Andy and I visited Surrey and brought along photos of Colleen at her best—and worst—from which we all made selections for a DVD and a memory board. Remembering Colleen's life was important, but so was being honest. When a person has had happy and productive years on earth it is so logical to memorialize that person with a "celebration of life". For Colleen we held a "recognition"—of the cuteness of her childhood, the ravages that refusing help for her BPD had wrought upon her, and the wonderful gift she has contributed to the world in Jaimie. Supportive friends, ours and some of Lisa's, packed the sanctuary. For her mom's sake, Jaimie summoned sufficient composure to deliver a riveting rendition of Hilary Duff's hit song *Someone's Watching Over Me*, with a picture of Colleen's face projected on the screen behind her. Almost all viewers of the memory board commented upon how pretty Colleen had been—something her own eyes had never for a moment seen in a mirror. Sadly, not a single one of Colleen's peers made an appearance.

Dear Linda and Gordon Hunter (who both joined us in eulogizing our daughter) were by our sides throughout, including at the subsequent interment of our half of the ashes in our church's Memorial Garden. Linda shed as many tears as we, saying, "Colleen called me not long ago. She left a message that she was going through a bad patch and needed to talk. I wasn't home so I didn't get back to her right away. If only…!" But Linda knows as well as we that "if only" was one of the tragic pervasive themes of Colleen's existence.

My diary sums up that day's events with these words: *God bless you, Colleen. We never stopped loving you and hurting for your torment. But you are tormented no more.* Indeed, she lies beside fragrant flowers and a cool fountain and she is overlooked by plaques on the sheltered west-facing wall naming many distinguished departed friends we knew and loved who now share that resting place with her. That she is in such good company at last is a great comfort to us.

The following March we took Jaimie to Hawaii for her school break and we three had a very relaxing and thoroughly enjoyable time there. At fourteen, our granddaughter was a truly beautiful young woman, inside and out. Evenings we had many heart-to-hearts while eating supper out on the lanai. It was then that she finally opened up enough to tell us her mom had known Brad wasn't her father. Her father was someone Colleen knew by first name only—and maybe even *that* wasn't accurate. It doesn't matter.

Jaimie also specified the "unspeakable things" her mom used to tell her about us when she was little (and used to tell others as well): "Mom said that, on a regular basis, you would hold her down by force, Grandma, while Grandpa raped her." Andy and I had been expecting tales of beatings or other punishments perceived as unfair; this made us gasp. It is absolute proof of how rampant Colleen's untreated mental illness was.

Did our daughter actually come to *believe* we'd done those unspeakable things to her? I don't think so. What I do think is that Colleen's overwhelming fear of abandonment made her desperate to own exclusive rights to her child's love and loyalty. And she sought that exclusive ownership by alienating or shutting away her child from any other relationships—with family or at school—that might potentially pose a threat to it. That is classic BPD behaviour.

"But," continued Jaimie, "as terrified as I was the day you took me away, something in me knew, Grandma, that those stories of Mom's weren't true. Both you and Grandpa were always much too kind to me." Bless her heart!

As to the details of our daughter's death, did Colleen intentionally die by her own hand, having finally been swallowed up by those feelings of abandonment? Did the brutal frankness of our answer to her last letter convince her that she had, indeed, lost our love forever? She left no suicide note, so we'll never be sure of the answers.

We do, however, have the coroner's post-mortem examination report and toxicology report. Both list the immediate cause of death as "acute Oxycodone, Amitriptyline (prescription medication for depression) and Methadone toxicity". The levels of these (and other anti-depressants) present in her blood were more than high enough to stop her heart. Andy and I didn't need the coroner's report to know that an overdose is what killed her, but confirmation in writing from a medical expert settles the matter for good.

Here is my considered opinion as Colleen's mother. My daughter's severe and unchecked BPD, which led her into deep drug addiction, ultimately brought her to the point where, when she took her last hit, she honestly didn't care whether she lived or died. That is what severe and unchecked BPD does to a person.

And that is why sufferers of BPD—mild, moderate or severe—*must* seek treatment. It is too late for my daughter. It is not too late for BPD sufferers today.

44. Identifying BPD

Modern thinking attributes a lot of the old stories about people being "possessed by the devil" to mental illness. Mason and Krieger mention in their book the reaction of non-BPD people toward BPD behaviour: the sense—identical to mine about Colleen—that the loved one's body has been taken over by an alien. It would be accurate to say that our family lost Colleen and grieved her loss long before the day she actually died.

How does one prevent such a loss before it's too late? It is a question being probed more and more today by the medical profession from both a medicinal and a psychiatric perspective.

As previously mentioned, various imaging techniques have shown subtle anatomical differences in the BPD brain as compared to the normal brain. PET scans, which measure brain activity, have shown irregularities and "blocks" in the neural pathways between one area of the brain and another, so that the two areas literally don't communicate. This may explain the "splitting" or black-and-white thinking symptomatic of the disorder: places are either wonderful or horrible; people are either villains or saints, and so forth. The day may come when a doctor is able to say to a newborn's parents, "Mr. and Mrs. Smith, your baby cries excessively and shows an abnormally high startle response, which could indicate a predisposition to mental illness. We'd like to do some imaging and scanning of her brain so that we can repair those indicators if we find them." That day is not yet here.

However, even though as far back as three-thousand years ago notes about individuals with BPD-like behaviour have been found in the writings of Homer, Hippocrates and others,[18] huge strides have *lately* been made towards recognizing and treating the specific symptoms of BPD—lately, as in since Colleen's birth in 1978. As stated in an earlier chapter, the term "borderline personality disorder" came into official use in 1980 with its inclusion as an identifiable illness in the third edition of the *Diagnostic and Statistical Manual* of the American Psychiatric Association (DSM-III). More mental health professionals began to pay

---

18 Friedel, Robert O., M.D. 2004. *Borderline Personality Disorder Demystified: The Essential Guide to Understanding and Living with BPD.* New York, NY: Marlowe & Company, Avalon Publishing Group Inc.: 46

attention to educating themselves about the disorder. Speculation that such famous figures as Abraham Lincoln (who suffered rampant mood swings and periods of deep depression), Virginia Woolf (whose feelings of emptiness and loneliness led her to commit suicide), Vincent Van Gogh (who in the throes of perceived rejection cut off his own ear) and most recently Princess Diana (whose binge eating and other self-destructive behaviours have led biographical author Sally Bedell Smith to say Diana demonstrated "compelling evidence" of having BPD)[19] has also brought the condition to public attention.

Princess Diana provides an excellent example of just how poised, well-adjusted and capable BPD sufferers can appear for limited periods of time. Colleen too was such a superb actress that McMan Centre's Darlene Petrie, who found her so many places to live over the years, says: "I never saw that side of Colleen. Of course I knew there were problems because landlord after landlord evicted her, but to me she was always pleasant and charming. I loved her." Darlene tells me she still can't read this book without crying.

It is that ability on the part of BPD sufferers to present a good public face that causes well-meaning people like Maureen Pysklywec to conclude the sufferer must be the victim—in Colleen's case, of faulty parenting. Author and mental-health educator Valerie Porr labels this the "raised eyebrow effect": *What are you talking about? I've never seen her like that.*[20] Because their own observations give them a contrary picture, outsiders like social workers—and even judges ruling on child guardianship cases—often distrust the claims of those close to BPD sufferers.

If I hadn't had a "normal" child in Lisa, I might well have completely bought into the intimation that Colleen's troubles were all to do with my incompetent parenting. To a degree I bought into that anyway. It is the reading that has become available since Colleen's death that has at last alleviated, if not removed, my self-blame.

BPD sufferers come closest to achieving the happiness that so eludes them when they are the focus of attention—as Colleen was the day she pulled the Lite-Brite swallowing stunt. They crave the spotlight and seek ways to grab it, probably because it temporarily fills up that great hole

19 Bedell Smith, Sally. 2000. *Diana in Search of Herself: Portrait of a Troubled Princess.* New York, NY: Signet Books

20 Porr, Valerie, M.A., *Overcoming Borderline Personality Disorder: A Family Guide for Healing and Change* (New York, N.Y.: Oxford University Press, 2010): 12-13

of emptiness and isolation inside them. When the spotlight shifts from them to others they become testy and upset (as did Colleen at Disneyland after Goofy and Pluto had shaken her hand and moved on) and they seek to regain it. Because they view their offspring as extensions of themselves, having their children in the spotlight (as when Jaimie sang at Lisa's wedding) achieves for them the same result. This accounts for Colleen's dotingly fond expression in the video, which disappeared moments after the song was over. The doctor on call the night our daughter had her stomach pumped—the one who irritated me by referring to Colleen as a "drama queen"—had a point after all. In fact it has been postulated that Hollywood, and the theatre in general, contain a considerably higher percentage of BPD sufferers than the two percent ascribed to the general population.

That very acting ability is often the worst enemy of BPD sufferers. Because they present such a poised and competent outer façade, others who associate with them for any length of time are bewildered and shocked when the façade collapses. And because the disease has no effect on intelligence, parents, partners or employers of BPD sufferers often become angry and succumb to a "you ought to know better" approach in dealing with them. The fact is, BPD sufferers *do* know better. They know their conduct is frequently considered inappropriate, harmful, even immoral. Their intellect tells them that. But they can't get the part of their brain that controls their impulses and emotions to fall into line. It's not that they won't. It's that they *can't*.

Years ago when my dad was hospitalized for heart bypass surgery, his roommate during recovery was a man who'd had a stroke. Sometimes the man would spontaneously burst into tears even while apologizing for the behaviour. "I know I shouldn't be crying," he would protest, "but I just can't help it." The stroke's damage had done a "disconnect" on the neural pathways between the area of his brain controlling rational thinking and the area controlling impulse and emotion. A BPD sufferer has that "disconnect" in those pathways from birth.

Shame is mortal enemy number one for BPD sufferers. Hopelessness is mortal enemy number two. They make frantic efforts to appear "normal" and keep people from discovering their true selves. Mason and Krieger talk of the "flat facial expression" (Colleen's brittle smile) and the insistence that "everything's fine" even when it obviously isn't.

They also make frantic attempts to *be* normal. This makes them especially prone to heavy street drug, opiate prescription and alcohol use, because these substances stimulate higher levels of dopamine and serotonin in their brains (which are abnormally low in these chemicals), temporarily relieving their severe emotional pain and giving them better control over their impulses. They are *self-medicating*.

Of course this relief is short-lived. Even worse, says Dr. Robert Friedel (Distinguished Clinical Professor of Psychiatry at Virginia Commonwealth University, professor emeritus at the University of Alabama at Birmingham, and author of the book *Borderline Personality Demystified: An Essential Guide for Understanding and Living with BPD*), the habitual use of these substances drastically decreases their reasoning ability and ultimately leads to a dramatic worsening of the symptoms of BPD.

Andy and I were angry with Colleen for her addictive behaviour. In our response to her letter, we refer to the "long string of bad decisions" she made. The more of this post-Colleen research I read, the more I realize that tendency to alcohol and drug abuse isn't so much a "bad decision" as a predictable outcome of having the disease: a continual effort to make themselves feel better. Soon they are in a Catch 22. Rationally they know they are killing themselves but emotionally these substances fill the void inside them. *That* is their reality.

"Get real!" is a phrase we often hurl at those we're engaging in an argument. It's a phrase I hurled at Colleen many a time. While she was growing up, numerous psychologists, psychiatrists and concerned friends advised Colleen that she had better learn how to deal with reality. In our own response to Colleen's last letter (the response that will forever plague me with questions about the role it played in her death), Andy and I told her forcefully that she'd never succeed in moving on with her life unless she faced reality. And then we brutally spelled out for her what reality was.

But we were talking about *our* reality. BPD reality is entirely different. It is, indeed, like living in the Land of Oz. It has no frame of reference to "normal" reality because it has never known "normal" reality. When Colleen said she didn't agree with parts of our letter, she couldn't explain why and she didn't even try.

Colleen, I think I now know why. Every time I scolded you while standing in Kansas, I assumed you were standing in Kansas beside me. I assumed our frame of reference was the same, which is the reason your acting so differently from what *I* considered logical and right made no sense to me at all. Now I realize that no matter how loudly or angrily I scolded you from Kansas, you couldn't begin to understand me—because you lived in Oz.

Photograph montages on the following pages represent the miniscule percentage we possess where the growing child and the adult Colleen is actually smiling. They have been chosen first, to illustrate how lovely, though often forced or empty-eyed, that smile could be; second, to show how her weight fluctuated with negative consequences to her general health; and finally (despite that Colleen never for a moment believed it about herself) to portray how pretty BOTH our daughters are!

1. *One of many such photos: Lisa, aged 4 holding a screaming one-month-old Colleen*
2. *Colleen, age 2*
3. *Thrilled to be walking with Minnie Mouse in Disneyland: a rare REAL smile*
4. *At Lisa's elementary school graduation, age 7*
5. *Brief interlude as a Brownie, age 10*

6. Colleen (left) with Lisa and our Sheltie "Marmite"
7. Colleen's elementary school graduation, age 11
8. School photo from her brief time at Okotoks Junior High, age 13
9. Colleen (left), age 14, with Mom and Lisa in Stratford, Ont.

10. *School photo for Alternative High School, age 15*

11. *Colleen (left), age 17, with Mom and Grandma*

12. *Colleen, age 19, at Jaimie's baptism*

13. *Family photo; Colleen (left), age 20*

14. *Colleen, age 21, with Jaimie*

15. *A rare happy expression captured as bride and groom kiss while Jaimie looks on*

16. *Walking down the aisle at Lisa's wedding*

17. Colleen (left), age 27, in downward slide
18. Age 31: in and out of rehab
19. Colleen, age 32, just a few months before she died
20. Jaimie, age 15 with Grandma and Grandpa in Hawaii the following March
21. Jaimie, age 16, with her new family Lisa and Shawn: the 'happy ending'

45. Treating BPD

If I could talk to Colleen today, I would tell her how very sorry I am that I didn't understand her as well as I do now. But I would still insist she learned to help herself deal with "reality", and I would make the best effort I could to find some area of communication between her reality and mine. There are experts now who would be able to help me with that.

Ideally, I would start this process when she was very young, as soon as she began to demonstrate behaviours far outside the norm—behaviours like the Lite-Brite incident, the drawing she made of the gory accident, and her fascination with death. I would find her a mental-health specialist not so worried about stigmatizing labels as about instituting a plan of action for changing her thought processes, based on the possibility that she was mentally ill and aimed at helping her combat the illness. There are far more of those today than there were when Colleen was growing up.

The DSM-IV-TR (2004) states that children with borderline traits lasting over a year should be treated for BPD while the brain is still developing, and the earlier the better. Even when impaired in certain ways, the brain possesses an amazing quality known as *neuroplasticity*: that is, the ability to re-program itself. Experts now believe that a child born with a brain predisposed to develop BPD will have a much higher chance of developing the disease if certain *developmental risk factors* occur such as trauma, parental abuse, or abuse by peers at school. Colleen may have experienced the latter—just because of the way children are with anybody "different"—but it's more likely, in my opinion, that *her* reality perceived as trauma and abuse (at our parental hands as well as at the hands of other people) that which the rest of us don't, and she lacked the coping tools to help her normalize that perception. Ultimately her "emotional hemophilia" caused her to bleed to death.

I love Eleanor Roosevelt's saying: "No one can make you feel inferior without your consent." It's worthwhile that *everybody* remember that, not just sufferers of BPD. As Pavlov taught his dogs to salivate at the sound of a bell, so the BPD sufferer can be taught techniques to help regulate his thought processes and emotional dysfunction at times when they threaten to overwhelm him. (And before the sufferer concludes—as I know Coleen would—that I'm demeaning him by comparing him to dogs, I simply make the point that we all demonstrate certain Pavlovian responses. If the BPD sufferer can learn from a young age to apply Pavlov's principle to his disease, he can do a lot towards helping himself.) And suppose you teach such coping techniques to a person with a non-BPD brain? Where is the harm? They are good life-navigating strategies anyway.

Psychotherapy Techniques Aimed Specifically at BPD

As Kreisman and Straus point out in their book *I Hate You—Don't Leave Me*, it is important to remember that BPD is a serious illness, not a wilful attempt to get attention. It is useless to get angry or to cajole and plead with the borderline sufferer to change; without help and motivation he cannot easily modify his behaviour.[21] However, this does not imply that the borderline sufferer is helpless and should not be held responsible for his conduct. Actually, the opposite is true. Only by being held responsible and by being taught to accept that responsibility can he move towards leading a normal life. Psychotherapy targeted at achieving this end has recently come a long way.

The borderline sufferer's greatest obstacle to change is his tendency to evaluate in absolute extremes. Kreisman and Straus use a poker analogy: unwilling to play the hand he's dealt, the borderline sufferer keeps folding every time, losing his ante, waiting to be dealt four aces. If he cannot be assured of winning, he won't play out the hand. Improvement comes when he learns to accept the hand for what it is (as we all must do in life, no matter what hand we're dealt) and recognize that, skillfully played, he can still win.

Marsha Linehan, PhD, Professor of Psychology and Director of Behavioural Research Therapy Clinics at the University of Washington, has had a remarkable life. When I began to read about the experimental work she conducted in the nineteen eighties and nineties with hundreds of severe BPD patients tagged "hopeless", I asked myself how she arrived at knowing what to do and where to start. Many who tried to help Colleen, including medical professionals and trained psychotherapists, freely admitted they were unsure of what to do or where to start with our daughter. The way to helping her was blocked by too many smoke-screens through which they could not batter. Marsha Linehan seems to

21 Kreiseman, Jerold J., MD, and Hal Straus. 2010. *I Hate You—Don't Leave Me: understanding the borderline personality*. New York, NY: Penguin Group, 127

have found a way to batter through these obstacles.

Linehan's patients have been tracked by researchers since the eighties and nineties. Compared with patients not receiving her therapy, "significantly more" of them demonstrate that they have been able to overcome suicidal thoughts and feelings; far fewer of them are hospitalized. Some even claim they are "cured". Her treatment, known as *dialectical behaviour therapy* (DBT) has been applied to other types of mental illness as well but was developed especially for people with BPD and is today regarded as the "gold standard" in BPD treatment.

Why did Linehan focus on BPD? Why did she pursue a patient group consisting of the very worst cases? In a *New York Times* article published on June 23 2011, she bares her soul. "I was in hell," she is quoted as saying, "And I made a vow: when I get out, I'm going to come back and get others out of here." Linehan is to the BPD world what Helen Keller was to the world of deafness and blindness: she suffers from it herself.

This is huge. She brings to patients a background much like their own: rebellious, often in trouble, inclined to tantrums in which she banged her head hard against walls and floors, prone to slashing her own arms, institutionalized, given electroshock treatments—and declared *hopeless* unless she stopped putting up smokescreens and decided to accept help.

And what made her suddenly able to do the impossible: to pull herself up by her own bootstraps? She attributes it to a flash of insight, like a blinding vision—a vision that suddenly made her able to accept herself as she was, yet also able to visualize working towards achieving the functional self she wanted to become. Some might call that a miracle. No matter what we call it, it resulted in her doing extensive formal study in the behavioural sciences and becoming an expert on her own disorder. She does not call herself "cured" but she has learned how to keep the symptoms at bay, so that she is able to lead not only a normal productive life but a highly distinguished one.

Linehan's *preoccupation* with her disorder has led to her making it her *occupation*, her life's work. This indeed, in simplest terms, is the principle behind her dialectical behaviour therapy: to make it one's life's work to keep the symptoms of BPD at bay. The more practiced one becomes at doing this by applying the techniques she teaches, the more the impaired but neoplastic brain re-programs itself. It isn't so very different from teaching oneself to do intricate tasks with one's feet if one is born without hands. As a non-BPD person, I can only say that I'm sure it is just as challenging, maybe more so. Yet if we do them over and over enough times, certain skills or tasks tend to become easier and easier for all of us, until the brain ultimately files them in its "second nature" category. And at that point we can ease up with concentrating on them quite so hard and get on with living our lives.

Dr. Blaise A. Aguirre, M.D., in his 2007 book *Borderline Personality in Adolescents* cites a 2006 study made by Knut Schell, M.D. and Sabine Herpertz, M.D. that investigated brain changes after BPD patients who showed significant improvement had undergone dialectical behaviour therapy. Five MRI brain scans were applied to each of six female BPD patients while the patients attended a twelve-week inpatient treatment program. The results were compared to the MRIs of six non-BPD female subjects. They found that patients who got better on DBT showed less activity—or closer-to-normal activity—in the parts of their brains associated with high arousal levels (the amygdala and the hippocampus). In other words their brains showed a decrease of activity in the parts that overreact to stress. DBT, states Aguirre, provides the best hope at this time for the treatment of adolescents with BPD, especially at the hands of a skilled, compassionate, and flexible treatment team.[22]

Auckland University psychiatrist Roy Krawitz cites a 2005 study by Zanarini *et al* that followed for six years people attending a private U.S. mental health service known for its BPD treatment. At six-year follow-up, 68% of those initially diagnosed with BPD no longer met diagnostic criteria for BPD, and only 6% of those had ever relapsed! The overwhelming majority (94%) of those that recovered *stayed* recovered.[23] Again, this is huge.

Essentially, Dialectical Behaviour Therapy teaches clients to accept themselves as they are—which then enables them to start work on making changes to their behaviour. It involves weekly group skills training sessions to learn how to tolerate distress, improve interpersonal skills,

22 Aguirre, Blaise A., M.D. 2007. *Borderline Personality Disorder in Adolescents: A Complete Guide to Understanding and Coping when Your Adolescent has BPD*. Beverly, Massachusetts: Fair Winds Press, 167

23 Krawitz, Roy and Wendy Jackson. 2008. *Borderline Personality Disorder: All the Information You Need, Straight from the Experts*. New York: Oxford University Press, 41 - 42

and become more *mindful* or introspectively aware, on an objective level, of your emotions without letting them consume you. Many eastern religions such as Buddhism practice mindfulness as a discipline and BPD sufferers find this practice tremendously helpful, as international speaker and advocate for BPD recovery Kiera Van Gelder points out in her 2010 book *The Buddha and the borderline: a memoir*. Clients also meet weekly with an individual therapist and fill out daily diary forms. The term *dialectical* refers to the bringing-together of apparently conflicting views, an attempt at resolution between the two worlds of Kansas and Oz. Rather than colliding, these two worlds try to find a middle ground and work out an understanding of one another. Clients who for years may have felt invalidated and somehow *bad* through being told things like "you ought to know better" or "get real" at last come to terms with their identity as people with the biological predisposition to experience emotion more intensely than the rest of the population—which is neither "good" nor "bad". It just *is*.

I talked to two DBT specialists in Calgary. Donna Hughes, registered psychiatric nurse and Executive/Clinical Director of Inner Solutions (a private clinic in the southwest, established in 2003) refers to the emotional log jam experienced by BPD sufferers, which overpowers and severely impedes the functional efficacy of the prefrontal cortex. Learning to control the logs in such a jam before they pile up to the point of blocking the river-flow of reason is the aim of DBT treatment: an effective analogy.

Early treatment is the most desirable, says Donna, but it is never too late. And when someone asks for help, *immediate* treatment is called for, not the frustration of being put on a waiting list. Inner Solutions has a staff of six highly-trained specialists and no waiting list. The clinic offers DBT to anyone suffering with emotional dysregulation, regardless of diagnosis. It also offers research-based MBSR (Mindfulness Based Stress Reduction), ongoing skills-practice sessions for "DBT Graduates", and an eight-week support and educational program for "Family and Friends of Persons with BPD". Some of these programs require a single diagnostic assessment session first, to determine where the client is most suitably placed. All come at a substantial cost, befitting the training and expertise of the specialists.

Cost, however, should not necessarily be a deterrent. Yes, financial constraints do impose a limitation on prospective clients of a private clinic. Without insurance coverage, the fees involved may indeed be a daunting prospect. But most insurance companies nowadays, thank heaven, treat mental illness in the same way as any other illness and will offset or totally cover the fees. Inner Solutions has a fine reputation and is well worth pursuing as a treatment option.

The second clinic I visited offers services covered under Alberta Health Care. Janice Wingrave, Clinical Supervisor of the Dialectical Behaviour Therapy Program at downtown Calgary's Sheldon M. Chumir Health Centre, paints for me an inspiring picture of the help and support available today under our Health Care system. "We began in 2002 and were a full clinic by 2004," says Janice. "We provide individual therapy on a once-a-week basis and there are four skills groups running continuously, offering twenty-four weeks of skills training. There are ten individual therapists and four psychiatrists attached to the team. Each client has an individual therapist as well as a psychiatrist who monitors any medications required and enhances skills acquisition and generalization. Yes, there's a waiting list—about four months at present—but we're trying to whittle it down more and more." That's impressive.

"No one would deny that recovery is a time-consuming process requiring dedication and hard work, especially at first," continues Janice with a lovely smile. "But take a look at some of the testimonials we've received since we began this. It brings tears to the eyes."

She handed me a book full of informal notes, most of them handwritten. I found it very moving that she would share these with me, and even more moving that she would offer to obtain from their authors permission to use some of them in this book. And yes, it does bring tears to the eyes, especially to *my* all-too-vulnerable and sorrow-drowned eyes. Allow me to introduce you to the brightness and the eloquence of the BPD mind: a mind so worth being *rescued* instead of ravaged! Read on about what has emerged on the scene just a fraction too late to save my baby:

I started off feeling the world was nothing and I was worth nothing. I gained the world and learned to accept myself and others.

I can't find words to express what a difference DBT has made in my life. The skills I've learned will stay with me forever.

I want to thank you all. I never thought it was possible, but I honestly DO have a life worth living. I am forever grateful.

I came to this program without hope of ever getting better. I didn't think life would

*ever be OK. Now, having gone through the DBT process, I understand that I don't
have to REACT to my emotions all the time; I can just sit and experience them.*

*Before I came, I was a mere shell of the fully-functioning person I now am. For
the first time, I have found stability.*

*I had all the borderline traits when I came. DBT made me feel connected and
grounded.*

*My life has changed profoundly. Thank you for helping me find peace and joy
and for teaching me what I needed to learn to develop a foundation of Mindfulness,
Emotional Regulation, Distress Tolerance, and Interpersonal Relationship Skill. I
continue to have challenges but I now have the tools within me to troubleshoot and to
effectively take care of myself.*

*I was told when I came that the DBT team would help me build a life worth living.
I thought that was a laugh. Nothing had ever worked before. Now, two-and-a-half
years later, there has actually come a day when I can say I'm HAPPY. I DO have
a life worth living now. I can never thank you enough.*

This group saved my life…

*When you first met me, I was a blubbering mess who could have self-destructed at
any time. Now I feel self-assured and able to face whatever life throws at me.*

*To anyone just entering the program: stick with it! DBT really does work. I no
longer have to take any medications; I can control and manage my emotions on my
own.*

*I did quite a bit of research on BPD before starting DBT. In my wildest dreams
I never thought it would change my life so much.*

*When I came, back in 2007, I was desperate. I felt guilty and angry. I hated myself
and wanted to die. I did not want to attend DBT classes, but forced myself. Thanks
to the tools they provided me, I have created a new, healthy and positive me. I feel in
control. I know about boundaries: something foreign to me before. I've learned how to
laugh and have fun and feel REALLY happy. Thanks to DBT, my children have
been returned to my care. It's okay to be diagnosed with BPD if it helps a person to
get into DBT and learn to create a better, healthier life.*

And lastly, from a departing therapist:

*It has been nine years of hard work and I would not trade it for the world. The
transformations that I have witnessed are truly rewarding and inspiring. I believe in
DBT and the team of professionals that deliver it. The spirit of the skills will live
on as I promise to share, educate and advocate for the program and clients everywhere
I go.*

Such testimonials evoke a visceral reaction that all the dry clinical treatment-advocacy statements in the world cannot achieve. Understandably, there are the doubting Thomases among medical professionals who say DBT has been around too short a time for any *real* long-term evidence of permanent recovery to exist. Yet while the stubborn empiricist in all of us craves sufficiently longstanding and concrete scientific evidence—some of which is certainly now being collected—the hopeful mother or spouse or child of a sufferer truly rejoices in declarations like those quoted above.

Therapies other than DBT have also appeared on the scene, and I give them less space only because I know less about them. *Mentalization Based Therapy* (MBT), developed by British psychoanalyst Peter Fonagy and professor of psychoanalysis Anthony Bateman, is designed to help BPD sufferers focus on distinguishing between *their* thoughts and those of others, recognizing how thoughts, feelings and desires are linked to behaviour. Its goals include achieving better relationships with others through improved control over emotions and behaviours. Then there is *Schema Therapy*, developed by psychologist and author Dr. Jeffrey E. Young. "Schemas" are entrenched self-defeating patterns which the therapy trains patients to access and then turn off. And popular in the Netherlands is the group-treatment program *STEPPS*, which stands for "Systems Training for Emotional Predictability and Problem Solving". Like DBT, *STEPPES* has a skills-training approach in which family members equally participate, learning how to reinforce and support the patient's new skills.

Regardless of the therapy a patient pursues or the clinic he attends, it is encouraging to know that resources aplenty exist today for those living with mental illness and those trying to adapt to living with a mentally ill person. It was Janice Wingrave who told me about TARA (Treatment and Research Advancements, National Association for Personality Disorder). Its online home page is full of the latest information on BPD, as well as on available reading materials, upcoming support workshops, and rapidly-growing branch chapters, both in the U.S. and Canada. She also referred me to NEA-BPD (National Education Alliance for Borderline Personality Disorder) which works to raise public awareness, provide education, and promote BPD research. At Donna Hughes's clinic—displaying brochures on publicly-funded help organizations right alongside its own—I picked up a folder on the United-Way-sponsored PSA (Parent Support Association) Calgary, which has been assisting parents with parent-youth conflict since 1982, and which currently offers parenting workshops, parent coaching, and abundant mental health information. *Knowledge* is ultimately the greatest BPD treatment of them all. Knowledge is power! And the borders limiting knowledge about BPD are daily being bulldozed in momentous proportions.

Medications

Expert agreement at present, states Roy Krawitz, is that psychotherapy is the primary treatment for BPD. The patient, along with the therapist, must take a proactive role in his own recovery, with medication to assist. No single magic pill works for all sufferers, but a range of medications, taken as prescribed, *have* been shown effective in reducing the BPD brain's difficulty with regulating impulsivity, anger, and emotional instability. Patient response to medication treatment is variable, but no one would dispute that a sufferer can engage far more capably in his recovery process if the edge is taken off some of his disabling symptoms.

The medications in common current use that have been shown statistically to be of some benefit in research studies are SSRIs (selective serotonin reuptake inhibitors, the most commonly prescribed antidepressants), newer antipsychotic medications such as olanzapine and aripiprazole, the anticonvulsant topiramate, and the dietary supplement omega 3.[24] Of all these, I fall on omega 3 with a glad cry. What scares me most about the others is that they are prescription mood-altering drugs put directly into the hands of those most inclined to abuse prescription mood-altering drugs. Is it just my English teacher's warped sense of black humour or is there a flabbergasting irony there?

Far be it for me to say a patient should be deprived of a substance with the capacity to alleviate his distressing symptoms, or to make any blanket statements at all about medication usage for helping the mentally ill. I am not an expert. I will say this, however: that there is controversy about the medication question even amongst those who *are* experts. And I will further say that, as an anguished mother reading a toxicology report that confirmed her worst nightmares, I have black-and-white proof that prescription mood-altering drugs are what killed my baby.

As for omega 3, the fact it is a dietary supplement rather than a prescription drug makes one feel far more comfortable. Indeed, certain fatty acids found in omega 3 are thought to render brain cell membranes more

24 Ibid, 43 - 45

fluid and to improve communication between brain cells.[25] A 2003 study by Zanarini and Frankenburg, cited in the *American Journal of Psychiatry*, states that "omega 3 fatty acids such as eicosapentaenoic acid (EPA) and docosahexaenoic acid (DHA), which are commonly found in seafood, have beneficial effects and none of the adverse side effects commonly associated with pharmacotherapy."[26] The authors conducted an eight-week, placebo-controlled, double-blind study on thirty female patients with moderate to severe BPD. Twenty subjects were randomly assigned one gram of EPA a day; ten subjects were given a placebo. Ninety percent of those in both groups completed all eight weeks of the trial. And what was the result? EPA was shown to be significantly superior to the placebo in diminishing aggression as well as severity of BPD symptoms. This particular omega 3 fatty acid, conclude the researchers, may be a safe and effective form of therapy for women with moderate to severe BPD. And Dr. Rod Densmore, in a recent conversation with me, declared himself an omega 3 proponent, stating his opinion that those with a familial tendency to BPD and/or other mental illness should, ideally, take regular doses of omega 3 from as early an age as possible.

More studies are being done, and some problems exist. For one thing, those with seafood allergies would require an alternative source. For another—as Dr. Densmore points out—the omega 3 capsules one buys at a regular pharmacy contain not only EPA (in a much smaller dosage than one gram, typically 180 mg.) and DHA but also a number of non-medicinal ingredients such as gelatin, glycerin, and tocopherol (vitamin E). Depending on the brand bought, one might have to take anywhere from six to ten capsules a day (the label directions read two) to get the same amount of EPA given to patients in the test and found to be effective. Mega-dosing to that degree risks producing other conditions that can compromise one's general health.

In my view, the moral of the story is this: unless part of a program carefully supervised by medical experts, one shouldn't monkey around with mega-doses of omega 3. Studies and trials are still too few and too new. But one *should* be hopeful that continuing research in the omega 3

25 Aguirre, Blaise A., M.D. 2007. *Borderline Personality Disorder in Adolescents: A Complete Guide to Understanding and Coping when Your Adolescent has BPD.* Beverly, Massachusetts: Fair Winds Press, 198

26 Zanarini, Mary C., Ed.D. and Frances R. Frankenburg M.D. *American Journal of Psychiatry*, Jan. 2003 Vol. 160, No. 1: 167 - 169

area will yield some safe alternative, symptom-relieving treatment courses for sufferers of BPD and related mental illnesses.

As a mother profoundly affected by the results of unchecked BPD in her child, my final words on treatment begin with this self-evident but necessary statement: neither the patient nor those close to him will get better without being *proactive*. No amount of counselling—whether one suffers directly or by association from BPD—will do any good if one resists getting actively involved with the recovery process and *sticking with* the recovery regimen. God knows, that's easier said than done. Grief and despair generate the desire for pat answers that don't involve any exertion at all on one's own part. They also make one want to curl up and retreat into a cocoon. Periodic resistance to help, as well as cocoon dwelling in times of crisis can be part of human tendency in general, never mind BPD tendency. But nature demonstrates that those who fail to break out of cocoons are destined not to survive.

Current North American society offers unfortunate *encouragement* of exactly that unhealthy cocoon-dwelling habit. Gone are the days when most people lived in small extended-family towns or villages and everybody looked out for everybody else. Today it is the norm to dwell in a high-rise condo, habituate the workplace from dawn till dusk, keep one's doors locked at all times, and never see one's neighbours. Even in suburbia, where *we* live, establishing any sort of regular neighbourly contact takes a major effort.

And the workplace itself is very different from what it once was; employees typically spend the entire day closeted in cubicles and interacting mainly with computers. Not long ago, Andy and I sat in a restaurant, adjacent to a table full of workers on their lunch break. Did they relax and engage one another socially? No. Most sat hunched over, madly texting cyber-buddies or business associates on their cell phones. The multi-lane, instant-access information and communication highway spawned by today's technology is marvellous, amazing—and very conducive to *actual* isolation (not just feelings of it), less face-to-face, flesh-and-blood contact, and an "always-in-a-hurry, no-time-to-talk" general attitude.

Will this contribute to a higher percentage and a greater severity of mental health problems in future populations? I fear it might, and I know I am not alone in my fear.

An effort must be made to seek out an environment that provides the missing "it-takes-a-whole-village-to-raise-a-child" philosophy that used to be present in mellower, kinder social eras. Andy and I found it in our church, in Peter O'Brien's Parent Support Group, and in some of the resources and facilities I have listed in Appendix II of this book. Where to find it will differ for individuals to the same degree individuals themselves differ.

An effort must also be made to find self-validating avenues and activities in order to combat the inevitable frustration, bitterness and guilt produced by dealing with BPD, whether directly as a patient or indirectly as family members of a patient. Again, those avenues will differ for individuals to the same degree individuals themselves differ. One of *my* avenues has been to research and to write this book. Its writing hasn't cured my grief over Colleen's death or my episodic self-blame over the final letter we wrote her. But it *has* been immeasurably therapeutic. It has renewed my appreciation for a family and for friends who have stood by me through it all. It has increased my knowledge about, and empathy for, what my poor darling child suffered throughout those years. And most importantly, it has made me realize that sometimes you have to create your own happy endings.

The lovely young woman Jaimie has become would make Colleen proud. She is well-adjusted, thoughtful, and grateful for every day. Two summers ago, when we made what is now our annual visit to Lisa and Shawn in Surrey, she shared with us a speech she wrote in response to a school assignment on someone who has greatly influenced her life. She was then age fourteen; it was four months after our trip with her to Hawaii. That speech made us all wipe our eyes. With her permission, I share it with you here:

A person to whom I owe much gratitude and admire greatly is my mother. Although she died of cardiac arrest last summer, she has left an indelible imprint on both my life and my heart. She taught me to read at a very young age, and much of my skills in the language arts I owe to her. She was a loving woman with a great sense of humour. She taught me to laugh at my mistakes and carry on. She taught me to be strong and never let anyone push me around. Although drugs clouded her mind towards the end, she was a very intelligent woman who would devour books at a rapid rate. She was a good mother when I was young, always feeding me healthy foods and passing on knowledge to me. She always told me that if I had not been born, she might not still be alive. As soon as she knew she was with child, she stopped the drugs and the smoking to ensure my life was safe. Though there were rough times later, where money was scant and living in squalor became the norm, I remember the woman past the pills, a woman who loved me so much but thought so little of herself. The rough patches in my life have made me stronger and the good times have made me smarter. I can see past the heartache and pain I've endured and realize just how lucky I was to have a mother like her.

Wow! What an epitaph! How amazingly resilient and stubbornly optimistic in the face of the worst possible occurrences the young can be! Colleen's BPD reality perceived her positive contribution to the world to be nonexistent. It further perceived that she had lost her beloved child for good. Jaimie's eloquent tribute offers conclusive proof—if Colleen could only have known it!—that neither was ever the case.

And there's a lesson to be had there, as well.

Pulling our precious granddaughter from the wreckage of Colleen's last few months on this earth cost us twenty thousand dollars in legal fees. Stepping into the role of Jaimie's new parents—as they unhesitatingly did—cost Lisa and Shawn a major lifestyle adjustment, an immense sacrifice of time and lost wages fighting Colleen for custody, and untold emotional stress. Once again I must end where I began: with my dear departed mum's words to me upon Lisa's birth nearly forty years ago now—words about the huge outlay of time, emotion and money involved with raising a child. They are words I have never forgotten, and words that apply in spades to the rescue of our precious Jaimie.

It was worth every tear, every minute, and every penny.

Acknowledgements

Without help from the following people, this book could not have been written.

I shall forever be indebted to our good friends Rev. Gordon Hunter and Rev. Linda C. Hunter. These people were always willing to go "above and beyond" in reaching out to offer help to our troubled daughter. They have been by our sides offering continual support, right up to and throughout, Colleen's memorial service and the interment of the ashes. When they told me they'd both be honoured to write separate "Foreword" passages for this book, each from his/her own distinct perspective, I was thrilled.

Similarly, I was thrilled to re-make the acquaintance of Darlene Petrie, Program Manager of McMan Youth, Family, and Community Services. Darlene deserves her own special medal for persistence in searching out, over and over, compatible and kind landlords for our daughter.

Peter J. O'Brien, MSW, RSW, family therapist for the Foothills Hospital Young Adult Program and coordinator/facilitator of its affiliated Parent Support Group, consented to visit with us recently and to share his memories of Colleen as a patient there—including her statement, as a young teen, that she didn't expect to remain very long in this world. We shall always appreciate Peter's frankness with us, his kindness to us during those difficult days, and the coping strategies we learned at his Parent Support Group.

Family physician Dr. Rod Densmore, who runs the Primary Care Social Medicine Clinic for Complex Neurodevelopmental Conditions in Salmon Arm B.C., has willingly taken time out of his busy life and has shared with us his professional opinions, his "take" on upcoming research, and the perspectives lent him by his specific expertise, for which I am most grateful.

For providing insights on the BPD mind and opinions about ways to help control emotional dysregulation, I owe thanks to Donna R. Hughes, Executive/Clinical Director of Inner Solutions. As well, I salute with gratitude Janice Wingrave, Clinical Supervisor of the DBT Program at the Sheldon M. Chumir Health Centre, who went out of her way to provide me with information, and to gain me permission to use some of the patient testimonials included herein. Janice's obvious devotion to her calling and her encouragement to me as I pursued mine has been a true inspiration.

To publisher Tina Crossfield for her faith in my book, I express my sincerest thanks. And to artist Larry Stilwell, who designed such an effective front cover, I tip my hat to your artistic and graphics-management capabilities. Thank you also to artist Harald Kunze, for layout design and photo collages. All who offered their commitment to us and to Colleen along the way deserve acknowledgment, and I hope those many people will find recognition and tribute for their efforts within these pages.

Lastly, there is Andy, my husband and my rock, who told me he read this book with a box of tissues by his side. He has helped me immeasurably when my memory of certain details needed a boost. And his faithful photographic record of our family's life over the years has supplied the photo montage selection included here. Without you, my love, I think I would have thrown in the towel a long time ago. You have my eternal devotion, admiration, and respect.

Appendix I End Notes

Chapter 17

1. Manning, Shari Y., PhD. 2011 *Loving Someone with Borderline Personality Disorder: how to keep out-of-control emotions from destroying your relationship.* New York, NY: The Guildford Press: 28

2. Porr, Valerie, M.A. 2010 *Overcoming Borderline Personality Disorder: A Family Guide for Healing and Change.* New York, N.Y.: Oxford University Press: 54

3. Mason Paul T. and Randi Kreger. 2010 *Stop Walking on Eggshells: Taking your life back when someone you care about has borderline personality disorder.* Oakland, CA: New Harbinger Publications

4. Ibid. 170

5. Eric Lis, Brian Greenfield, Melissa Henry, et al., "Neuroimaging and Genetics of Borderline Personality Disorder: A Review", *Journal of Psychiatry and Neuroscience* 32 (2007): 162-173

6. Jerold J. Kreisman, M.D. and Hal Straus, *I Hate You—Don't Leave Me: understanding the borderline personality* (New York, N.Y.: Penguin Group, 2010): 12

7. Ibid, 127

8. Paul T. Mason and Randi Kreger, *Stop Walking on Eggshells: Taking your life back when someone you care about has borderline personality disorder* (Oakland, CA: New Harbinger Publications, 2010) 168

Chapter 22

9. Van Gelder, Kiera. 2010. *The Buddha and the borderline: a memoir.* Oakland, CA: New Harbinger Publications

Chapter 25

10. Paul T. Mason and Randi Kreger, *Stop Walking on Eggshells: Taking your life back when someone you care about has borderline personality disorder* (Oakland, CA: New Harbinger Publications, 2010) 205, 206

Chapter 27

11. J. Christopher Perry, Elizabeth Banon and Floriana Ianni, "Effectiveness of Psychotherapy for Personality Disorders", *American Journal of Psychiatry 156 (1999)*: 1312 – 1321

Chapter 29

12.   Paul T. Mason and Randi Kreger, *Stop Walking on Eggshells: Taking your life back when someone you care about has borderline personality disorder* (Oakland, CA: New Harbinger Publications, 2010) 42

13.   Ibid, 180

14.   Aguirre, Blaise A., M.D. 2007. *Borderline Personality Disorder in Adolescents: A Complete Guide to Understanding and Coping when Your Adolescent has BPD.* Beverly, Massachusetts: Fair Winds Press, 126

Chapter 30

15.   Friedel, Robert O., M.D., 2004. *Borderline Personality Disorder Demystified: The Essential Guide to Understanding and Living with BPD.* New York, NY: Marlowe & Company, Avalon Publishing Group Inc. 87, 88

Chapter 39

16.   Spungen, Deborah. 1983. *And I Don't Want To Live This Life.* Toronto, Canada: Ballantine Books, 323

17.   Ibid, 391

Chapter 44

18.   Friedel, Robert O., M.D. 2004. *Borderline Personality Disorder Demystified: The Essential Guide to Understanding and Living with BPD.* New York, NY: Marlowe & Company, Avalon Publishing Group Inc.: 46

19.   Bedell Smith, Sally. 2000. *Diana in Search of Herself: Portrait of a Troubled Princess.* New York, NY: Signet Books

20.   Porr, Valerie, M.A., *Overcoming Borderline Personality Disorder: A Family Guide for Healing and Change* (New York, N.Y.: Oxford University Press, 2010): 12-13

Chapter 45

21.   Kreiseman, Jerold J., MD, and Hal Straus. 2010. *I Hate You—Don't Leave Me: understanding the borderline personality.* New York, NY: Penguin Group, 127

22.   Aguirre, Blaise A., M.D. 2007. *Borderline Personality Disorder in Adolescents: A Complete Guide to Understanding and Coping when Your Adolescent has BPD.* Beverly, Massachusetts: Fair Winds Press, 167

23.   Krawitz, Roy, and Wendy Jackson. 2008. *Borderline Personality Disorder: All the Information You Need, Straight from the Experts.* New York: Oxford University Press, 41 - 42

24. Ibid, 43 - 45

25. Aguirre, Blaise A., M.D. 2007. *Borderline Personality Disorder in Adolescents: A Complete Guide to Understanding and Coping when Your Adolescent has BPD.* Beverly, Massachusetts: Fair Winds Press, 198

26. Zanarini, Mary C., Ed.D. and Frances R. Frankenburg M.D. *American Journal of Psychiatry*, Jan. 2003 Vol. 160, No. 1: 167 – 169

Appendix II:
List of Resources and Facilities Mentioned in this Book

AARC: Alberta Adolescent Recovery Centre (aarc.ab.ca)

Address: 303 Forge Rd. SE, Calgary, AB T2H 0S9

Tel: (403) 253-5250

Alternative High School (alternative@cbe.ab.ca)

Address: 5003 – 20 Street S.W., Calgary, AB T2T 5A5

Tel: (403) 777-7730

Avenue 15 Youth Shelter (www.boysandgirlsclubsofcalgary)

Address: 938 15 Avenue S.W., Calgary, AB T2R 0S3

Tel: (403) 229-3408

BPD Central (www.bpdcentral.com) – established by Randi Kreger in 1995 and offering a wide variety of BPD basic and advanced information, including articles, essays, interviews with experts, book and booklet excerpts, links and resources, and answers to common questions

Calgary Academy www.calgaryacademy.com

Address: 1677 93 St. S.W., Calgary, AB. T3H 4A6

Tel: (403) 686-6444

Crossroads Treatment Centre (info@xrdstc.net)

Address: 123 Franklyn Road, Kelowna B.C. V1X 6A9

Tel: (250) 860-4001

Dialectical Behaviour Therapy Program – Sheldon M. Chumir Health Centre (www.albertahealthservices.ca)

Address: 7th Floor, 1213 4 Street S.W., Calgary, AB T2R 0X7

Tel: (403) 943-1500 Ext. 2 (Intake)

Densmore, Dr. Rod, M.D. (drdensmore@shaw.ca) - Primary Care Social Medicine Clinic for Complex Neurodevelopmental Conditions

Mailing Address: Box 10006, Salmon Arm B.C. V1E 1H6

Street Address: Unit 2, 161 2nd Ave N.E., Salmon Arm, B.C.

Tel: (250) 833-4922

Glory House Recovery

Address: 1559 Grant Ave., Port Coquitlam, B.C. V3B 1P1

Tel: (604) 464-0475

Inner Solutions (www.innersolutions.ca)

Address: Sloane Square, Suite 106, 5920 1A st. S.W. Calgary, AB, T2G 0G3

Tel: (403) 714-4199

Kitchur, Maureen, MSW, RSW (maureen@kitchur.com)

Address: 1305 7 St. S.W., Calgary, AB. T2R 1A5

Tel: (403) 270-0652

Louise Dean School (louisedean@cbe.ab.ca)

Address: 120 – 23 Street S.W., Calgary, AB T2N 2P1

Tel: (403) 777-7630

McMan Youth, Family & Community Services (calgary@mcman.ca)

Address: #1 4004 19 St. N.W., Calgary, AB. T2L 2B6

Tel: (403) 508-6259

NEA-BPD (www.neabpd.org) – an extensive web site containing information about upcoming conferences, grants, family programs, video resources, and interviews with experts

Pediatric Centre for Weight and Health, Alberta Children's Hospital (pcwhcalgary@albertahealthservices.ca)

Address: Alberta Children's Hospital, 3rd Floor, 2888 Shaganappi Trail N.W., Calgary, AB T3B 6A8

Tel: (403) 955-7133

PSA (Parent Support Association) Calgary (www.psa.calgary.ab.ca)

Address: 200, 609 35 Ave. N.E., Calgary, AB. T2E 2L2

Tel: (403) 270-1809

Renfrew Recovery Detoxification Centre (www.calgaryaddiction.com)

Address: 1611 Remington Rd. N.E., Calgary, AB. T2E 5K6

Tel: (403) 297-3337

Step by Step Recovery House

Address: 12442 78A Ave., Surrey, BC. V3W 7X2

Tel: (604) 591-3153

Stepping Stones Recovery House for Women (www.steppingstonesrecoveryhouse.ca)

Address: 1571 Burgess Rd., Courtenay, B.C. V9N 5R8

Tel: (250) 897-0360

TARA Association for Personality Disorder (www.tara4bpd.org)

Address: 23 Greene St. NYC 10013

Welcome to Oz (www.bpdcentral.com) – an online community for family members with a BPD loved one, founded by Randi Kreger in 1995 and now with over 16,000 members

Woods Homes (www.woodshomes.ca)

Address: 805 37 St. N.W., Calgary, AB. T2N 4N8

Tel: (403) 270-4102

Young Adult Services – Mental Health – Foothills Medical Centre (formerly Foothills Hospital) (mental.health@albertahealthservices.ca)

Address: Unit 26, 1403 29 Street N.W., Calgary, AB T2N 2T9

Tel: (403) 943-1500 (Access Mental Health)

Appendix III: List of References

American Psychiatric Association. 2004. *Diagnostic and Statistical Manual of Mental Disorders* (DSM-IV). Washington, D.C.: American Psychiatric Association

Aguirre, Blaise A., M.D. 2007. *Borderline Personality Disorder in Adolescents: A Complete Guide to Understanding and Coping when Your Adolescent has BPD.* Beverly, Massachusetts: Fair Winds Press

Bedell Smith, Sally. 2000. *Diana in Search of Herself: Portrait of a Troubled Princess.* New York, NY: Signet Books

Chapman, K.L., and K.L. Gratz. 2007. *The Borderline Personality Disorder Survival Guide: Everything You Need To Know About Living with BPD.* Oakland, CA: New Harbinger Publications

Friedel, Robert O., M.D. 2004. *Borderline Personality Disorder Demystified: The Essential Guide to Understanding and Living with BPD.* New York, NY: Marlowe & Company, Avalon Publishing Group Inc.

Krawitz, Roy, and Wendy Jackson. 2008. *Borderline Personality Disorder: All the Information You Need, Straight from the Experts.* New York: Oxford University Press

Kreisman, Jerold J., M.D., and Hal Straus. 2004. *Sometimes I Act Crazy: Living with Borderline Personality Disorder.* Hoboken, N.J.: John Wiley & Sons, Inc.

Kreisman, Jerold J., M.D., and Hal Straus. 2010. *I Hate You—Don't Leave Me: understanding the borderline personality.* New York, NY: Penguin Group

Lawson, C.A. 2000. *Understanding the Borderline Mother: Helping Her Children Transcend the Intense, Unpredictable, and Volatile Relationship.* Northvale, N.J.: Jason Aronson Inc.

Linehan, M.M. 1993. *Skills Training Manual for Treating Borderline Personality Disorder.* New York: The Guilford Press

Manning, Sheri Y, PhD. 2011. *Loving someone with borderline personality disorder: how to keep out-of-control emotions from destroying your relationship.* New York, NY: The Guilford Press

Mason, Paul T. and Randi Kreger. 2010. *Stop Walking on Eggshells: taking your life back when someone you care about has borderline personality disorder.* Oakland, CA: New Harbinger Publications

Monks, Millicent. 2010. *Songs of Three Islands: A Story of Mental Illness in an Iconic American Family.*
New York, NY: Atlas & Co. Publishers

Perry, J. Christopher, Elizabeth Banon, and Floriana Ianni. "Effectiveness of Psychotherapy for Personality Disorders",
American Journal of Psychiatry 156 (1999): 1312 – 1321

Porr, Valerie, M.A. 2010. *Overcoming Borderline Personality Disorder: A Family Guide for Healing and Change.*
New York, NY: Oxford University Press

Roth, K. and F.B. Friedman. 2003. *Surviving a Borderline Parent: How to Heal Your Childhood Wounds and Build Trust, Boundaries, and Self-Esteem.*
Oakland, CA: New Harbinger Publications

Spungen, Deborah. 1983. *And I Don't Want to Live This Life.* Toronto, Canada: Ballantine Books

Van Gelder, Kiera. 2010. *The Buddha and the borderline: a memoir.*
Oakland, CA: New Harbinger Publications

Reviewer's reference: A. E. Jongsma, L. M. Petersen, W. P. McInnis, 2011. *Adult, Adolescent & Child Psychotherapy Treatment Planners,* Hoboken, NJ: John Wiley & Sons, Inc.

CROSSFIELD
PUBLISHING